Praise for *Reality Check*

"The key word in describing this book is useful. Like a good travel guide, it's packed with smart and current advice that you can actually apply. Easy to navigate and fun to read, this is the perfect manual for business today!"
—Emanuel Rosen, author of *The Anatomy of Buzz Revisited*

"Now I know what they mean when they talk about 'encyclopedic knowledge.' They mean Guy Kawasaki. This book is the proof." —Dan Roam, author of *The Back of the Napkin: Solving Problems and Selling Ideas with Pictures*

"Buy two copies of this book. One to rip pages out of, mark up, copy, and tack on the wall. And one to give away to your clueless colleague. Oh, better make that three copies. Four?" —Seth Godin, author of *Linchpin* and *The Dip*

"*Reality Check* is a very practical, yet highly entertaining book. If you're looking for a self-help book that coddles your entrepreneurial fancies, this book is not for you. If you're starting a business and looking to understand the world you're walking into, you won't find a better, more honest and enjoyable guide than Guy Kawasaki." —Jack Covert, 800 CEO READ

"[Kawasaki's] come up with a gem. In a way, this compendium is like MBA in a box, another compilation of wisdom by sundry sages and savants. In other ways, it's like a cocktail party, as Kawasaki effortlessly glides from table to table, chatting with his guests, who offer very bright and pithy comments in response to the host's queries. . . . Of value to most readers are the portions dealing with job seeking. The advice, both from the perspective of employee and employer, is realistic and sound. The chapters covering the vagaries and realities of the corporate world are also quite funny and true."
—*Miami Herald Tribune*

"Kawasaki more than meets his stated goal of providing 'hardcore information to hardcore people who want to kick ass.'" —*Time*

"Some of the chapters are quick, pithy, and direct with practical advice (How to Kick Butt on a Panel), others are interviews with people Kawasaki finds interesting, and there are often nuggets of information to be had in them (Chip and Dan Heath, The Sticking Point). All in all, an easy to read book, and probably the only person who couldn't find something useful to take away from this book would be Guy Kawasaki himself." —*Sacramento Book Review*

ABOUT THE AUTHOR

Guy Kawasaki is a founding partner and entrepreneur-in-residence at Garage Technology Ventures. He is also the cofounder of Alltop.com, an "online magazine rack" of popular topics on the Web. Previously, he was an Apple Fellow at Apple Computer, Inc. Kawasaki is the author of eight books including *The Art of the Start*, *Rules for Revolutionaries*, *How to Drive Your Competition Crazy*, *Selling the Dream*, and *The Macintosh Way*. He has a BA from Stanford University and an MBA from UCLA as well as an honorary doctorate from Babson College. Portfolio/Penguin will publish his book *Enchantment: The Art of Changing Hearts, Minds, and Actions* in 2011.

Reality Check

{ The Irreverent Guide to
Outsmarting, Outmanaging, and
Outmarketing Your Competition }

GUY KAWASAKI

PORTFOLIO/PENGUIN

PORTFOLIO/PENGUIN

Published by the Penguin Group

Penguin Group (USA) Inc., 375 Hudson Street,
New York, New York 10014, U.S.A.
Penguin Group (Canada), 90 Eglinton Avenue East,
Suite 700, Toronto, Ontario, Canada M4P 2Y3
(a division of Pearson Penguin Canada Inc.)
Penguin Books Ltd, 80 Strand, London WC2R 0RL, England
Penguin Ireland, 25 St Stephen's Green, Dublin 2, Ireland
(a division of Penguin Books Ltd)
Penguin Group (Australia), 250 Camberwell Road, Camberwell,
Victoria 3124, Australia
(a division of Pearson Australia Group Pty Ltd)
Penguin Books India Pvt Ltd, 11 Community Centre,
Panchsheel Park, New Delhi – 110 017, India
Penguin Group (NZ), 67 Apollo Drive, Rosedale, North Shore 0632,
New Zealand (a division of Pearson New Zealand Ltd)
Penguin Books (South Africa) (Pty) Ltd, 24 Sturdee Avenue,
Rosebank, Johannesburg 2196, South Africa

Penguin Books Ltd, Registered Offices:
80 Strand, London WC2R 0RL, England

First published in the United States of America by Portfolio,
a member of Penguin Group (USA) Inc. 2008

This paperback edition published 2011

10   9   8   7   6   5   4   3   2   1

Portions of this book first appeared in the author's blog.

THE LIBRARY OF CONGRESS HAS CATALOGED THE HARDCOVER EDITION AS FOLLOWS:

Kawasaki, Guy, 1954–
Reality check : the the irreverent guide to outsmarting, outmanaging,
and outmarketing your competition / Guy Kawasaki.
p.   cm.
Includes index.
ISBN 978-1-59184-223-1 (hc.)
ISBN 978-1-59184-394-8 (pbk.)
1. New business enterprises. 2. Entrepreneurship. 3. Competition.
4. Management. I. Title.
HD62.5.K382 2008
658—dc22   2008024954

Printed in the United States of America
Set in Warnock Pro
Designed by Amy Hill

To my four startups:

Nate, Nohemi, Noah, and Nic.

You four check me every day of my life.

The Reality of Planning and Executing

The Reality of Innovating

The Reality of Marketing

The Reality of Selling and Evangelizing

The Reality of Communicating

The Reality of Beguiling

The Reality of Competing

The Reality of Hiring and Firing

The Reality of Working

The Reality of Doing Good

Imagine the American Dream on steroids and Red Bull and you have some idea of what life is like in Silicon Valley. Sure, Frank Sinatra called New York "the city that never sleeps," but that's only because Frank never visited the Valley. This strip of land stretching from San Francisco to San Jose is another place where nobody ever seems to sleep. You know why? Because everybody is up all night working. And hoping. And dreaming.

Yes, there's the money. But there's something else, something much more powerful and seductive. There's the chance to change the world. The chance to catch a wave just as it's building and go for that once-in-a-lifetime ride. Ever wonder why these people who've already struck it rich on one tech company always go back and try to do it again? They can't help themselves. It's too much fun. And if they fail, who cares? Now think about that. Where else in the world can you fail at something—and I mean utterly *fail*—and still get another chance? And another one after that?

The Valley is a place like no other place on earth. It's the last true meritocracy in America, a place where a great idea and a willingness to work ridiculously hard can turn a bunch of unknown kids into a bunch of billionaires. This isn't Wall Street, or Washington, D.C., or Hollywood, where success depends largely on which people you know and what college you went to. The Valley doesn't care where you went to college or even if you didn't go to college at all. The Valley is simply about ideas. Think you've got a good one? Code it up and give it a shot.

If you're reading this book chances are you've been bitten by that bug and you're dreaming of making it as an entrepreneur. There's a lot you'll need to learn. How to raise money. How to build a team. How to sell. How to schmooze. How to make presentations. How to influence people and make them believe in you. There is no better guide to the Valley than Guy Kawasaki, the legendary evangelist and venture capitalist who seems to know everyone out here. To put it another way—he's the guy who marketed the original Macintosh, back in 1984. Have you heard of it?

Maybe you've dreamed of meeting a mentor, a wise Valley veteran who would take you under his wing and share his insider's knowledge of how the Valley works. Well, now you've found one. My advice to the aspiring entrepreneur goes like this: Read this book. Study it. Listen to Guy. Take his advice. Then put down the book and get to work! There's no time to waste. There's already another guy in the Valley chasing the same thing you are. Maybe more than one. Whoever gets it right, and gets it first, wins. Oh, and there's probably some luck involved, too.

Good Luck.

DANIEL LYONS, aka FAKE STEVE JOBS

June 2008

What follows is the best foreword in the history of business books. It came about because shortly after Dan wrote the first foreword, he announced that he was discontinuing Fake Steve Jobs. I begged him to write one last piece as Fake Steve Jobs—what an honor that would be for my book! Fortunately, he agreed, and so Reality Check has not one but two forewords.

You know what I think about whenever I hear the name *Guy Kawasaki*? Motorcycles. It's true. It's the first thing I think about when I hear his name, even though I've been told again and again that Guy actually has nothing to do with motorcycles. So then I try not to think about motorcycles, but come on, the dude's name is Kawasaki. What else are you going to think about? And don't say Vietnam because he's a VC because that is not cool, people. Not cool at all. Guy was just a friggin' *kid* when all that shit was going down.

Anyway, since Guy is not a motorcycle designer, and also no longer a member of the Viet Cong, I try to think about something else, and usually what I think about is the fact that he worked for me at Apple back in the eighties. To be honest, he didn't make much of an impression on me back in those days, and I didn't really remember anything about him, but I asked HR to pull his records and apparently the only notes we have on him are that he had a habit of cutting the line in the cafeteria and that a lot of people did not like him.

Anyway, Guy worked here for about fifteen minutes, but he's been dining out on that for the past twenty years, and whatever, more power to him. His big claim to fame is that he created this notion of technology evangelism and he created this huge community of weirdo Apple fanboys who would camp out overnight to get our products and who would attack anyone who dared to criticize Apple. To this day these freako Apple kooks still worship me like a god and never let me have a moment of peace or privacy. They steal license plates from my car. Some even show up outside my house hoping to catch a glimpse of me as I drive through the gate. Basically, they've made my life a living hell.

So, um, thanks, Guy Kawasaki. Thanks a friggin' million for that. Great job. I mean it. You dick.

So what is Guy's new book about? To be honest, I have no idea. I didn't read it. I didn't even pretend to read it. I told Guy, "Dude, look, I don't read books, okay? Books are a technology of the last century. If you want to make your book into a movie, or a podcast, and if you want to download that video or audio content onto a totally sweet iPod or iPhone, then maybe you will have created some modern content that I will consume, although, to be honest, probably not even then because I don't need to hear your frigtarted ideas about startups or marketing or raising money or whatever, because I am already the greatest businessperson in the entire history of the planet, and I've forgotten more about marketing than you'll ever know. Besides that, I'm super, super busy and important, and I've got so much money that I could wipe my ass with hundred-dollar bills every day for the rest of my life and I'd still have more money than almost everyone on the planet, including you, since the last time I checked, you haven't exactly been setting the world on fire as a venture capitalist."

But I digress.

Anyway, Guy is craven enough that he doesn't really care whether I read his book or not. As he put it to me, all he wants is a famous name to put on the cover, and pretty much everyone else turned him down and so he had to resort to calling me, and so, fine, I let him beg a little bit and then I made him do some humiliating things like stand on one leg for half an hour and jump up and down and make strange noises, and then I said, Okay, okay, enough already, you total freak, I'll write you something.

So this is it—my official endorsement. *Reality Check* is by far the best book ever written about the Valley. It's an important and necessary work, one that should be required reading in every business school in the country. I wish this book had been around when I was starting Apple in my garage back in 1976. I'm sure I wouldn't have read it, but still it would have been nice if it had been around back then to help out all those other people who wanted to start companies but couldn't figure out some of the more subtle aspects of business, like the fact that you need to charge more money for your products than it costs you to make them.

That's a really super-important lesson, yet one that so many people overlook, especially here in the Valley. Anyway, if these incredibly super-obvious things aren't already super-obvious to you, then you probably need to read a book like this and have someone like Guy Kawasaki teach you how to start a business in terms that a child could understand.

And now I'm thinking about motorcycles again. Dammit! *Namaste,* poorly informed wannabe business people. I honor the place where your imbecilic gaze and my incredibly wise words become one. Much love. Peace out.

FAKE STEVE JOBS

July 2008

{ ACKNOWLEDGMENTS }

First, my thanks to Rick Kot, editor extraordinaire, for suggesting this book, and second, to the rest of the awesome crew at Portfolio, including Allison McLean, Laura Tisdel, Will Weisser, and Sharon Gonzalez.

Third, a big "domo arigato" to Sloan Harris, agent extraordinaire, because, among other things, he made Rick pay a lot for it.

Fourth, "you the man" to Noah Stid, because he kick-started this book for me.

Fifth, my eternal gratitude to Bill Meade, who is the best beta tester of a business book in the history of man. If only I could meet his lofty expectations.

Sixth, my admiration to Glenn Kelman for his contributions to my thinking and my blogging—both of which ultimately ended up as big components of this book.

Seventh, a big, sweet tweet to all my buddies on Twitter who beta tested the manuscript on very short notice: John Atkinson, Eric Byers, Patrick Byers, Ori Cohen, Russell Cooper, Gilbert Corrales, David Damore, Shirley de Rose, Michael Dorausch, Michael Falkner, John Frenette, Lauren Goddard, Alfonso Guerra, Patricia Handschiegel, Mike Harris, Chris Hong, Greg Hughes, Pokai Liao, Violet Lim, Christine Lu, Darren Lui, Keran McKenzie, Drew McLellan, Amanda Magee, Marina Martin, Patricia Mayo, Gordie Meyer, Mitch Mitchell, Bram Pitoyo, Sharon Richardson, John Saddington, Maria Santoyo, Ayat Shukairy, Hjörtur Smárason, Paul Steketee, Patricia Skinner, Alex Strand, John

Swartz, Don Tamihere, Frank Watson, Thomas White Jr., David Yack, Scott Yoshinaga, and Jason Zagar.

Eighth, a big "Mahalo" to Neenz "the bloggin' Samoan" Faleafine for all the top stuff that she did to help me with this book and Alltop.

Ninth, my thanks to Gary Stimeling, the masochist who copyedited the manuscript. To his credit, he tried, albeit unsuccessfully, to make me stop using the term "bull shiitake."

Tenth, my love to my wife, Beth, and my four kids ("Nononina"). Like the Joker said in *Dark Knight*—though in a much more positive way—"You complete me." And I can't forget Tessie Dagarag, the world's greatest nanny, for all she does for all of us.

A truly good book teaches me better than to read it.
I must soon lay it down, and commence living on its hint.
What I began by reading, I must finish by acting.

⁓ HENRY DAVID THOREAU

When entrepreneurs ask me for my opinion of their ideas, I give them the choice of the truth or "feel good" pablum. Most opt for the truth, and they usually thank me because they learn something from the tough love. Apparently, politeness and expedience ("It's very interesting. Let me get back to you") are more common than information and feedback ("Your financial projections are insanely optimistic"). This led me to conclude that there is a shortage of candid and straightforward information for entrepreneurs and would-be entrepreneurs.

At the same time, I grew frustrated with the shortcomings of blogging, which I began to do in earnest in 2006 with my blog "How to Change the World." I quickly learned that people rarely scroll past the home page of a blog or search for previous material. However, I wanted my blog to serve as a constant reference source for a wide range of topics of entrepreneurial interest. The reality is that blogs and online sources don't do this very well for everyone.

These two forces inspired me to publish *Reality Check*. That is, I wanted to provide hardcore information to hardcore people who want to kick ass, and I wanted this information in something you can hold in your hands—aka, a book. Why? Because a book boots up faster than a blog, and a book has better copyediting and fact-checking than a blog. Also, a book is not dependent on Internet connectivity, battery life, or the ineptness of HTML printing. And best of all, because you can write in a book, stick stickies in a book, and dog-ear its corners.

In short, *Reality Check* is a tweaked, updated, and supplemented compilation of the best of everything I've done and seen that pertains to starting and operating great organizations. My focus is only on the stages of the creation and operation of an organization, but you can use this book's lessons in all stages of an organization's life span except senility. My hope is that *Reality Check* makes you act—in other words, that it passes the Henry David Thoreau test for a "truly good book." This I say to you: There is no greater validation of an author's work than to see his readers make the world a better place because of it.

GUY KAWASAKI

Silicon Valley, California

The Reality of Starting

Here's the fairy tale: Two guys or gals in a garage come up with a great idea. They approach investors who quickly fund the idea. They launch on time to universal acclaim and unprecedented customer adoption. The company is immediately profitable and goes public more successfully than Google. Then, the company innovates and thrives for decades. Fairy tales don't happen, but this section explains what does happen in those first years of starting up, which entails a lot of floundering and flailing.

CHAPTER 1

Flounders (*sic*) at Work

All the best things I did at Apple came from (a) not having money, and (b) not having done it before, ever.

⌒ STEVE WOZNIAK

So we went to Atari and said, "Hey, we've got this amazing thing, even built with some of your parts, and what do you think about funding us? Or we'll give it to you. We just want to do it. Pay our salary, we'll come work for you." And they said, "No." So then we went to Hewlett-Packard, and they said, "Hey, we don't need you. You haven't got through college yet."

⌒ STEVE JOBS

Flailing, grinding, thrashing, and getting lucky are why companies succeed. Not knowing you're doing something that's "impossible" helps, too. Jessica Livingston's book, *Founders at Work: Stories of Startups' Early Days* (Apress, 2007), is a gold mine for stories about the reality of starting an organization. In particular, these will delight and inspire you:

- **James Currier (Tickle)** "When we started the company, we wanted to change the world, and we had all these tests on the site to help people with their lives. We had the anxiety test, the parenting, relationship, and communications tests. And no one came. . . . 'Let's do a test for what kind of breed of dog you are.' We put it online, and eight days later we had a million people trying to enter our site."

- **Catarina Fake (Flickr)** "So Flickr started off as a feature. It wasn't really a product. It was kind of IM in which you could drag and drop photos onto people's desktops and show them what you were looking at."

- **Paul Graham (Viaweb)** "Neither of us knew how to write Windows software, and we didn't want to learn. It seemed like this huge steaming turd that was best avoided. So the main thing we thought when we first had the idea of doing Web-based applications was, 'Thank God we don't have to write software on Windows.'"

- **Ann Winblad (Open Systems and now venture capitalist)** "So I get in front of these sixty or seventy guys, and these guys are probably all in their fifties and I'm in my twenties, and we had a 'blue light special,' where we said, 'If you give me a check today for $10,000, you can have unlimited rights to one of our modules.' . . . I went home with, I think, like twelve or fifteen of these $10,000 checks in my purse."

- **Tim Brady (Yahoo!)** "The funniest thing I can remember was when there was a huge storm in May '95, and the power grid went down for a few days. We had to go rent a power generator and take turns filling it with diesel fuel for four days. 24/7. We were laughing: 'How many pages to the gallon today?'"

- **Mitch Kapor (Lotus Development)** on how much money he wanted to raise from Sevin-Rosen: "I think I said probably $2 to $3 million. We had nothing. We had an early-stage, under-development spreadsheet, and me and Jon Sachs. So that was the biggest number I felt I could ask for without being totally absurd."

- **Chuck Geschke (Adobe)** on the reaction of the spouses of Xerox execs to a demonstration of PARC technology in 1977: "They loved this stuff. They sat down and played with the mouse, they changed a few things on the screen, they hit the print button and it looked the same on paper as it did on the screen. They said, 'Wow, this is really cool. This would really change an office if it had this technology.'" (Unfortunately, the Xerox execs didn't listen to their wives, and that's why Adobe and Apple exist today.)

- **James Hong (Hot or Not)** on his first beta site: "My dad was the first person that ever saw Hot or Not besides Jim [his cofounder] and me, and he got addicted to it! Here's my dad, a sixty-year-old retired Chinese guy who, as my father, is supposed to be asexual, and he's saying, 'She's hot. This one's not hot at all.'"

On using his parents to moderate the pictures: "I originally had my parents moderating since they were retired, and after a few days I asked my dad how it was going. He said, 'Oh, it's really interesting. Mom saw a picture of a guy and a girl and another girl and they were doing . . .' So I told Jim, 'Dude, my parents can't do this anymore. They're looking at porn all day.'"

These stories depict what happens in startups. Success takes crazy, passionate people who believe they can change the world. Success doesn't take "professional" and "proven" people. I'm not alone in this sentiment; I once heard Michael Moritz (he funded Google) of Sequoia Capital explain what kind of entrepreneurs he wanted to invest in. I'm paraphrasing: Guys under thirty who are building a product that they themselves want to use. Amen!

The Problem with Serial Entrepreneurs

Unfortunately, Mike Moritz is the rare venture capitalist who looks beyond the lack of a "perfect background" in entrepreneurs. Most venture capitalists want a proven team with a proven technology and a proven business model. Indeed, one popular theory is that these "serial" entrepreneurs, wealthy from their previous smashing success but restless and too young to die, are the best bets for starting the next big thing.

However, it is unproven entrepreneurs who start the great world-changing companies such as Hewlett-Packard, Apple, eBay, Microsoft, Google, Yahoo!, and YouTube. My theory is that serial entrepreneurs fail in subsequent attempts for these reasons:

- **Serial entrepreneurs try to prove that their first success wasn't a fluke.** Rather than starting from the basis of technology ("isn't this cool?") or customers ("there must be a better way"), the reason for existence is "I'm going to prove that I'm talented." This is a bull-shiitake reason for starting a company, compared to solving people's problems or changing the world.

- **Serial entrepreneurs cannot distinguish between causation and correlation.** The actual cause of previous success may have been blind, dumb luck, but few people realize this and even fewer admit it. Thus, they have the hollow arrogance of people who just got lucky instead of being people who have been truly tested, and arrogance is a bad thing in entrepreneurs.

- **Serial entrepreneurs use the same methods again.** How can you fault them for using the same methods that made them successful the first time? For example, if they built a high-end computer the first time, then they build a high-end computer the next time. If they used dealers the first time, then they use dealers the second time. If they gave away content to get eyeballs and sold the company to a bigger, dumber, and richer company, then they try that path again.

- **Serial entrepreneurs use the same people again.** How can you fault them for hiring their buddies from a previous success? After all, they've proven that they can achieve success. However, to make lightning strike twice, you need people who don't know what they don't know, to push the edge of what's possible and to use new methods to address new markets. Ignorance is not only bliss; it's also empowering.

- **Serial entrepreneurs don't (or can't) work as hard as before.** When you have kids, a 5,000-square-foot house, a second house in Montana, and a car made by a company whose name ends in *i*, your attitudes and priorities change. Indeed, attitudes should change or people never grow up. However, it's one thing to work to survive and another to work for fulfillment. They can say they're just as hungry this time, but no one had to ask if they were hungry the first time.

- **Serial entrepreneurs don't get smacked around enough.** Life is good for serial entrepreneurs: They strut in, tell people that their last company was sold for a bazillion dollars, and now they're starting another one. Who's going to poke holes in their strategy? They're "proven." No one. And that's to their detriment, because no one plays the role of devil's advocate.

- **Serial entrepreneurs fill new roles in their next companies.** For example, in the first company the person was an engineer who became the vice president of engineering. In the next company, she is the CEO and founder. Just because you are good at designing chips doesn't mean you're CEO material. You may end up not doing what you're good at and doing what you're not good at.

"The Banality of Heroism"

Instead of pursuing professional entrepreneurs, we should figure out how and why ordinary people can do heroic things. Dr. Philip Zimbardo of Stanford University and Zeno Franco of the Pacific Graduate School of Psychology wrote an article called "The Banality of Heroism" (Google "Banality of Heroism" to find it) about this very subject.

The short explanation is that heroism requires the presence of a "heroic imagination," which the authors describe as "the capacity to imagine facing physically or socially risky situations, to struggle with the hypothetical problems these situations generate, and to consider one's actions and the consequences." According to Zimbardo and Franco, heroes do five things:

1. Maintain constant vigilance for situations that require heroic action.

2. Learn not to fear conflict because you took a stand.

3. Imagine alternative future scenarios beyond the present moment.

4. Resist the urge to rationalize and justify inaction.

5. Trust that people will appreciate heroic (and frequently unpopular) actions.

This is a good checklist for entrepreneurs, too: watching for opportunities, willing to compete with the status quo, imagining that there is a better way, refusing to settle for the status quo, and building a product or service based on the hope that people will love it. The bottom line is that if you exhibit these qualities, you're probably as qualified as anyone to achieve heroism.

CHAPTER 2

The Inside Story of Entrepreneurship

The great liability of the engineer compared to men of other professions is that his works are out in the open where all can see them. His acts, step by step, are in hard substance. He cannot bury his mistakes in the grave like the doctors. He cannot argue them into thin air or blame the judge like the lawyers. He cannot, like the architects, cover his failures with trees and vines. He cannot, like the politicians, screen his shortcomings by blaming his opponents and hope the people will forget. The engineer simply cannot deny he did it. If his works do not work, he is damned.

~ HERBERT HOOVER

This is a guest chapter by Glenn Kelman. He is the CEO of a company called Redfin that enables people to buy homes online. I include it here to provide the inside story of a startup from someone who is in the middle of the fray right now.

Lately I've been thinking how hard, not how easy, it is to build a new company. Hard has gone out of fashion. Like college students bragging about how they barely studied, startups today take care to project a sense of ease. Wherever I've worked, we've secretly felt just the opposite. We're assailed by doubts, mortified by our own shortcomings, surrounded by freaks, testy over silly details.

And now, having been through a few startups, I'm not even sure I'd want it to be that easy. Working two hours a day on my own wasn't my goal when I came to Silicon Valley. Does anybody remember the old video of Steve Jobs launching the Mac? He had tears in his eyes. And even though Jobs is Jobs and I am nobody, I knew how he felt. I had the same reaction—absurdly—

to portal software and more recently to Redfin, a fledgling real estate Web site.

"The megalomaniac pleasure of creation," psychoanalyst Edmund Berger wrote, "produces a type of elation which cannot be compared with that experienced by other mortals." Jobs wasn't just crying from simple happiness but from all the tinkering, kvetching, nitpicking, wholesale reworking, and spasms of self-loathing that go into a beautiful product. It was all being paid back in a rush.

Like the souls in Dostoevsky who are admitted to heaven because they never thought themselves worthy of it, successful entrepreneurs can't be convinced that any other startup has their troubles, because they constantly compare the triumphant launch parties and revisionist histories of successful companies to their own daily struggles. Just so you know you're not alone, here's a top ten list of the realities of startups.

1. **True believers go nuts at the slightest provocation.** The best people at a startup care too much. They stay up late taking support calls, snapping at bureaucracy, citing Joel Spolsky on Aerons, and Paul Graham on cubes. They are your heart and bones, so you have to give them what they need, which is a lot. The only way to get them on your side is to put them in charge.

2. **Good people need big projects.** If you aren't doing something worthwhile, you can't get anyone worthwhile to work on it. I often think about what Ezra Pound once said of his epic poem, *The Cantos*, " . . . if it's a failure, it's a failure worth all the successes of its age." We're not writing poetry, but it matters to us that we're trying to compete with real estate agents rather than just running their ads. You need a big mission in order to recruit people who care about what you're doing.

3. **Startups are freak-catchers.** To join a startup, to leave a Microsoft, you have to be fundamentally unhappy with the way things are and unrealistic enough to believe the world can change. This is a volatile combination that can result in group mood swings and a motley crew, so don't worry if your startup seems to have more than its fair share of oddballs.

4. **Good code takes time.** One great software engineer can do more than ten mediocre ones, especially when starting a project. But great engineers still need time: Whenever we've thought our talent, sprinkled with the fairy dust of some new engineering paradigm, would free us from having to schedule time for design and testing, we've paid for it. To make something elegant takes time, and the cult of speed sometimes works against that. "Make haste slowly."

5. **Everybody has to rebuild.** The shortcuts you have to take and the problems you couldn't anticipate when building version 1.0 of your product always mean you'll have to rebuild some of it in version 2.0 or 3.0. Don't get discouraged or shortsighted. Just rebuild it. This is simply how things work.

6. **Fearless leaders are often terrified.** The CEO of the most promising startup I know of recently used to anonymously ask his Facebook friends if we thought his idea was any good. Just because you're worried doesn't mean you have a bad idea; the best ideas are often the ones that scare you the most. And don't believe the after-the-fact statements from entrepreneurs about how they "knew" what to do.

7. **It's always hard work.** Most startups find an interesting problem to solve and then just keep working on it. At a recent awards ceremony, Microsoft CEO Steve Ballmer tried to think of the secret of Microsoft's success and could only come up with "hard, hard, hard, hard, hard, work." This is an obvious cliché, but most entrepreneurs remain fixated on the Eureka! moment. If you don't believe you have any reliable competitive advantage, then you're the kind of person who will work your competition into the ground, so keep working.

8. **It's not going to get better—it already is.** In the early days, people in startups focus on how great it's going to be when they succeed, but the moment they do, they start talking about how great it was before they did. Whenever I get this way, I remember that the Venerable Bede (a Benedictine monk born in the late seventh century) complained that his eighth-century contemporaries had lost the fervor of seventh-century monks.

Even in the darkest of the Dark Ages, people were nostalgic for . . . the Dark Ages. Startup folks are like medieval monasteries: always convinced that paradise is just ahead or that things only recently got worse. If you can begin to enjoy the process of building a startup rather than the outcome, you'll be a better leader.

9. **Truth is the only currency.** At lunch last week, an engineer said the only thing he remembered from his interview was our saying the most likely outcome for Redfin—or any startup—was bankruptcy, but that he should join us anyway. It's odd, but the more we've tried to warn people about the risks, the more they seem to ignore them. And since you have to keep taking risks, you have to keep telling people about them.

10. **Competition starts at $100 million.** A Sequoia partner once told me that competition only starts when you hit $100 million in revenues. Maybe that number is lower now. But if you do something worthwhile, someone else will do it, too. Since you can't see what's going on behind a competitor's pretty Web site, it's natural to assume that all the challenges we just went over only apply to your company. They don't, so keep the faith.

I've started four companies and served on the boards of directors of three others, and Kelman speaks the truth. Don't get us wrong: Starting an organization is a wonderful experience, but it's also a difficult and scary one. If it were easy, more people would do it, and that means more competition. Also, only the things that scare you make you stronger.

CHAPTER 3

The Art of Intrapreneurship

The people who get on in this world are the people who get up and look for the circumstances they want, and, if they can't find them, make them.

~ GEORGE BERNARD SHAW

There are lots of guys and gals inside established companies who are as innovative and revolutionary as their bootstrapping, soy-sauce-and-rice-subsisting, external entrepreneur counterparts. This chapter is for these brave souls, who face a different kind of reality and must practice the art of entrepreneurship inside a company—or "intrapreneurship."

From the outside looking in, entrepreneurs think intrapreneurs have it made: ample capital, infrastructure (desks, chairs, Internet access, secretaries, lines of credit, etc.), salespeople, support people, and an umbrella brand. Guess again. Intrapreneurs don't have it better; they simply have it different. Indeed, the reality is that they probably have it worse, because they are fighting against ingrained, inbred, and inept management. This is the real-world list of what you have to do to succeed as an intrapreneur.

- **Kill the cash cows.** This is the best perspective for both intrapreneurs and their upper management. Cash cows are wonderful—but you should milk them but not sustain them until, pun intended, the cows come home. Truly brave companies understand that if they don't kill their cash cows, two guys/gals in a garage will do it for them. Macintosh killed the Apple II: Do you think Apple would still exist if it tried to "protect" the Apple II cash cow ad infinitum? The purpose of cash cows is to fund new calves. If you can't openly kill the cash cow, then ignore it, circumvent it, or work parallel to it—somehow shorten its journey to the slaughterhouse.

- **Reboot your brain.** Just about everything you learn and do inside a large company is wrong for intrapreneuring. For example, in a large company, you survey customers, check with the sales force, build consensus, conduct focus groups, test, test, test, ensure backward compatibility, test, test, test, and then ship. When you ship, you buy ads because that's what you always do. Forget these practices. Generally, you should do everything the opposite from the tried-and-true existing way of large companies.

- **Find a separate building.** One of the best ways to stay intrapreneurial is to work in a separate building. Ideally, it is between 440 yards and a mile from the main corporate campus—that is, close enough to steal stuff but far enough so that upper management is not in your face. This building should be a piece of crap with lousy furniture, because intrapreneurs need to build cohesiveness, and the best way to build cohesiveness is to suffer, and you can't suffer if your butt is sitting in a $700 Herman Miller Aeron chair in a beautiful building.

- **Hire infected people.** What's the most important characteristic of an intrapreneurial team (and entrepreneurial team, too, for that matter)? It's being infected with a love for what the team is doing. It's not work experience or educational background. I would pick an Apple II repair department engineer over a PhD from MIT if he "gets it," loves it, and wants to change the world with it. Of course, you understand that you're reading the book of a jewelry schlepper who went to work for Apple.

- **Give hope to the hopeless.** My prediction for when you begin your intrapreneurial quest and hire infected people is that other believers will come out of the woodwork to support you. This is because you are giving hope to the hopeless—in other words, the folks inside the company who knew there was a better way but could not make it happen. Thank your lucky stars if this happens, because you're going to need all the support you can get.

- **Put the company first.** Intrapreneurs must put the company, not themselves, first. As long as you're an employee, you have to do what's right for the company. However, many employees will think it's wrong to kill the cash cow and so think you're *not* putting the company first, but they just don't get it. You can't have it both ways—the security of existing employment and the financial rewards of entrepreneurship. Also, unfortunately, the very bozo who stood in your way may get some of the credit for what you did.

- **Stay under the radar.** Speaking of bozos who get in your way, you need to stay invisible as long as practical. Your initial reaction to an innovative idea may be to seek upper-level and peer buy-in (although rebooting your brain should have taken care of this problem). Not a good idea. Seek forgiveness (if it comes to this), not permission. As soon as you appear on the radar, the flak will start flying. Let the vice presidents come to *you*. When they appear and start suggesting new product, that's the time to tell them you're already working on it. Even better: Make them believe it was their idea.

- **Collect and share data.** Trust me, you will get in trouble if you are a good intrapreneur. This is because the higher you go in many organizations, the thinner the air, and the thinner the air, the more difficult it is to support intelligent life. At some point, a bean counting, status-quo-preserving milkmaid is going to criticize you for wasting corporate assets on something that no customer is asking for. At that point, you need to already know how much your project has cost. If you have to spend weeks retracing your steps to figure this out, you'll occupy a much weaker position. If there's anything a bean counter respects, it's someone who's already counted the beans.

- **Dismantle when done.** If your intrapreneurship is successful, then your product and team will move into the mainstream of the company. That insanely great team of pirates must now integrate into the system. Hopefully, they will improve the system and not become the scum of a new bureaucracy, but integrate they must. I laugh about it now, but at one time we thought the Macintosh Division would never be larger than one hundred people.

Intrapreneurship has its own advantages and disadvantages. It takes an extra dose of courage because if you are successful, you will often cannibalize the current cash cows of your company. However, if you are not successful, your company could die when your cows wither and die.

CHAPTER 4

The Art of Commercialization

None can love freedom heartily, but good men;
the rest love not freedom, but license.

~ JOHN MILTON

Commercialization is the flip side of intrapreneuring. In this case, an organization (company, laboratory, or university) that owns some technology decides to let others run with it. The organization's logic goes like this:

The technology we invented for satellite imaging can be used for amateur video, so we could have created YouTube and sold to it to Google for $1.6 billion. Let's find an investor to fund this. How hard could it be to create a better YouTube?

I've been on the other side of the table when these organizations try to negotiate a deal to spin off, license, or sell their technology. It's almost always a *Mission: Impossible* to get a deal done, because most organizations try to stipulate conditions like these:

• You can't hire any of our employees. You cannot even talk to them, because we don't want our employees distracted from our Department of Defense contract work.

- Our sole contribution is a DVD containing research findings. We will mail it to you when the deal is done.

- Our technology is so great that we aren't offering any kind of exclusivity or perpetual license, because we might find a better deal.

- We want to own 80 percent of the spin-off, because our technology "is the company." In addition, we want a 50 percent royalty structure with a $5 million advance.

- We want to restrict the markets that you can sell into because we know best who should use our technology and for what purposes. (Did you know that the inventor of Novocain insisted that only doctors use it for operations? He thought it was too important a discovery to be used by mere dentists for mere tooth extraction.)

There are four flaws in most attempts to commercialize technology via a startup. First, organizations think that starting a successful company is easy and that the hard part—that is, the research—is already done. The truth is that it's not easy to productize technology and start a company; if it were, then these organizations would do it themselves. You heard it here first:

Those who can, do. Those who can't, license.

Second, patents are nice—in particular, they impress parents—but they aren't products, and they don't make people buy products. When is the last time you bought a gadget from Best Buy based on its patent? Unfortunately, these organizations think that patents are the endgame, not a means to an end. The last time I checked, an effective strategy for a company is not "Patent, sue, collect."

Third, the value of technology is not directly related to how long it took to develop it. In actuality, the longer it took to create something that no one has already commercialized, the less it's worth. Technology developed in a cost-plus environment by cost-plus scientists usually has difficulty succeeding in a market-driven market.

Fourth, for most organizations commercialization isn't about doing good. It's about *looking* good, where looking good equals having lots of meetings, dragging out negotiations so that management cannot accuse you of leaving money on the table, and focusing on doing as little for the licensee as possible.

Sorry to be the bad guy, but it won't be easy to commercialize most technology. If you can do it, you'll need these conditions:

- **The right attitude.** Something is better than nothing. It might gall an organization to learn that its science is the basis for a multi-billion-dollar exit "that it could have done itself," but that's a high-quality problem. More or less, its research is a sunk cost—if not, indeed, something that taxpayers underwrote—so anything it gets is upside. Thus, the licensor should expect no more than royalty in the 10 to 20 percent range with no upfront payments and a 10 percent ownership position.

- **A product or a tactical path to a product.** Customers buy products, not technology, science, or research findings. Technology, science, and research findings are a long way from a product. The closer the technology is to an actual product the better. The more the licensor can help the licensee, the better.

- **Warm bodies.** Simply providing DVDs or white papers doesn't cut it. The company needs the brains behind the science, because it's one thing to discover something in a lab, and it's quite another to ship a product on a large-scale basis. These employees will have to reboot their brains, so they may choose to stay in their current jobs. (Or the startup may choose not to take them.) Here's why:

  a. They have to choose revenue over peer acclaim in scientific journals. The choice boils down to being famous or rich—although if you make enough money, you can be both.

  b. They have to pick "good enough" over "best possible." Most customers don't care about being at the bleeding edge of technology and are happy if something simply works dependably. Computer operating systems, for example, fit in this category.

c. They have to listen to customer feedback. This isn't the same as submitting research findings to a journal, because at the end of the day, the customer is king.

d. They have to understand that investors don't invest on a cost-plus basis. The size of the bank account is limited, and the clock is ticking. And there's no politician who is trying to protect jobs by influencing budgets and cost overruns.

- **A hands-off attitude.** The final ingredient is that organizations should either actively help or get out of the way of the startup. It's tough enough dealing with customers, competition, investors, and the government. To add another stakeholder might be the straw that breaks the camel's back. It might look like it's fun to start a company, but it's hard work. Harder, in fact, than doing research on company time.

If all else fails, you can try to find a member of the organization's team who understands the technology, believes that she can improve it, and is willing to bet her life that she can make it into a product or service. She has to quit cleanly and legally—leaving everything at the office except her brain—but this path may be faster, cheaper, and easier than the commercialization process.

CHAPTER 5

Mantras for Dummies

Brevity is the soul of wit.

~ WILLIAM SHAKESPEARE

A mantra is three or four words that explain why your product, service, or company should exist. A mission statement is a fifty-word tome that no one can remember or believe, which is supposed to impress readers of your business plan. Unfortunately, most people work for an organization with a mission statement. Who among us has not had the horrible experience of a management offsite to build teamwork and to craft a mission statement? The offsite went like this:

Day 1: Teambuilding. First, form cross-functional teams so that engineering has to work with sales. Then tolerate a day of exercises such as, "Each of you will come up to the front of the group, turn your back to the group, close your eyes, and fall backward into the arms of your colleagues. This will teach you to communicate with and trust your fellow employees."

Day 2: Crafting the mission statement. In a hot, crowded room with a pad of white paper and a facilitator who knows nothing about your business, you are going to collectively craft a mission statement. Everyone who is at director level and above in the company is there—that's sixty people. You each figure you get one word, so at the end of the day, you have a sixty-word mission statement that is good for the customers, shareholders, employees, whales, and dolphins:

The mission of Wendy's is to deliver superior quality products and services for our customers and communities through leadership, innovation, and partnerships.

Don't get me wrong. I love Wendy's, but I've never thought I was participating in "leadership, innovation, and partnerships" when I ordered a hamburger there. I have given up on trying to get people to create short, different, and meaningful mission statements, so go ahead and spend the $25,000 for the offsite, facilitator, and consultants to create one. However, you should also create a mantra for your organization. A mantra is three or four words long—tops. Its purpose is to help employees truly understand why the organization exists.

If I were the CEO of Wendy's, I would establish a corporate mantra of "healthy fast food." End of story. Here are more examples of corporate mantras to inspire you:

- Federal Express: "Peace of mind"
- Nike: "Authentic athletic performance"
- Target: "Democratize design"
- Mary Kay: "Enriching women's lives"
- eBay: "Democratize ecommerce"

The ultimate test for a mantra (or mission statement) is whether your telephone operators can tell you what it is. If they can, then you're on to something meaningful and memorable. If they can't, then, well, it sucks.

If you still insist on doing a mission statement, then at least let me help you save a lot of time and money. Just Google "Dilbert Mission Statement Generator." There, without a consultant, facilitator, and offsite, you can get the mission statement of your dreams. Meanwhile, you still need a mantra, so get to it.

The Reality of Raising Money

The closest real-world analogy to raising money, whether you are seeking it from venture capitalists, angel investors, or the three Fs (friends, fools, and family), is speed dating. That's right: In five minutes, people decide if they are interested in you, just as in bars and nightclubs. This isn't right, and it isn't fair, but it's reality.

[CHAPTER 6]

The Investor Wish List

FINANCE, n. The art or science of managing revenues
and resources for the best advantage of the manager.

~ AMBROSE BIERCE

You may never try to raise money from a venture capitalist, but unless you're a trust-fund brat, you'll probably have to raise money
from someone to fund a business. Two pieces of advice before you
begin:

- First, don't confuse fundability with viability. Only a few thousand companies a year raise venture capital. These companies are "fundable" in the
sense that they have fooled a venture capitalist into believing that they can
achieve sales of at least $100 million per year within five years. Thousands
of other companies failed this fundability test—or, more likely, didn't bother
trying to raise venture capital.

  Many of these companies are perfectly viable; they simply aren't fundable, because they probably won't achieve sales of $100 million/year, which
is what venture capitalists are looking for. This applies to restaurants, book-
stores, consultancies, blogs, and design firms. Venture capitalists are trying
to fund the next Google, Apple, Microsoft, Cisco, and YouTube. Venture
capitalists are not trying to help you build a nice $10 million business.
However, angels, friends, fools, and family might think this a whopping
success.

- Second, don't ask any potential investor to sign a nondisclosure agreement (NDA), because asking them to do so will make you look clueless. Venture capitalists and angel investors are often looking at three or four similar deals, so if they sign an NDA from one company and then fund another, they expose themselves to legal action.

  I've never heard of a venture capitalist or angel investor ripping off an idea—frankly, few ideas are worth stealing. Even if your idea is worth stealing, the hard part is implementing the idea, not coming up with it. Finally, continuing the dating analogy, if the first thing out of your mouth is "Will you sign a prenuptial?" you probably won't get very many dates.

These are the characteristics of an attractive and fundable "date" for a venture capitalist or angel investor.

- **Realness.** This seems like a "duh-ism," but few entrepreneurs do it. Most entrepreneurs focus on quick flips to an IPO or acquisition. Don't get me wrong: Venture capitalists and other investors aren't necessarily good guys who want to make meaning and change the world. A simpler explanation is that entrepreneurs who make meaning and change the world usually also make money. Nothing is more seductive to venture capitalists than a company that may have a big impact on the world.

- **Traction.** The easiest way to prove that you have a real business is to already generate revenue. It's one thing to believe your bull-shiitake pitch; it's another to have customers and cash flow. You show traction, and investors will suspend disbelief. Fundamentally, you're asking them to take a leap of faith, and it's easier to get people to jump off a diving board than the Golden Gate Bridge. If you can't show traction, then at least line up customer references who will really say, "If they build this, we'll buy it."

- **Cleanliness.** Investors are busy, so you need to present a clean deal to them. "Clean" means that there isn't a lawsuit by your former employer contesting the ownership of the intellectual property, or a disgruntled founder who owns 25 percent of the company but doesn't do anything but sit around and complain. The more crap that an investor has to clean up, the less likely he'll be interested in your deal.

- **Forthrightness.** If you have crap that you simply cannot clean up, then disclose it right away—not necessarily in the first meeting, but soon thereafter. Also, have a plan ready to fix the problems. The worst thing you can do to an investor is surprise her with bad news, like a messy deal with lawsuits and conflicts beneath the surface of the company.

- **Enemies.** Woe unto you who claims that there is no competition. It means you're clueless or pursuing a market that doesn't exist. Investors like to see some competition because it validates that a market exists. Then it's your problem to explain why you have an unfair advantage. If you truly have no competition (and I doubt it), then either say that Microsoft or Google might go after you because these companies want it all or provide potential competitive threats.

In everything that you say, ensure that your results exceed expectations. Deliver a prototype early. Deliver your list of references early. Sign up your first customers early. Close a partnership deal early. Launch early. The only thing you shouldn't do early is run out of money.

CHAPTER 7

The Art of Getting the Attention of Investors

Have you ever observed that we pay much more attention to a wise passage when it is quoted than when we read it in the original author?

~ PHILIP G. HAMERTON

E ven if you fulfill the investor wish list, don't be naïve: Investors will not beat a path to your door. These deals are sold—not bought—but they are sold through indirect and informal paths. This chapter explains how to attract the attention of investors.

The Art of the Introduction

An old boss once told me that public relations is better than advertising because advertising is when you talk about how good you are and public relations is when other people talk about how good you are. The public-relations approach is the key to getting the attention of investors, because they want to hear from others about a hot new company, not from the founders of the company itself. This is the art of the introduction.

- **Ensure that your company is in the right market.** No matter how you get to the investor, make sure that she is the right one for you. For example, if you have the cure for cancer, contacting a firm's enterprise software guru isn't the brightest idea, so get on the Web and do your homework so that you are targeting the right venture capitalists.

- **Get an introduction by a partner-level lawyer.** Next, ask your lawyer for help. He should work at a firm that does a lot of financings, like my buddies at Wilson, Sonsini, Goodrich, and Rosati. Best case e-mail/voice mail: "This is the most interesting company I've seen in my twenty years of legal work for startups." Investors dream about calls like this—it's the equivalent of a scoring shot that knocks the goalie's water bottle off the top shelf.

  Incidentally, this is part of the reason why you should pay top dollar and use a well-known corporate finance attorney instead of Uncle Joe the divorce lawyer (even if he handles many investors' divorces). You're paying for connections, not only expertise.

- **Get an introduction by a professor of engineering.** Best case e-mail/voice mail: "These students are the smartest ones I've ever had in twenty years of teaching computer science. Larry and Sergei would have carried their backpacks for them." Arguably this is better than the lawyer's call if the school, like Stanford, has a history of engineering students starting successful companies.

- **Get an introduction by an executive of a company in the investor's portfolio.** Best case e-mail/voice mail: "My buddies are starting a new company, and I think it's really cool." Obviously, it would help if the company is a successful one. A service like LinkedIn can help you find acquaintances in the investor's portfolio.

Suppose you can't get any of the introductions mentioned above. A compelling e-mail/voice mail would sound like this:

My buddy and I have been working in our garage, taking no pay, and with MySQL we built a site that is doubling in traffic every month. Right now, we're at 250,000 page views a day after thirty days.

With two sentences, you've shown that you can make a little bit of money go a long way, create a product that scales to large volume, get the word out to attract customers, and make these customers keep coming back. "Wow! Be still my heart. I need to learn more about these guys" is what most venture capitalists would think, and they'll ask you for an executive summary, which is the subject of the next chapter.

CHAPTER 8

The Art of Executive Summary

**Don't fear failure so much that you refuse to try new things.
The saddest summary of a life contains three descriptions:
could have, might have, and should have.**

~ UNKNOWN

Your executive summary is probably the most important document you will write for your company. You send it to the investor after the introduction in order to get a meeting and to determine if there is any investor interest. If it works, the potential investor will contact you to set up a meeting. The components of an effective executive summary are:

1. **Problem.** What pressing and important problem are you solving or opportunity are you addressing?

2. **Solution.** How are you solving this problem or tapping this opportunity?

3. **Business model.** Who are your customers and how will you make money?

4. **Underlying magic.** What makes your company special?

5. **Marketing and sales strategy.** What is your go-to-market strategy?

6. **Competition.** Whom do you compete with? What can you do that they can't? What can they do that you can't?

7. **Projections.** What are your financial projections for the next three years? What are key assumptions and metrics to achieve these projections?

8. **Team.** Who is on your team? Why are they special?

9. **Status and time line.** Where are you now and what are the major, close milestones?

Your executive summary should not exceed two pages in length because its purpose is to sell, not describe your company. Indeed, if it takes you more than two pages to sell your idea, your idea isn't very good. These are more recommendations to help you create a masterful executive summary:

- **Craft a compelling subject line.** Essentially, your subject line is your "pickup line." And like a good pickup line, it has to be different, interesting, and short. Writing "$100 million opportunity" to a venture capitalist is as common and effective as saying "I drive a Corvette" to an intelligent woman.

- **Do not attach a presentation.** Save your presentation for the face-to-face meeting. It probably sucks anyway, so you're only burying yourself if you attach it.

- **Do not use the word "patented" more than once.** No good venture capitalist believes that patents make a company defensible. They just want to learn (once) that there might be something worth patenting.

- **Do not claim that you're in a multi-billion-dollar market.** Isn't every company in a multi-billion-dollar market according to some study? I have yet to read an executive summary for a company that isn't in a market of this size.

- **Do not claim you'll create the fastest-growing company in the history of capitalism.** Most projections that I see are for companies that will grow faster than Google—and the entrepreneur is "being conservative." My advice is that it's better to be too low than too high, because if the investor likes your idea, he'll convince himself you can do more. If the investor doesn't like your idea, it doesn't matter what your projection is.

- **Do not brag about an MBA degree.** Most venture capitalists want to invest in hardcore engineers, not overhead—also known as MBAs. The MBAs can come later, so focus on engineering and sales experience, because in the beginning, all you need is someone to make a product and someone to sell it.

- **Do not try to create the illusion of scarcity.** Many entrepreneurs claim that "Sequoia is interested," thinking that this will scare a venture capitalist into investing immediately. Dream on. If Sequoia is interested, then you should take its money. If it isn't, the venture capitalist you're pitching will find out you're lying.

Stop reading for a bit in order to craft your executive summary. Spend a good couple of days on this, because your executive summary is the foundation of a successful fund-raising campaign. In the next chapter, we'll discuss the next step: how to make a pitch.

CHAPTER 9

The 10/20/30 Rule of Pitching

**Make sure you have finished speaking
before your audience has finished listening.**

— DOROTHY SARNOFF

I have a strange medical condition called Ménière's disease—don't worry, you cannot get it from reading my book. The symptoms of Ménière's are hearing loss, tinnitus (a constant ringing sound), and vertigo. There are many medical theories about its cause: too much salt, caffeine, or alcohol in one's diet, too much stress, and allergies.

However, I have another theory. As a venture capitalist, I have listened to hundreds of entrepreneurs pitch their companies. Most of these pitches are crap: sixty slides about a "patent pending," "first mover advantage," "all we have to do is get 1 percent of the people in China to buy our product" startup. These pitches are so lousy that I'm losing my hearing, there's a constant ringing in my ears, and every once in while the world starts spinning.

In order to prevent an epidemic of Ménière's in the venture-capital community, I am proselytizing the 10/20/30 Rule of PowerPoint. It's quite simple: A pitch should contain ten slides, last no more than twenty minutes, and use no font smaller than 30 points. This rule is applicable for any presentation to reach agreement: for example, raising capital, making a sale, or forming a partnership.

10 Slides

Ten is the optimal number of slides in a pitch because a normal human being cannot comprehend more than ten concepts in a meeting—and venture capitalists are at best normal and perhaps even a little attention deficient. The content of these slides is the same as the sections in your executive summary explained in the previous chapter, plus a title slide that contains your contact information.

20 Minutes

You should give your ten slides in twenty minutes. Sure, you have an hour time slot, but you're not using a Macintosh, so it will take forty minutes to make it work with the projector. Even if setup goes perfectly, people will arrive late and leave early. In a perfect world, you give your pitch in twenty minutes, and you have forty minutes left for discussion.

Your opening line is the most crucial part of the pitch. What should you say? First let me tell you what you shouldn't say and why.

You say:	Investor thinks:
"I'm bright and ambitious."	"That's a relief, because I usually invest in stupid and lazy people. Why are you wasting my time?"
"I'm a blue-sky thinker."	"You have no business model, and you don't know how to ship. Why are you wasting my time?"
"I don't know much about your firm, but I thought I'd contact you anyway."	"You're a lazy idiot—why are you wasting my time?"
"I love to think of new ways to solve problems."	"Is this a high school science fair? Why are you wasting my time?"
"I have lots of great ideas, but I have trouble figuring out which one to try. Let me tell you about a couple."	"I want to know which idea you're going to kill yourself trying to make successful, not which ideas have crossed your idle mind. Why are you wasting my time?"

You say:	Investor thinks:
"I've always wanted to be an entrepreneur."	"I've always wanted to be a professional golfer. So what if you always wanted to be an entrepreneur? Why are you wasting my time?"
"I'm sure you are aware of the growing need for security. Web 2.0, Open Source, whatever."	"If you're sure I'm aware, why are you telling me you're sure I'm aware? Why are you wasting my time?"
"If you sign an NDA, I'll tell you my idea."	"How can you not know that venture capitalists don't sign NDAs? Why are you wasting my time?"
"The last time I contacted you, I . . ."	"I'm going to fire my secretary for putting this clown on my calendar again. Why are you wasting my time?"
"My goal is to build a world-class company."	"How about you ship and sell the first copy before we talk about world-class anything? Why are you wasting my time?"

"This is what my company does . . ." is how you should begin. It's that simple. The goal is to get investors thinking about the potential of your company and the size of your market. They can't think about this if they don't know what you do. And they don't want to be your friend, mother, or psychiatrist until they understand what you do, so cut the crap and explain what you do.

30-Point Font

Many presentations that I see use a 12-point font. Entrepreneurs use a small font in order to jam as much text as possible on their slides; then they read them aloud. Unfortunately, as soon as investors realize that entrepreneurs are reading, they read ahead of them. The result is that entrepreneurs and investors are out of synch.

The reason people use a small font is twofold: First, they don't know their material well enough. Second, they think more text is more convincing. Total bozosity. Force yourself to use no font smaller than 30 points. This will make your presentations better, because it requires you to find and comprehend the most salient points. If "30 points" is too dogmatic, then I offer you an algorithm: Find out the age of the oldest person in your audience and divide it by two. That's your optimal font size.

Using Pitching Beyond Fund-raising

Consider yourself lucky if you never have to pitch investors for money. However, this doesn't mean that this chapter isn't relevant to you. Sometimes you will pitch for money. Sometimes you will pitch for a sale. Sometimes you will pitch to sign up a partner. Sometimes you will pitch to recruit an employee. For entrepreneurs, life's a pitch, so practice the 10/20/30 rule.

CHAPTER 10

The Top Ten Lies of Venture Capitalists

If you want to know what God thinks of money, just look at the people He gave it to.

~ DOROTHY PARKER

The goal of the next two chapters is to foster greater understanding between the investors and entrepreneurs. I debated whether to call this chapter the top ten lies of investors or of venture capitalists. I chose "venture capitalists" because they lie more often and are better at it. If you can handle their lies, you can handle any investor's.

1. **"I liked your company, but my partners didn't."** In other words, no. The venture capitalist who is saying this is telling you that he's the good guy, the smart guy, and the guy who gets it; the "others" didn't, so don't blame him. This is a cop-out; it's not that the other partners didn't like the deal as much as the sponsor wasn't a true believer. A true believer would get it done.

2. **"If you get a lead, we will follow."** In other words, no. As the old Japanese say, "If your aunt had balls, she'd be your uncle." She doesn't have balls, so it doesn't matter. The venture capitalist is saying, "We don't really believe, but if you can get Sequoia to lead, we'll jump on the pile." In other words, once you don't need more investors, the venture capitalist would be happy to invest. What you want to hear is, "If you can't get a lead, we will lead the deal." That's a believer.

3. **"Show us some traction, and we'll invest."** In other words, no. This lie translates to "I don't believe your story, but if you can prove it by achieving significant revenue, then you might convince me. However, I don't want to tell you no because I might be wrong, and by golly, you may sign up a *Fortune* 500 customer, and then I'd look like a total orifice." As opposed to bull shiitake, this is chicken shiitake.

4. **"We love to co-invest with other venture capitalists."** Like the sun rising and Canadians playing hockey, you can depend on the greed of venture capitalists. Greed in this business translates to "If this is a good deal, I want it all." What you want to hear is "We want the whole round. We don't want any other investors." Then it's your job to convince them why other investors can make the pie bigger instead of reconfiguring the slices.

5. **"We're investing in your team."** This is an incomplete statement. While it's true that they are investing in the team, you are hearing, "We won't fire you—why would we fire you if we invested because of you?" That's not what the venture capitalist is saying at all. What she is saying is, "We're investing in your team as long as things are going well, but if they go bad we will fire you because no one is indispensable."

6. **"I have lots of bandwidth to dedicate to your company."** Maybe the venture capitalist is talking about the data line into his office, but he's not talking about his personal calendar, because he's already on ten boards. Including board meetings, an entrepreneur should assume that a venture capitalist will spend five hours a month on your company. That's it. Deal with it and don't be fooled.

7. **"Do you mind if one of our associates accompanies me to your board meetings?"** This isn't a lie per se, and it looks like a harmless request. However, it isn't what you might delude yourself into thinking: "These guys are so interested in our company that they want two people helping us." If you agree to the request, your board meetings will become a training class for an MBA who knows nothing about running a company but will nevertheless be offering his learned opinion.

8. **"This is a vanilla term sheet."** There is no such thing as a vanilla term sheet. Do you think corporate finance attorneys are paid $500/hour to push out vanilla term sheets? If venture capitalists insist on using a flavor of ice cream to describe term sheets, the only flavor that works is rocky road. This is why entrepreneurs need their own $500/hour attorney, too— as opposed to Uncle Joe the divorce lawyer.

9. **"We can open up doors for you at our client companies."** This is a double whammy of a lie. First, a venture capitalist can't always open up doors at client companies, because the management of that company may hate him. The worst thing in the world is a referral from him. Second, even if the venture capitalist can open the door, you can't seriously expect the company to commit to your product—that is, something that isn't much more than a slick pitch.

10. **"We like early-stage investing."** Venture capitalists fantasize about putting $1 million into a $2 million premoney company and end up owning 33 percent of the next Google. That's early-stage investing. Do you know why we all know about Google's amazing return on investment? The same reason we all know about Michael Jordan: Googles and Michael Jordans hardly ever happen. If they were common, no one would write about them. If you scratch beneath the surface, venture capitalists want to invest in proven teams (for example, the founders of Cisco) with proven technology (for example, the basis of a Nobel Prize) in a proven market (for example, growing 30 percent per year) with no competition. They are remarkably risk averse, considering it's not even their money.

What should you do when you hear these lies? First, for lies 1, 2, and 3, when a venture capitalist is telling you no, you should move on. A venture capitalist is either performing due diligence (calling references, talking to your customers, and meeting more of your team), or she isn't interested. If she's not interested, don't waste your time or hers.

Second, for lies 4–10, understand that when a venture capitalist tells you what a wonderful, supportive investor she'll be, she's lying. Truly, she may not even realize she's lying, but she is. The game shouldn't work like this, but it does. And don't get self-righteous on me, because we're about to discuss the lies that you tell.

CHAPTER 11

The Top Eleven Lies of Entrepreneurs

> Delusions of grandeur make me
> feel a lot better about myself.
>
> ∼ JANE WAGNER

Entrepreneurs lie just as much as venture capitalists. The difference is that they often don't even know they are lying. This is a list of the most common lies of entrepreneurs. I provide them not to increase the level of honesty of entrepreneurs (that's wishful thinking) but to help you understand when you are lying and to help you come up with new lies. At least new lies indicate a modicum of creativity! Incidentally, just about every entrepreneur who pitches me tells at least four of these eleven lies.

1. **"Our projections are conservative."** An entrepreneur's projections are never conservative. If they were, they would be $0. I have never seen an entrepreneur achieve even her most conservative projections. Generally, an entrepreneur has no idea what sales will be, so she guesses: "Too little will make my deal uninteresting; too big, and I'll look delusional." The result is that everyone's projections are $50 million in year four. As a rule of thumb, when I see a projection, I add one year to delivery time and multiply by 10 percent.

2. **"(Big name company) is going to sign our purchase order next week."** This is the "I heard I have to show traction at a conference" lie of entrepreneurs. The funny thing is that next week, the purchase order still

isn't signed. Nor the week after. The decision maker transferred to a different department; the CEO got fired; or there's a natural disaster. The only way to play this card is *after* the purchase order is signed, because no investor whose money you'd want will fall for this one.

3. **"Key employees are set to join us as soon as we get funded."** More often than not when a venture capitalist calls these key employees, who are vice presidents at Microsoft, Oracle, and Sun, he gets the following response: "Who said that? I recall meeting him at a cocktail party, but I certainly didn't say I would leave my cushy $250,000/year job at Microsoft to join his startup." If it's true that key employees are ready to rock and roll, have them call the venture capitalist after the meeting and testify to this effect.

4. **"No one is doing what we're doing."** This is a bummer of a lie, because there are only two logical conclusions. First, no one else is doing this because there is no market for it. Second, the entrepreneur is so clueless that he can't even use Google to figure out he has competition. Suffice it to say that the lack of a market and cluelessness are not conducive to success. As a rule of thumb, if you have a good idea, five companies are doing the same thing. If you have a great idea, fifteen companies are doing the same thing.

5. **"No one else can do what we're doing."** If there's anything worse than the lack of a market and cluelessness, it's arrogance. No one else can do what you're doing until the first company does it, and ten others spring up in the next ninety days. Did anyone else run a sub-four-minute mile after Roger Bannister? (It took only a month before John Landy did.) The world is full of smart people, so you're kidding yourself if you think you have a monopoly on knowledge. And on the same day that you tell this lie, the investor met with another company that's doing the same thing.

6. **"Hurry, because several other venture capital firms are interested."** The good news: At any given time there are one hundred entrepreneurs in the world who can make this claim. The bad news: The fact that you are reading this book means you're not one of them. As my mother used to

say, "Never play Russian roulette with an Uzi." For the absolute cream of the crop, there is competition for a deal, and an entrepreneur can scare other investors to make a decision. The rest of us cannot create a sense of scarcity when it's not true.

7. **"Oracle is too big/dumb/slow to be a threat."** Larry Ellison has his own jet. He can keep the San Jose Airport open for his late-night landings. His boat is so big that it can barely get under the Golden Gate Bridge. Meanwhile, you're flying on Southwest out of Oakland and stealing the free peanuts. There's a reason why Larry is where he is and you are where you are, and it's not that he's big, dumb, and slow. Competing with Oracle, Microsoft, and other large companies is a very difficult task. Entrepreneurs who utter this lie look, at best, naïve. You think it's bravado, but venture capitalists think it's stupidity.

8. **"We have a proven management team."** Says who? Because the founder worked at Morgan Stanley for a summer? Or McKinsey for two years? Truly "proven" in a venture capitalist's eyes is founder of a company that returned billions to its investors. But if you were that proven, then you (a) probably wouldn't have to ask for money and (b) wouldn't be declaring that you're proven, because it would be obvious. A better strategy for you is to state that (a) you have relevant industry experience; (b) you are going to do whatever it takes to succeed; (c) you are going to surround herself with directors and advisers who are proven; and (d) you'll step aside whenever it becomes necessary. This is good enough for a venture capitalist who believes in what you're doing.

9. **"Patents make our product defensible."** The optimal number of times to use the P word in a presentation is one. Just once, say, "We have filed patents for what we are doing." Done. The second time you say it, venture capitalists begin to suspect that you are depending too much on patents for defensibility. The third time you say it, you are holding a sign above your head that says, "I am clueless." Sure, you should patent what you're doing—if for no other reason than to say it once in your presentation. But at the end of the day, patents are mostly good for impressing your parents.

You won't have the time or money to sue anyone with a pocket deep enough to be worth suing.

10. **"All we have to do is get 1 percent of the $x billion market."** There are two problems with this lie. First, no venture capitalist is interested in a company that is looking to get 1 percent of a market. They want their companies to face the wrath of the antitrust division of the Department of Justice. Second, it's also not that easy to get 1 percent of any market, so you look silly pretending that it is. Generally, it's much better for you to show a realistic appreciation of the difficulty of building a successful company.

What do investors do when they hear these lies? There are three kinds of investors. First, some investors are too dumb to know that they are lies. You should avoid them. Second, some understand that you're lying, but are so used to it that they don't care, because they are going to pass on your deal anyway. You should learn what you can from this investor and write off this meeting as a learning experience. Third, some confront you, because they are actively engaged in the meeting and can't stand being lied to. This is the investor that might invest and might even add value to your company.

Don't get me wrong: I'm not suggesting that you lie in order to see investor reactions. In the best case, you should tell no lies. Incidentally, telling a lie that you don't realize is a lie is still lying. At the very least, tell new lies. If nothing else, it will be a more interesting meeting.

CHAPTER 12

The Art of Raising Angel Capital

We shall find peace. We shall hear the angels,
we shall see the sky sparkling with diamonds.

~ ANTON CHEKHOV

Venture capitalists aren't the only source of capital. There is also a large and active group of angel investors. They do not work for firms but are investing their own money. Raising angel capital is not easier than raising venture capital—it's simply different. The reality is that there is an art to raising angel capital.

- **Ensure they are "accredited" investors.** "Accredited" is legalese for "rich enough to never get back a penny." You can get into big trouble for selling stock to the proverbial "little old lady in Florida," because the law protects investors from unscrupulous entrepreneurs. So get a good corporate finance attorney to advise you about the process of seeking investments from angels. If he doesn't know what "Reg D" is, get another attorney.

- **Make sure they're sophisticated investors.** The least desirable angel investor is a rich doctor or dentist—unless you're a life sciences entrepreneur. They will drive you crazy, because they read how Ram Shriram made gazillions of dollars as an early investor in Google, and they want to know when *you're* going public, too. Sophisticated angel investors have expertise and experience in your industry. Sure, you want their money, but you also want their knowledge.

- **Don't underestimate them.** Try to meet the standards of the venture capitalist wish list provided earlier in this section because the days of angel investors as "easy marks" are gone forever. You can have an early-stage company but not a dumb-ass company, and angels care as much about liquidity as venture capitalists—maybe even more, because they're investing their personal, after-tax money. Angels do not consider investments to be "charitable contributions"—well, no angel whose money you'd want, anyway.

- **Understand their motivation.** Typically, angel investors have a triple bottom line. First, they've made it, so now they want to pay back society by helping the next generation of entrepreneurs. Second, they want to stay current with technology and tinker with interesting products and technologies. Finally, they want to make money. Thus, they are often willing to invest in less proven, more risky deals to provide entrepreneurs with the ability to get to the next stage. I know many nice venture capitalists, but I cannot tell you that many of them are motivated by the desire to pay back society or garner intellectual stimulation.

- **Enable them to live vicariously.** More on angel motivation: One of the rewards of angel investing is the ability to live vicariously through an entrepreneur's efforts. That is, angels want to relive the thrills of entrepreneurship while avoiding the firing line. Thus, you should frequently seek their guidance, because they enjoy helping you. By contrast, most venture capitalists only get involved when things are going really well or really poorly.

- **Make your story comprehensible to a spouse.** The investment committee for many venture capitalists works like this: "You vote for my deal, and I'll vote for yours." That's not how an angel investor makes decisions, because an angel's investment committee consists of one person: a spouse. So if you've got a "client-server open-source OPML carrier-class enterprise software" product, you must make it comprehensible to the angel's spouse when he asks, "What are we going to invest $100,000 in?"

- **Sign up people they've heard of.** Angel investors are also motivated by the social aspect of investing with buddies in startups run by bright, young people who are changing the world. Even if the other investors are not buddies, investing side by side with well-known angels is quite attractive. If you get one of these guys or gals, you're likely to attract a whole flock of angels.

• **Be nice.** More so than venture capitalists, angel investors fall in love with entrepreneurs. Often, the entrepreneurs remind them of their sons or daughters—or fill the role of the sons or daughters they never had. By contrast, venture capitalists will often invest in a schmuck if the schmuck is a proven moneymaker. If you're seeking angel capital, then you're probably not proven, so you can't get away with acting like a schmuck.

For more information about angels, Google these terms: "Ron Conway" (investor in Google, PayPal, and Ask Jeeves), "Andy Bechtolsheim" (cofounder of Sun Microsystems, and the first investor in Google), and "Ram Shriram" (investor in Google, still on Google's board). These are the überangels of Silicon Valley, and reading about them will help you further understand angels.

Think optimistically: Maybe you'll raise money from angels, bootstrap yourself to profitability, and never need venture capital. Or maybe you'll raise money from angels, finish your product or service, gain customer traction, and then raise venture capital on much better terms. Both are good paths.

CHAPTER 13

The Inside Scoop on Venture Capital Law

So act that your principle of action might
safely be made a law for the whole world.

⁓ IMMANUEL KANT

L et's assume that all the e-mailing and pitching works, and you're moving along to getting the money. Now you need to understand the legal issues of fund-raising, and there is no better person to explain this to you than Fred Greguras, a partner at the law firm of K & L Gates. His past clients include BioMarker Pharmaceuticals, Excite, Kintana, and Speedera Networks. I've served on the boards of several companies for which he was legal counsel, so I can tell you that his advice is sound—and because you're reading it in this book, it's also much cheaper.

Q: Can I start a technology company in the same business as my current employer?

A: Working completely outside an employer's premises and not using an employer's trade secrets or other resources may not be enough to avoid a taint on your technology and intellectual property (IP) for the new business. Investors will examine the creation of IP very carefully in such a situation because they don't want to buy into a lawsuit. While California law favors employee mobility, it also protects employers in Labor Code Section 2870, which is part of most employee invention assignment and confidentiality agreements that you sign before you begin to work for a company.

Basically, 2870 states that an employee owns an invention that he or she developed entirely on his or her own time without using the employer's equipment, supplies, facilities, or trade-secret information, except for those inventions that either relate—at the time of conception or reduction to practice of the invention—to the employer's business or to the actual or demonstrably anticipated research or development of the employer, or result from any work performed by the employee for the employer.

The taint to the new business can come from a founder who is trying to continue work with his/her current employer while trying to create technology and IP for a new business or from a consultant who is moonlighting from a business in the same space. Some business sectors, such as electronic design automation (EDA) software, are notorious for litigation against departed employees who try to start a new business in the same space.

Q: When should I incorporate?

A: The first step in starting a business is to test the business concept with prospective customers and to look carefully at potential market size to see if there really is a business opportunity. Timing of incorporation will be driven by the need to document the founders' ownership of the business, to secure ownership of preexisting intellectual property, to enter into contracts with customers, to grant stock options, and to accept investment. You usually don't want to delay incorporating until just before a Series A financing round, because such timing could cause tax problems for founders who want to buy their shares at a nominal price compared to the valuation of the corporation at the time of the financing.

Q: Why don't I use a Limited Liability Company (LLC), because it is cheaper to start?

A: An LLC is often used for consulting and smaller businesses, but not often for an operating business that will seek venture capital. You can decide whether to be taxed as a corporation or partnership when your business organization is an LLC. Losses and gains of the business flow through to the shareholders' individual 1040 tax returns when taxed as a partnership. Venture capitalists won't invest in an LLC, you can't grant stock options to employees and other service providers in an LLC, and an LLC can't be acquired tax-free in a stock-acquisition exit.

Q: Why does everyone incorporate in Delaware?

A: I still see some entrepreneurs using California corporations because they want to keep their costs as low as possible. Delaware incorporation advantages are venture capitalist preference, ease of dealing with regulatory authorities, flexibility in the law (such as the number of board members), and more helpful precedent in corporate law. Disadvantages are the corporation being taxed by and subject to two states' regulatory requirements.

You can't avoid California taxes if the corporation is operating in California. California advantages are lower cost and being subject to only one state's regulatory requirements, if the corporation is operating there. One major disadvantage of using California is the difficulty of dealing with regulatory authorities on corporate filings in a financing or other situation when articles of incorporation need to be amended. If a business has been incorporated in California, the venture capitalists will often want it to be reincorporated in Delaware as part of a round of financing.

Q: Should we incorporate as an S corp or C corp?

A: "S corp" and "C corp" are tax statuses rather than a type of corporation you would form in California or Delaware. An S corporation is taxed like a partnership. Gains and losses flow through to the shareholders, so it can provide tax advantages if, for example, there is a long product-development period with significant expenses that would flow through to individual tax returns.

There are restrictions on the number (one hundred) and types of shareholders in an S corp. Shareholders must be U.S. citizens or residents, and natural persons, not entities. Also, while you can make a decision at the end of a calendar year to switch to a C corp, you can't decide to turn S corp status off whenever you want to. A preferred stock financing will terminate S corp status because an S corp may not have more than one class of shares outstanding.

Q: Should I incorporate offshore if my business will focus on China or India?

A: This decision is driven by the likely exit strategy and the type of investors most interested in your business. Exit alternatives such as an IPO on the Indian or Hong Kong stock exchanges are not possible if you are a U.S. corporation. Some global investors will invest only in an offshore corporation such as a Cayman Islands exempted company, while some domestic U.S. venture capitalists will still only invest in a U.S. corporation.

You can reincorporate from one state to another, i.e., California to Delaware, on a tax-free basis, but you can't reincorporate outside the United States without tax consequences. Reincorporation offshore almost always will cause the corporation to remain subject to U.S. taxes under Internal Revenue Code Section 7874. If you initially incorporate offshore, you can reincorporate into the United States on a tax-free basis, so if in doubt, start offshore at the outset.

Q: Can I have everyone in my startup be contractors or consultants ("1099 services") rather than employees?

A: Many startups label service providers as consultants rather than employees prior to a round of financing to try to avoid employer obligations such as income tax withholding and unemployment taxes. This status depends on facts, however, not a label in an agreement. The basic test is the degree of control over the individual.

If he/she is tightly supervised and on the company's premises during regular working hours, the individual is really an employee. It is very hard for a startup to properly structure a contractor relationship because of the way the company must operate. For example, many times the company provides a "contractor" with business cards identifying them in an employee position such as VP Sales, which is not the right thing to do legally but is what the company believes it needs to do to be successful.

Q: How can I grant stock options to employees and consultants?

A: Your startup should adopt a stock-option plan at the time of incorporation that satisfies federal and state tax and securities law requirements. In California, the plan is often referred to as a "25102(0) plan," based on the California Corporations Code provision. Adopting such a plan will enable the corporation to grant tax-favorable options ("incentive stock options") and avoid securities-law violations, because the plan will have a securities-law exemption under state and federal law. If the plan is not created in accordance with securities laws, granting an option to an employee or other service provider requires the individual to qualify for the same type of securities-law exemption as an investor ("accredited investor").

Q: How does the corporation obtain ownership of the technology and IP from each of the founders that was developed before we incorporated?

A: Founders will usually assign ownership of technology and IP as payment for their shares of common stock of the corporation. This is documented in their founders stock-purchase agreement. Investors will almost always want technology and IP to be a transfer of ownership rather than a license in which the founders hedge on their commitment to the new business. Ownership provides more value to the business than a mere license. Ownership of technology and IP created after the corporation is established occurs through invention-assignment agreements or consulting agreements.

Q: Can I hire people away from my former employer?

A: Your employee invention-assignment agreement with your former employer will likely have a restriction on soliciting employees, usually for a period of twelve months. The restriction usually doesn't cover unsolicited hiring of your former employer's employees, but proving who solicited whom may be difficult. Even if the nonsolicitation period has expired, you still need to be careful to make sure the new hire does not use trade secrets of your former employer while working for you.

Q: Can I file a provisional patent application myself?

A: You can, but you need to be very careful to describe the invention and the best mode of practice as required by patent law. A patent attorney may be needed to help draft "claims language," because of increasing litigation over whether a provisional application covered these elements. The provisional patent application must contain a written description of the invention and "of the manner and process of making and using it, in such full, clear, concise, and exact terms as to enable any person skilled in the art to which it pertains, or to which it is most nearly connected, to make and use the same."

Q: If we have been issued a patent, won't that stop a Microsoft from copying us?

A: You cannot enforce a patent unless and until it is issued, and the costs to enforce a patent can be staggering—literally millions of dollars. Whether someone is infringing your patent usually isn't a one or zero case. The other party may claim it is not infringing your patent or that your patent is invalid—for example, because it is based on a defective provisional application. There may be good arguments on both sides that require a court to make a decision after a lengthy and expensive trial.

Q: Shouldn't prospective investors sign nondisclosure agreements (NDAs) so that they don't rip off our ideas?

A: Venture capitalists won't sign NDAs before hearing your pitch because they see so many companies that may be in the same business segment and overlap in what they are doing. NDAs with investors' patent counsel are usually feasible later, during IP due diligence for a financing, for example, when investors' counsel needs to review an unpublished patent application. I recommend "peeling the onion" in making disclosures to investors and others whenever feasible. This means disclosing only as much as you need to for the purpose of the meeting. This isn't helpful in many businesses, such as Internet Web 2.0 companies, where what you are doing may be obvious.

Q: If my buddies and I own more than half of the corporation, don't we control it?

A: You may, if it is prior to venture capital financing and you also control the board of directors of the corporation. Both the board of directors and shareholders have a right to approve key decisions of the corporation. Board decisions are made on the basis of one person, one vote, rather than on a percentage of ownership, so you need to be careful with the size and composition of the board. The preferred stockholders in a venture capitalist financing will have what are called protective provisions, which give them veto rights over key decisions, like a new round of financing or selling the corporation without regard for their percentage of ownership of the corporation.

Q: Why should founders vest?—we've already been working on the business for two years.

A: Vesting among founders avoids the "free rider" problem, whereby a founder gets shares and then leaves the corporation, while the other founders continue to make contributions. I recommend vesting schedules whenever there is more than one founder, to try to make sure all founders continue to contribute. While the investors may renegotiate vesting schedules for founders at the time of a financing, providing some up-front vesting is appropriate when founders have been working on the business for a while. The balance is between maintaining the "stickiness" of the founder and recognizing prior contributions. I usually tell founders to err on the side of more stickiness.

Q: Why does it cost $50,000 or more to do a round of financing?

A: The corporation receiving investment pays the legal fees of both its own legal counsel and the investor's legal counsel. The total tends to be higher than $50,000 in most Series A financings because of the number and complexity of the financing documents and the rate structures of the large law firms that tend to represent both sides in these deals.

You can manage these costs to a certain extent by having a clear and complete financing term sheet that covers all key points. The business people on each side should address the tough issues (such as founders vesting and option-pool size) at the term-sheet stage and make decisions on such issues themselves rather than have lawyers argue over them and increase legal fees. A vague term sheet may avoid confrontation for the moment, but it is likely to cause larger legal fees.

Greguras has kindly answered the most common questions that entrepreneurs ask their attorneys—or that they don't ask their attorneys and later regret not asking. This chapter alone should pay for this book.

CHAPTER 14

The Top Sixteen Lies of Lawyers

Lawyers spend a great deal of their time shoveling smoke.

~ OLIVER WENDELL HOLMES JR.

Although I like Fred Greguras, lawyers lie as much as venture capitalists, entrepreneurs, CEOs, marketers, and engineers. No matter who the source is, lies are lies, and you need to understand exactly what's going on when you talk to your lawyers.

1. **"I'm really excited about what you are doing and will give your company my personal attention."** Once someone gets to the partner level, "making it rain" is as important as doing work. This is part of a standard sales pitch, so don't let it go to your head.

2. **"Our firm is really excited about what you're doing, so we'd like to invest in your company, too."** Also part of the standard sales pitch. Most firms invest in most of their startup clients—it's simply the law of big numbers: Invest in enough dumb ideas, and one will be a Google.

3. **"We can work on the billing so that you pay us when you get financed."** The final flattery in a good sales pitch. As with the others, don't think you're special. This is a standard offer.

4. **"I'll have that to you by the end of the day."** The important question to ask when you hear this is, "End of which day?" Because every day has an

end. And you should find out how your lawyer defines the end of the day: 6:00 P.M. or 11:59 P.M., today, tomorrow, or next week.

5. **"Don't worry about the date on that option grant; it's not a big deal."** Unless you enjoy getting indicted, you should run from a lawyer who utters such stupidity.

6. **"The bill would be lower if it weren't for the lawyers on the other side."** The lawyers on the other side are saying this about your lawyers, too.

7. **"I thought you were more interested in getting it right rather than saving a few dollars."** In other words, the legal bill for your Series A funding may exceed the amount of capital raised.

8. **"Your case is much stronger than theirs; I'm sure we can convince them to see things our way."** If your position is so strong, you don't need lawyers. It's when your position is weak that you need them. Also, your opponent is hearing the same thing about their case.

9. **"We have relationships at the highest level in Shanghai/Munich/ Mumbai/New York/Los Angeles."** In other words, someone from the firm once flew in first class to Shanghai/Munich/Mumbai/New York/Los Angeles with the vice premier's uncle's sister's nephew.

10. **"We'd much rather be on the company side than on the investor side."** Let me get this straight: You believe your lawyer would rather be on the side of two guys/gals in a garage who are raising $500,000 than on the side of a venture capital fund managing $500 million whose partners play golf at the same country club?

11. **"We usually don't bill the full retainer; it only happens if there are unforeseen issues that come up."** One of two things is happening: Either you've been sandbagged with an artificially high estimate or your lawyer just passed the bar.

12. **"Sure we're busy, but I'll make sure you don't get handed off to a green associate."** Translation: Your main contact passed the bar a year ago.

13. **"I've done work with Google/Microsoft/Apple, so I know how to structure deals with them."** Translation: "My favorite search engine is Google, which I use on my Windows laptop while I'm listening to my iPod."

14. **"We think you will have a very strong patent."** If you hear this, ask this question: "So if Microsoft infringes on our patent, we'd win the lawsuit?"

15. **"We know the opposing attorneys, so we'll be able to work out something quickly and cheaply."** There is no such thing as quickly and cheaply. There are only good and expensive, quick and lousy, and cheap and lousy. Pick one.

16. **"I can call several venture capitalists to help you secure funding."** Actually, you *should* select your lawyer as much for his connections to the venture capital community as for his legal expertise. However, take this very literally: He "can" call. This is different from "will" call.

We've now covered the triple crown of lying: how investors will lie to you, how you will lie to investors, and how your lawyer will lie to everyone. You probably found these lies amusing—as you should. You won't be laughing, though, when you are the victim of them, and this is no lie: That day will come.

CHAPTER 15

The Venture Capital Aptitude Test (VCAT)

**What is youth except a man or a woman
before it is ready or fit to be seen?**

~ EVELYN WAUGH

T his is the Guy Kawasaki Venture Capital Aptitude Test (VCAT). It has little to do with raising venture capital, but I created it because I get several e-mails a week along these lines:

I'm about to graduate from college, where I majored in economics. I've always been interested [what does "always" mean for a twentysomething?] in business and entrepreneurship, and I ran my school's entrepreneurship club. I've been working as an analyst for Goldman Sachs, and now I'd like to get into the venture capital business to further my understanding of entrepreneurship and to help startups achieve success by tapping into my knowledge base. I am adept with Facebook and other social networks.

These punks and punkettes see a wonderful job: going to cocktail parties and networking events, flying in private jets, and getting sucked up to by entrepreneurs while pulling down a base salary of $500,000/year plus a piece of the upside of selling a YouTube for $1.6 billion. Who wouldn't want such a job? (Frankly, I would, too.) Here's my advice to all the Biffs, Sebastians, Brooks, and Tiffanys who want to be kingmakers:

Venture capital is something to do at the end of your career, not the beginning. It should be your last job, not your first.

My theory is that when you're young, you should work eighty hours a week to create a product or service that changes the world. You should not sit in board meetings listening to an entrepreneur explaining why she missed her numbers while you read e-mail on a BlackBerry and intermittently spew forth gems like, "You should partner with MySpace; I can also introduce you to a few of the losers in our portfolio."

Furthermore, entrepreneurs should view any young person who opted for venture capital over real-world experience with suspicion. Why would you want advice from someone whose background consists of cranking spreadsheets at an investment bank? Thus, I crafted the Venture Capital Aptitude Test (VCAT) to provide a reality check for people who think they should be venture capitalists.

Part I: Work Background

What is your background?

1. Engineering (add 5 points)

2. Sales (add 5 points)

3. Management consulting (subtract 5 points)

4. Investment banking (subtract 5 points)

5. Accounting (subtract 5 points)

6. MBA (subtract 5 points)

The ideal venture capitalist has an engineering or sales background. Engineering is useful because it helps you understand the technology that you're investing in—for example, is the entrepreneur trying to defy the laws of physics? Sales is useful because every entrepreneur has to introduce a product and sell it.

The three worst backgrounds for a venture capitalist are management consulting, investment banking, and accounting. Management consulting is bad because it leads you to believe that implementation is easy and insights are hard, whereas the opposite is true in startups. Investment banking is bad because it leads you to believe that you can reduce a company to cells on a spreadsheet and that entrepreneurs should create companies for Wall Street, not customers. Moreover, investment bankers are oriented toward doing deals, not building companies. Accounting is bad because it leads you to believe that history not only repeats itself, it predicts the future.

Finally, there is the issue of the pertinence of an MBA to venture capital. The upside is that such a degree can provide additional tools and knowledge (such as calculating that 25 percent of $1.6 billion is $400 million) to help you make investment decisions and to assist entrepreneurs. The downside is that earning this degree (and I have one) causes most people to develop the hollow arrogance of someone who has never been tested. All told, the downside of an MBA outweighs the upside.

Part II: Firsthand Experience

You may have been in the right places, but you also need the right experiences in those places.

1. Have you been kicked in the groin by a major, long-lasting economic downturn, so that you know how powerless you are? (add 1 point)

2. Have you worked at a successful startup, so that you have firsthand experience with the ecstasy of entrepreneurship? (add 1 point)

3. Have you worked at a failed startup, so that you understand three things: first, how hard it is to achieve success; second, that the world doesn't owe you anything; and third, what it's like to be fired or laid off? (add 3 points)

4. Have you worked at a public company, so that you know what the end goal looks like, warts and all? (add 1 point)

5. Have you held a CEO position, so that you have this fantasy experience out of your system and will not try to run the startup from a board position? (add 2 points)

6. Have you made investments with your own money, so that you understand the fiduciary responsibility of investing other people's money? (add 2 points)

Part III: Necessary Knowledge

Do you know enough about building companies, and do you know the right people to really help entrepreneurs? Your answer is important because this is the kind of advice that entrepreneurs need. (Don't worry: Many current venture capitalists would fail this part.)

1. Do you know how to introduce a product with no budget? (add 2 points)

2. Do you know how to determine whether there's really a market demand for a product? (add 1 point)

3. Do you know what to do if customers hate the first version of a product? (add 1 point)

4. Do you know how to get Walt Mossberg to return a call? (add 2 points)

5. Do you know how to get to the folks who run DEMO? (add 1 point)

6. Do you know how to get a plug in TechCrunch? (add 1 point)

7. Do you know how to get the folks at Fox Interactive to return a call? (add 1 point)

8. Do you know how to dominate a segment when there are already five other companies offering similar products? (add 2 points)

9. Do you know how much time, energy, and money a company should spend on patent protection? (add 1 point)

10. Do you know what to do if a company bet on the wrong architecture for its product? (add 2 points)

11. Do you know what kind of people a startup should hire (young, old, unproven, proven, cheap, expensive, local, remote)? (add 1 point)

12. Do you know how to get them to leave their current jobs without throwing a lot of money at them? (add 2 points)

13. Do you know how to tell a best friend that he can't be chief technical officer just because he was a cofounder? (add 2 points)

14. Do you know how to get the buyer at Best Buy to return a call? (add 1 point)

15. Do you know how to handle a customer who wants to send back his purchase for a full refund? (add 1 point)

16. Do you know how to fire people? (add 2 points)

17. Do you know how to lay people off? (add 2 points)

Results

Here's how to assess your readiness to become a venture capitalist:

- 40 or more points: Call CalPERS and tell them you're raising a new fund.

- 35 to 39 points: Call Sequoia and Kleiner Perkins and tell them that you're available.

- 25 to 34 points: Send your résumé to 2,000 venture capitalists and pray.

- 24 points or less: Work until you can score higher and keep flying on Southwest Airlines.

When I published the VCAT in my blog, I received dozens of hate comments from venture capital associates who insisted that they added value to their clients and firms. That's when I first knew that the VCAT was an effective test.

The Reality of Planning and Executing

If you think that raising money was the hard part, you're in for a surprise. Raising money is easy and fun. The real work begins when you have to deliver the results that you promised. Execution separates great companies from great ideas. This section explains the reality of planning and executing.

CHAPTER 16

The Paradox of Strategy: How Apple Blew It and Microsoft Got Lucky

I get up every morning determined to both change
the world and have one hell of a good time.
Sometimes this makes planning my day difficult.

— E. B. WHITE

In the first half of my career, I thought that coming up with a great idea was the hard part and that implementation was the easy part. In the second half of my career, I've come to believe that the idea is the easy part and that implementation is the hard part. The purpose of this section of the book is to provide a reality check on implementation—that is, planning and then executing the plan.

Michael Raynor has a doctorate of business administration from Harvard and works for a big-name consulting firm, so I had to overcome several deep-seated prejudices to read his new book, *The Strategy Paradox: Why Committing to Success Leads to Failure (and What to Do About It)*. I'm glad that I did, because his book goes a long way in explaining how strategy makes or breaks a company. This interview with Raynor gives you a picture of how execution is messy, brutal, and perplexing.

Q: Why did Windows kick Macintosh's butt and VHS kick Beta's butt?

A: Apple continued along the path that it had blazed with the Apple II and the Macintosh: very cool, very high-performing products built around a proprietary architecture of hardware-software integration. This was a perfectly reasonable bet to continue, but it happened to be the wrong one in the personal computer market of the late 1980s. Even a broken clock is right twice a day, though statistically it is wrong more often than not. The iPod is Apple's latest hit, and it's more of the same: a cool device built around a proprietary architecture. Apple's clock hasn't changed; it still reads twelve o'clock. It's just that it happens to be noon again.

By contrast, Microsoft built a series of strategic options that positioned the company for success under a variety of different outcomes. Microsoft had what turned out to be a better strategy only because it didn't commit itself to a single strategy. For example, when IBM began aggressively creating a competitor to MS-DOS and Windows, OS/2, Microsoft collaborated with IBM. The Windows development effort is evidence of Microsoft's belief in GUI OSs, but Microsoft was also getting a foothold in applications development for GUI-based systems by writing Excel and Word for . . . Apple! Corporate customers seemed to think that UNIX had a promising future, and so Microsoft was investing in UNIX, too, even as it released new versions of the by then venerable menu-driven MS-DOS.

Sony, like Apple, similarly suffered the fate of a reasonable, but wrong, commitment. It positioned the Betamax as a high-fidelity video recording device for time-shifting broadcast TV programs. In contrast, Matsushita's VHS was a lower-performing, lower-cost device. Much to everyone's surprise, using VCRs to view rented movies turned out to be the "killer app," and recording fidelity became a secondary consideration.

Sony couldn't adapt by cutting costs and hence price because Matsushita was, by the mid-1980s, millions of units ahead of Sony on the VCR experience curve. Any move by Sony would have been easily countered. In other words, much as Apple had done in the PC market, Sony made a perfectly reasonable bet that turned out to be the wrong one. Matsushita didn't end up on the right end of this battle because it had a more strategically flexible stance than Sony as in the Microsoft/Apple case. Rather, Matsushita made a different bet that simply turned out to be the right one.

Q: So Apple and Sony didn't do anything wrong per se?

A: You could say that Apple's and Sony's strategies were great strategies that simply happened to fail. They failed not because of any shortcomings in the strategies, but because of shortcomings in each firm's ability to predict what sort of strategy would succeed. Trying harder to craft the perfect strategic moves won't work; companies need to more effectively manage the uncertainty that necessarily colors every strategic decision.

Q: What is the explanation for Toyota's success?

A: A big part of it was being well positioned for the oil crisis of the mid-1970s. Toyota was influenced by its origins in the Japanese market, where size and fuel economy mattered, and in the United States, it was focusing on the second-car market, where the need for low prices similarly rewarded smaller, more fuel-efficient cars. When the oil crisis hit, Toyota happened to have products that were much better suited to the suddenly changed environment.

As Louis Pasteur said, "Fortune favors the prepared mind," so this bit of luck would have been useless to Toyota if it made inferior cars. But of course customers quickly noted Toyota's vehicle quality. This reflected its tradition of manufacturing excellence, of defect and cost reduction and quality improvement, a system that is known today as the Toyota Production System, or TPS.

By the way, Toyota has been selling cars in the United States since the mid-1950s. They're number two and threatening to become number one [Toyota took the top spot less than a year after this interview], but it took fifty years. GM overtook Ford as the number one automaker in the early 1930s, less than twenty years after Alfred Sloan created GM. Toyota's accomplishment is remarkable, but it took a long time.

Q: You make it sound confusing: damned if you do, damned if you don't— what's a company to do?

A: This is what I call the strategy paradox. That is, the same strategies that have the highest probability of extreme success also have the highest probability of extreme failure. In other words, everything we know about the linkage between strategy and success is true, but dangerously incomplete. Vision, commitment, focus . . . these are all in fact the defining elements of successful strategies, but they are also systematically connected with some of the greatest strategic disasters.

For example, Apple's strategy sometimes works great, and sometimes fails miserably. It's not that Apple sometimes "forgets" what makes for greatness. It's that what makes for greatness also exposes you to catastrophe. The same goes for Sony.

To succeed, vision, commitment, and focus must be linked to an accurate view of what lies ahead, and nobody can adequately predict the future. If you can guess right on a regular basis, my hat's off to you . . . and can I buy your stock? But no one—no one—has any legitimate claim to an ability to make predictions relevant to true strategic planning.

Q: Why can't companies predict the future better?

A: Companies might be able to predict the future better than they can now, but for me the question is whether they will ever be able to predict the relevant future accurately enough for the purposes of strategic planning and avoid, or at least mitigate, the strategy paradox. I don't think that's going to happen anytime soon, for some deep, structural reasons—for example, randomness.

Prediction requires the identification of a pattern that repeats, because a pattern is what allows you to use what has happened to infer what will happen next. Randomness is the enemy of pattern-based prediction because randomness means that there is no pattern, no way to use the past to predict the future.

In *A New Kind of Science* (Wolfram Media, 2002), Stephen Wolfram identifies three sources of randomness, the first two of which are relevant here. First, any system must have boundaries that define it, because any system without boundaries would be the universe itself. Second, no system is entirely closed. Therefore, every system is subject to exogenous, and necessarily unpredictable, shocks that introduce randomness into it. And if you keep on expanding the boundaries to encompass the various externalities, you will need a theory of everything to have a theory of anything.

Q: But what if there was a system that was self-contained and orderly?

A: Unless we can specify the initial conditions precisely enough, we cannot exploit that orderliness for the purposes of prediction. The problem is that we never really know what counts as "initial." Exogenous shocks make it impossible to know where to stop defining a system, and sensitivity to initial conditions makes it impossible to know where to start.

Q: What's the proper role in strategy formation for each level in a hierarchy?

A: I've found that it helps to think about strategy in two halves: the commitments that all successful strategies entail, and the uncertainties attendant to those commitments. Commitments and uncertainties are only half the answer. The rest of the solution lies in calibrating the focus of each level of the hierarchy to the uncertainties it faces. It is common sense—if not common practice—that the more senior levels of a hierarchy should be focused on longer time horizons. What hasn't been as widely recognized is that with longer time horizons come greater levels of uncertainty, and strategic uncertainty in particular. This fact has some profound implications for how each level in an organization should act.

Board members should ask: What is the appropriate level of strategic risk for a firm to take? What resources should be devoted to mitigating risk? What sacrifices in performance are acceptable in exchange for lower strategic risk? This allows the board to be involved in strategy without getting involved in strategy making, which is correctly the purview of the senior management team.

CEOs should ask: What strategic uncertainties does the company face? What strategic options are needed to cope with those uncertainties? In other words, it falls to the CEO, and the rest of the senior team, to find ways to create the strategic-risk profile the board has mandated for the firm.

Divisional or business-unit vice presidents should ask: What commitments should we make in order to achieve our performance targets? For these folks, it's no longer about mitigating strategic risks, but making strategic commitments. Someone has to take the actions that create wealth, after all.

Managers should ask: How can we best execute the commitments that have been made in order to achieve our performance targets? To put it on a bumper sticker, they have to "show us the money." There are no strategic choices to make at this level, because the time horizons are too short—six to twenty-four months. Strategies simply can't change that fast.

Q: How does your answer change with respect to a startup?

A: Startups tend to be enormously resource constrained. Typically they are not able to devote money and time to the problems of strategic uncertainty. As a result, startups tend to be "bet the farm" propositions: high risk, with the potential of high reward. Such firms don't manage strategic risk—they accept it.

Q: Are you saying that by definition a startup is resource constrained, so it should/has to bet the farm on one approach?

A: The degree to which you manage risk will be a function of your ability to bear risk and recover from setbacks. On the continuum from the archetypal two people in a garage to Johnson & Johnson, I take the counterintuitive view that startups are much better able to bear risk: If the venture fails, the people and other resources involved are typically far more easily redeployed than is the case with large corporations.

Q: So if a startup fails for other than poor execution and implementation, it's OK because betting the farm is the way to go?

A: I wouldn't go that far. There is always room for thinking carefully about the risk you face and how to mitigate it effectively. You've suggested, for instance, that startups can think about betting on sectors, or customers, then trying to adapt their products, or betting on products, then adapting things like marketing or distribution to find the right customers. Either approach involves a core bet and a series of options on contingencies. Which approach makes the most sense will be a function of the risk involved and the cost of mitigating it.

Q: So startups are wrong to simply accept strategic risk?

A: Although accepting strategic risk is not necessarily bad, it can be unwise to just accept it without doing your homework first. It's possible to go to the opposite extreme and squander resources on multiple investments that are styled as strategic options, only to find that they actually undermine your primary strategy without securing the desired options. The common problem is not adequately assessing your firm's risk profile and shaping it appropriately.

This is what I learned from this interview. First, I'm not so smart if a company that I invest in succeeds. Second, I'm not so dumb if a company that I invest in fails. Third, you take your best shot at analysis, place your bet on the table, work your ass off, and don't look back. That's how you build a great company.

CHAPTER 17

The Zen of Business Plans

Plans are worthless, but planning is everything.

~ DWIGHT D. EISENHOWER

Before you dedicate your life to crafting a business plan the length of a book, read this quotation from an article called "Enterprise: Do Start-ups Really Need Formal Business Plans" (*Wall Street Journal,* January 9, 2007):

> A study recently released by Babson College analyzed 116 businesses started by alumni who graduated between 1985 and 2003. Comparing success measures such as annual revenue, employee numbers and net income, the study found no statistical difference in success between those businesses started with formal written plans and those without them. . . .

"What we really don't want to do is literally spend a year or more essentially writing a business plan without knowing we have actual customers," says the author of the study, William Bygrave of Babson College. He advocates that entrepreneurs "just do it." He also cautions that entrepreneurs are apt to stick with a flawed plan they spent months drafting.

Don't conclude from this study that analysis, planning, vision, communication, and teamwork are not necessary. This isn't true. What is true is that a business plan should not take on a life of its own. It is a tool but not an end in itself. In order to effectively write a business plan, you now need to learn the Zen of writing business plans.

- **Focus on the executive summary.** The executive summary, all one or two pages of it, is the most important part of a business plan. If it isn't fantastic, eyeball sucking, and pulse altering, investors won't read beyond it to find out who's on your great team, what your business model is, and why your product is curve jumping, paradigm shifting, and revolutionary. Even if the plan is purely for internal use, you should still spend 80 percent of your effort on writing a great executive summary. Most people spend 80 percent of their effort crafting a one-million-cell Excel spreadsheet that no one understands, much less believes.

- **Write for all the right reasons.** Most people write business plans to attract investors, and while this is necessary to raise money, most venture capitalists make a gut-level go or no-go decision during pitch. Receiving (and possibly reading) the business plan is a mechanical step in due diligence. The more relevant and important reason to write a business plan, even if you're not raising money, is to force the management team to solidify the objectives (what), strategies (how), and tactics (when, where, who).

- **Make it a solo effort.** While creation of the business plan should be a group effort involving the management of a company, one person, ideally the CEO, should do the actual writing of the plan. Take it from an author, it's very difficult to cut, copy, and paste several people's sections and come out with a coherent document.

- **Pitch, then plan.** Most people create a business plan, and it's a piece of crap: sixty pages long, fifty-page appendix, full of buzzwords, acronyms, and superficialities like "All we need is 1 percent of the market." Then they create a pitch from it. The correct sequence is to perfect a pitch and then write the plan from it. A good business plan is an elaboration of a good pitch; a good pitch is not the distillation of a good business plan. Why? Because it's much easier to revise a pitch than to revise a plan. Give the pitch a few times, see what works and what doesn't, change the pitch, and then write the plan. Think of your pitch as your outline and your plan as the full text. How many people write the full text and then the outline?

- **Keep it clean.** The ideal length of a business plan is twenty pages or less, and this includes the appendix. When it comes to business plans, less is more. For every ten pages over twenty pages, you decrease the likelihood that the plan will be read, much less funded, by 25 percent. Many people believe that the purpose of a business plan is to shock and awe investors into begging for wiring instructions. The reality is that the purpose of a business plan is to get to the next step: continued due diligence with activities such as checking personal and customer references. The tighter the thinking, the shorter the plan; the shorter the plan, the faster people will finish reading it.

- **Limit yourself to a one-page financial projection plus key metrics.** Many business plans contain five-year projections with a $100 million top line and such minute levels of detail that the budget for pencils is a line item. Everyone knows that you're pulling numbers out of the air. Do everyone a favor: Reduce your Excel delusions to one page and provide a forecast of the key metrics of your business—for example, the number of paying customers. These key metrics provide insight into your assumptions. For example, if you're assuming that you'll get 20 percent of the *Fortune* 500 to buy your product in the first year, I would suggest checking into a rehab program.

- **Write deliberate, act emergent.** I borrowed this from my buddy Clayton Christensen, the author of *The Innovator's Dilemma* (Harvard Business School Press, 1997). It means that when you write your plan, you act as if you know exactly what you're going to do. You are deliberate. You're probably wrong, but you take your best shot. However, writing deliberate doesn't mean that you adhere to the plan in the face of new information and new opportunities. As you execute the plan, you act emergent—that is, you are flexible and fast moving, changing as you learn more and more about the market.

Here are your marching orders. Take your pitch and give yourself one week to write a plan from it. Consult with your team as you write it (you'll find how different your perspectives of the business are). Consider it a working document, and don't let it run your business. If you do these things, you'll have a better business plan than 90 percent of your competitors.

CHAPTER 18

The Art of Financial Projections

Finance is the art of passing currency from hand to hand until it finally disappears.

∼ ROBERT W. SARNOFF

Most entrepreneurs struggle with the financial projection part of a business plan. If they're providing the plan to investors, they want to show that their business is interesting, if not the next Google. Even if the plan is for internal use, you still want employees to have a challenging but achievable goal. Truly, crafting a projection is an art, and these tips will help you master this art.

1. **Underpromise and overdeliver.** I have never seen a company meet or exceed its initial forecast. Entrepreneurs come up with numbers that they guess investors want to hear, and everything goes downhill from there. As a rule of thumb, dividing sales forecasts by one hundred and adding one year to the projected shipping date is about right for startups without a prototype. For startups with a prototype, dividing by ten and adding six months is about right.

2. **Forecast from the bottom up.** Figure out how many business development and sales meetings you can get per week—that is, four or five. Then multiply this number by the percentage that will be successful. Then add six months to close the deal. This forecasting method yields a much

smaller number than the "conservative" method of assuming that you can get at least 1 percent market share.

Once you're done with the plan, show it to the rest of the management team and demand honest feedback. This is the only way to make a bottom-up plan truly bottom-up. Don't let anyone make the company sign up for a plan that isn't achievable with at least 80 percent certainty.

3. **Don't go beyond twelve to eighteen months.** Anything beyond that is a waste of everyone's time, because you really don't know when you'll ship, and you can only fantasize about customer adoption. If you're into five-year forecasts, go to work for a nice consumer packaged-goods company that's been around for fifty years.

4. **Reforecast every three months.** Otherwise, forecasting is a joke: You get approval for an annual budget and then reforecast it in the following board meeting. It's better to know that reforecasting is necessary once a quarter than to pretend that "this time we got it right."

   However, there is a danger in the rolling three-month forecast: Employees will start to believe that investors don't mind constant shortfall (I hope you're not this clueless). In a startup, everything is "near term," or in the long term the company will die.

5. **Don't let costs get in front of revenue.** I know, I know: Your startup is going to be the fastest-growing company in history, so you need to build an infrastructure to support the onslaught of customers. Dream on. Always run leaner than you think is necessary, because your challenge will be *creating* demand, not fulfilling it. Just once in my career, I would like to hear, "We ran too lean and sacrificed growth" instead of what I hear all the time: "Costs got ahead of revenue, so we need to cut back, but we'd prefer that you just give us more money because it will harm morale to lay people off."

6. **Collaborate with your investors.** It's just plain dumb to show your fantasy forecast to investors for the first time at a board meeting. You should feel them out in advance, and never get in the position of guessing what

you think they want to see. Collaboration is especially important if you have bad news. Surprising investors with good news is never a problem.

7. **Think in terms of per-unit profitability.** It may be acceptable to lose money on every unit for a time, but at some point you have to make money on every unit. And don't count on a big company buying you out, because "getting lucky" is not a viable strategy. Also, you need to know exactly how much you're losing on every unit so that you can measure progress toward profitability.

8. **Plan for marketing costs.** Don't depend on wishful-thinking marketing based on virality, buzz, TechCrunch, and DEMO. It's true that some companies do achieve success this way, but we've heard of them because they are few and far between. To use a sports analogy, we all know who Michael Jordan and Wayne Gretzky are because they are rare examples, not because their story is common.

   You need to explain your demand-creation process in a mechanical, not magical, way: ad rates, click-through rates, unique visitors per month, conversion rates, revenue per customer, etc. Ultimately, the underlying assumptions in your marketing model are the key to the fundability and viability of your startup.

9. **Create a one-page report and stick to it.** It seems as though thirty minutes of most board meetings are spent explaining a new way to report revenues, costs, and metrics. You would think that you could pick a few numbers that indicate what's happening at the startup and see the historical trends—but not if you change reporting methods every month. One innovative way to fix this might be to reduce the CEO's and CFO's stock options by 10 percent every time they change the report.

   You'll impress investors if you present your projections and your results in the same format. For example, if you use QuickBooks categories for your general ledger, then use these same categories for your projections. The good news is that your numbers will be much easier to understand; the bad news is that you'll be a lot more accountable.

   Finally, you'll astound investors if you show up with what's called a

Waterfall Forecast, a report that shows how your forecast changed over time. (Google "waterfall forecast" to find more details.) If you force yourself to show when your revenue forecasts are slipping but your costs aren't, you'll be a much stronger company.

10. **Never miss a cost projection.** It's relatively OK to miss a revenue projection because sales forecasting for a startup is truly a crapshoot. If you miss a cost projection, however, then you're entering the realm of cluelessness. There is no excuse for it, barring an act of God, like a factory burning down that produces the raw material you need. Even then, you should have had a backup source.

And you thought financial projections require a spreadsheet jock. I hope you understand why this is wrong. Truly, strategic management decisions and the communication of these decisions to all employees determine the quality of financial projections—not the ability of a finance type to crank a spreadsheet.

Incidentally, while writing this chapter, I used a book by Bob Prosen called *Kiss Theory Good Bye: Five Proven Ways to Get Extraordinary Results in Any Company* (Gold Pen Publishing, 2006). It's a very helpful resource if you're interested in this topic.

CHAPTER 19

Financial Models for Underachievers

We didn't actually overspend our budget.
The allocation simply fell short of our expenditure.

~ KEITH DAVIS

Glenn Kelman of Redfin decided to bare his financial soul so that other entre-
preneurs could get greater insight into the witchcraft called financial modeling.
In this chapter, he reveals his numbers and his lessons in 2007. By the time you
read this, who knows what market conditions will be, but the difference between
budget and real is instructive.

Part I: Numbers

Startups face one primary challenge: to never run out of cash. So when projecting costs, we heeded Guy's advice that "the three most powerful words you can utter at a board meeting are 'We beat projections.'" This convinced us to develop the worst possible financial model that could still be used to raise money.

We're glad we did. True underachievers, we've performed at or just a bit better than this worst-case plan almost every month, raising revenue projections only when forced to in December 2006. We've been able to stick to our plan mostly because absurd assumptions in opposite directions canceled one another out. As the real estate market tanks, we may not be so lucky in the future.

When first putting together our financial model, we looked online to calibrate spending assumptions. So many people have blown venture capital that we thought there must be a manual somewhere on how to do it, at what rate, avoiding which follies. We couldn't find anything. So we took some wild guesses and figured we'd see how they turned out. And now, two years later to the day since we built our first model, here are the projections and actual results. I hope you can learn from our experiences.

Rent per Employee per Month: Redfin Model, $250; Actual Redfin Cost (Last Month), $336

Our actual costs are high because last month we moved into an office with room to grow, which seems to happen every eighteen months. When people were sitting in hallways at the old space, we were paying about $200 per employee per month. Class B space on well-traveled mass-transit lines is roughly $20 per square foot per year in Seattle, $30 in the Bay Area. You need 165–200 square feet per person or more.

At the extremes, Adobe supposedly allocates 435 square feet per person, while Yahoo! allocates 220 square feet per person. The startup cult of cramming people into small spaces is counterproductive: People are what's really expensive, not space. The cost Redfin really didn't anticipate was for tenant improvements, which you mostly have to fund yourself when signing sub-three-year leases. In September, we spent more than $100,000 to add private offices for our engineers in the hope that our current office will last us longer. It was probably too much money.

Initial Equipment Cost per Employee: Redfin Model, $6,500; Actual Redfin Cost: $5,700

Computers, 20-inch monitors, IKEA desk, decent chair, VOIP telephone, and cell phones for field employees. Our first phone system came from craigslist, and we had to upgrade after a year.

Monthly Benefits, per Employee: Redfin Model, $600;
Actual Redfin Cost, $471

Redfin benefits are competitive, but many employees are Seattle-based. Costs are 10 percent higher in California.

Annual Payroll Tax: Redfin Model, 12.5%;
Actual Redfin Percentage: 8.5%

We added 4 percent to our plan here, just to pad costs per employee. In ways you can't anticipate, people cost money. Payroll taxes aren't the same nationwide. California's state payroll tax is, for example, negligible.

Quarterly Bonus Payout, as a Percentage of the Total Possible:
Redfin Model, 85%; Actual Redfin Cost: ~85%

We pay quarterly bonuses, mostly based on customer satisfaction objectives. Maintaining discipline on bonus payouts has been difficult. When business booms, everyone wants to be paid for it, even if you haven't yet turned a profit.

Annual Payroll Increase for Existing Employees: Redfin Model, 6%;
Actual Redfin Cost, "not available"

We can't disclose actual costs here, but they were higher than planned. When we set the plan, many employees were being paid below-market rates, which is not uncommon for startups; as a startup raises more capital and people go into their second year of sucking it up, you have to pay the piper at the employees' annual review.

Percentage of Candidates for Whom Redfin Paid a Recruiting Fee:
Redfin Model, 35%; Actual Redfin Percentage, 20%

If you can't build an engineering team through your own network, recruiting fees can become a significant expense at an early stage. Most of the folks

Redfin paid a recruiting fee to hire still came through our own employees, who got a $2,000 bonus for every recruit they brought on board.

I assumed colleagues would encourage friends to apply to Redfin without a fee, but for $2,000, people start nagging their cousin's friend's wife to apply. We saw an immediate increase in candidates. The occasional party, done on the cheap with kegs and pizza, has also worked well for us.

For Employees Recruited for a Fee, the Recruiting Fee as a Percentage of Annual Salary: Redfin Model, 20%; Actual Redfin Percentage, 4.5%

Because we want top-of-the-stack candidates, we do pay 20 percent to professional headhunters, but most recruits only required a $2,000 employee referral bonus. We've also experimented with in-house recruiters working on an hourly wage, but they tend to focus on managing the hiring process rather than adding candidates to the pipeline.

What really wrecks the budget is a retained search for executives ($30,000–$50,000), a cost we didn't even include in our calculations above. A retained search, an agreement to work exclusively with one search firm, is reasonable, but we recommend negotiating aggressively to defer most payment until placement.

Incremental Amount Paid to Contractors, as Percentage of Payroll: Redfin Model, 5%; Actual Redfin Percentage, 3%

Our contractors have mostly been an in-house recruiter, a graphic designer, and a Web programmer—no big-shot consultants.

Monthly Travel Costs per Field Employee: Redfin Model, $300; Actual Redfin Cost, $369

The $369 includes mileage for field agents who drive clients to listings, as well as travel between our San Francisco and Seattle engineering offices. Your costs may be lower. Or not: On the road, some of us still stay with friends.

Monthly Telephone Costs per Field Employee: Redfin Model, $125; Actual Redfin Cost, $261

We've started equipping real estate agents with cellular modems, so costs are unusually high here, too.

Monthly Legal Costs: Redfin Model, $12,500; Actual Redfin Cost, $9,406

The $9,406 per month excludes legal costs for a round of financing, usually about $50,000 for company counsel and investors' counsel (more in late stage, less in early stage). We have saved money by dividing the monthly work between a more expensive tech-focused firm (Orrick, very good) for board resolutions, minutes, and stock administration and a general corporate practice (Lasher, also quite good) for employment and real estate law.

We also handle on our own most of the repetitive paperwork, like option grants and, perhaps unwisely, vendor contracts. We don't spend much on patents. Incidentally, we pay a service $14,000 per year to set a quarterly price for our stock options. This is a cost that we didn't anticipate and didn't project as part of our legal costs.

Annual Accounting Costs: Redfin Model, $45,000; Actual Redfin Cost, $32,912

Once you've raised money, your investors will want a year-end audit of financial statements. This can be done for less money when the business is small and if you keep your books in good order, but we commissioned our first audit only after Redfin had generated over $1 million in revenues. Your accounting expenses will also be a bit higher (and your payroll significantly lower) if you can hire a bookkeeper to come in twice a month to pay your bills, which makes sense for the first year or two, until you need someone permanent.

All-Company Meeting Cost, per Meeting per Employee:
Redfin Model, $350; Actual Redfin Cost, $560

Almost half of Redfin works outside Seattle, so our meeting costs are unusually high. But we can't avoid meeting at least once a year, which is a significant expense that we forgot to plan for in our original model.

There are, of course, all sorts of other costs that are unique to our business as an online real estate broker: how much we spend to attract a home buyer to our site, for example, or what it costs to sell a listing. What you see here are just the costs common to every startup.

And now, looking this over, I worry at every turn that we've spent too much money. When I first worked at a venture-backed company, someone told me that Sequoia liked to see entrepreneurs "dive in the toilet for nickels." I'm not even sure that's true, but it was an image that always stayed with me. At the time it was actually comforting. I couldn't do anything else right but, thinking about the toilet and the nickels, I said to myself, "This I can do."

Part II: Lessons

Here are a few other tips for building a financial model:

- **Focus on head count.** Outside of marketing programs, the basis for all cost in Internet software is head count. Just figure out whom you'll hire and how much you'll pay and you can't go far wrong.

- **Plan slow, run fast.** The most likely scenario is that you won't be able to hire engineers fast enough, and that revenues will come more slowly, too. Investors expect their money to drive artificially accelerated growth rates, but signing up for that sometimes just blows a company up before you've had a chance to figure everything out. At least in the financial model, give yourself as much time to grow as you can.

- **Run top-down sanity checks.** To estimate what a company is likely to spend each year, try doubling the average salary and multiplying it by the number of employees. A hundred-person company might spend as much as $15 million per year.

- **Forget economies of scale.** The biggest whopper is that a business will magically become more efficient as it grows. If you really believe this, just walk into the headquarters of Amazon or eBay. Bureaucracies grow. Salaries float away. Straining to make a model work, I always forget that costs per employee rise every year.

- **Admit that revenues are a mystery.** If you don't have any revenues yet, you can't say what they'll be. The point of a model is to prove you can make money if people buy your product, not to insist that they will. By developing different scenarios based on different levels of demand, you can later calibrate hiring and spending according to which scenario fits reality best.

- **Build with building blocks.** Nearly every model is the sum of smaller units. In Redfin's case, our unit is a market like the San Diego real estate market, which we plan to grow to a certain size in a certain number of months, returning, we hope, a certain amount of profit to the overall business. We can then gauge whether the model works by just looking at whether San Diego works, and then asking, "Now what if we had twenty San Diegos?" For another company, it may be a user-created Web site, with so many page views and so many ads, or it may be the productivity of a single salesperson with a million-dollar quota per year.

- **Take out "hope."** Think about what is most likely to happen, so that a bookie would say you're as likely to outperform the plan as underperform it. Generally speaking, hope is not a strategy.

- **Flag your assumptions.** Rather than burying your assumptions in Excel formulae, call them out in a separate tab of the workbook, so that you have a control panel for adjusting the model. This is especially important if you plan to share your model with potential investors.

- **Hit $100 million in revenues within five years.** The premise of most venture investments is the possibility of generating tenfold returns in five to seven years, which is hard to do if you spend $5 million to build a $25 million company.

- **Keep market share under 20 percent.** Most startups reach a jillion in projected revenues by assuming that the business grows by leaps and bounds for five years. Since there's a natural limit on growth, be ready for the question, "What would your market share be in year five?" If it's over 20 percent, take the jillion-dollar projection down a notch. You'll be lucky to come close to 20 percent of any market.

Kelman is a real pal to bare his numbers to the world. He did it because advice is nice but a real company's data provides much greater insights into how things work. If you want to repay the favor, go buy a house at Redfin.com so that he can make his numbers.

CHAPTER 20

The Art of Execution

**When a man tells you that he got rich
through hard work, ask him: "Whose?"**

∼ DON MARQUIS

In the movie *The Candidate*, the Robert Redford character mouths "Now
what?" after he gets elected. Most entrepreneurs ask the same question
after they get funded. The answer is, "Now you have to deliver." And the
next question is, "How do we deliver?" This is where the art of execution
comes in.

- **Create something worth executing.** You're going to get tired of my
  obsession with great products and services, but pitching, demoing, bootstrapping, and executing are a lot easier if you've created something meaningful. It's hard to stay motivated and excited about executing crap. It's easy
  if you're changing the world. So if you and your team are having a hard time
  executing, maybe you're working on the wrong thing.

- **Set goals.** The next step is to set goals. Not just any kind of goals, but goals
  that embody these qualities:

  - **Measurable.** If a goal isn't measurable, it's unlikely you'll achieve it. For
    a startup, quantifiable goals are things like shipping deadlines, down-
    loads, and sales volume. The old line "What gets measured gets done"
    is true. This also has ramifications for the number of goals, because

you can't (and shouldn't) measure everything. Three to five goals measured on a weekly basis are plenty.

- **Achievable.** Take your "conservative" forecasts for these goals and multiply them by 10 percent; then use that as your goal. For example, if you think you'll easily sell a million units in the first year, set your goal at 100,000 units. There is nothing more demoralizing than setting a conservative goal and falling short; instead take 10 percent of your forecast, make this your goal, and blow it away. You might think that such a practice will lead to underachieving organizations, because they aren't being challenged—yeah, well, check back with me after you don't sell a million widgets.

- **Relevant.** A good goal is relevant. If you're a software company, it's the number of downloads of your demo version. It's not your ranking in Alexa, so telling the company to focus on getting into the top 50,000 sites in the world in terms of traffic is not nearly as relevant as 10,000 downloads per month.

- **Rathole resistant.** A goal can be measurable, achievable, and relevant and still send you down a rathole. Let's say you've created a content Web site. Your measurable, achievable, and relevant goal is to sign up 100,000 registered users in the first ninety days. So far, so good. But what if you focus on this body count without regard to the stickiness of the site? So now you've gotten 100,000 people to register, but they visit once and never return. That's a rathole. Ensure that your goal encompasses all the factors that will make your organization viable.

- **Postpone, or at least de-emphasize, touchy-feely goals.** Touchy-feely goals like "create a great work environment" are bull shiitake. They may make the founders feel good. They may even make the employees feel good. But companies that reach on measurable goals are happy. Those that don't, aren't. As soon as you start missing the measurable goals, all the touchy-feely stuff goes out the window.

- **Communicate the goals.** Many executive teams set goals but don't communicate them to the organization. For goals to be effective, they have to be communicated to everyone. Employees should wake up in the morning thinking about how they're going to help achieve these goals.

- **Establish a single point of responsibility.** If you ask your employees who is responsible for a goal, and no one can answer you in ten seconds, there's not enough accountability. Good employees accept responsibility. Great employees seek responsibility. Lousy employees avoid responsibility.

- **Follow through on an issue until it is done or irrelevant.** Many organizations set goals and even measure progress toward them. However, after a short time, some goals are no longer on the radar because people start focusing on the coolest and most interesting stuff. For example, fixing bugs in the current version of a software application is not as interesting as designing a new, breakthrough product—but your current customers think it is. Legend has it that Pat Riley, the coach of the Los Angeles Lakers, measured stats of his players and posted each player's progress on his locker.

- **Reward the achievers.** Rewarding the people who achieve their goals has two positive effects. First, the achievers become even more excited about doing their job. Second, the under- and nonachievers know that the company takes execution very seriously. The form of the reward can be money, stock options, time off—whatever works to serve notice to everyone that "this person delivered."

- **Establish a culture of execution.** Execution is not an event—a onetime push toward achieving goals. Rather, it is a way of life, and this way of life is set in the early days of the organization. The best way to establish this culture is for the founders, particularly the CEO, to set an example of meeting goals, responding to customers, and heeding and measuring employees. This obsession should include the CEO's answering e-mails and responding to phone calls.

- **Heed your Morpheus.** Morpheus is the character in *The Matrix* who gave Neo the choice between the blue pill and the red pill. He was, essentially, the adult supervision. Cold, brutal reality is the ally of execution, so find a Morpheus who distributes the red pills and enables employees to see things as they really are.

When the hype dies down, a company either executed or it didn't. Put aside the brilliance of your idea, the qualifications of your world-class team, and the hype surrounding your launch. Either you ship a product and customers buy it, or not. That's execution, and execution is why you get the big bucks and stock options.

CHAPTER 21

After the Honeymoon

Love is an ideal thing, marriage a real thing.

~ JOHANN WOLFGANG VON GOETHE

The reality of most businesses is that after a short honeymoon period, there are personnel issues, product issues, sales issues—everything seems to go wrong. And this is for a successful company. This chapter provides insight (and hope) for the major problems that you're likely to encounter. When you do, don't feel as though you're making history; every company experiences these problems.

Problem: A founder isn't delivering.

How you got here: In the early days of many organizations, the primary qualifications for key positions are being around and believing in the story. For example, your college roommate became "chief technical officer" because he was the only programmer you knew. However, now that he has to build a scalable product and implement serious engineering discipline, he's lost, and some employees want him off the island.

What to do now: You could simply get rid of him. This isn't very humanitarian, but neither is keeping him around until he tanks the company. Let's keep termination as a last, desperate step, because losing a founder is usually traumatic for everyone.

Until then, let's assume that he is good at some functions. The thing to do is to move him into a position where he can succeed. This usually involves a demotion, but that's tough shiitake for him and a good precedent for everyone else to see. If he doesn't want to make this transition, then it's *aloha oe*. Remember: Founder status affords a person equity, not immunity.

Here's a news flash: The founder may be happy to change to a position with fewer management responsibilities. Perhaps all he wanted to do was code, and a management role was thrust upon him. Changing his role could be win-win for everyone.

Problem: The product is late.

How you got here: It could be because you hired your roommate. The other common reasons are inexperience, wishful thinking, and knuckling under to the real or imagined pressure of investors to ship by a certain date.

What to do now: Several things: (a) Gather the team and have a "come to Jesus" about the real status of the project. (b) Ruthlessly decide on any changes in roles of people. (c) Scale back the scope/complexity/coolness of the product. (d) Plead guilty to your investors—that is, admit that you screwed up. (e) Sandbag the investors—that is, tell them a shipping date that you know you can beat. And I do mean *know*, because your neck is on the chopping block. (f) Shut up and get to work.

Problem: Sales aren't meeting projections.

How you got here: Most likely you're in this position because you're too close to the product, so you thought that customers would leap to adopt your curve-jumping, paradigm-shifting, and patent-pending innovation.

In fact, your greatest fear was about the ability to ramp up and scale volume. You never anticipated that customers wouldn't demand an unproven product from a thinly capitalized startup in the middle of a buying cycle.

What to do now: Sales needs to have its own "come to Jesus" meeting with the goal of determining what's truly happening and what the correct roles are for everyone. Then get any kind of sale that you can. My reasoning is that (a) you never know who will turn into a big account; (b) closing smaller, easier accounts is good practice; (c) these little successes build confidence in the sales organization; and (d) beggars can't be choosers.

The clock is ticking. You need to prove that the dogs will eat the food. Sure, you can try for the AKC champion German shepherd, but I would recommend finding a few hungry mutts.

Problem: Our team is not getting along.

How you got here: You're in this position because this is what always happens. Companies don't ship on time, watch sales go the roof, go public, and kick back. Startups are messy. Things go wrong. People don't get along. If it was easy, everyone would do a startup and be rich. Welcome to the real world.

What to do now: You work things out. You keep talking. You try to get an experienced outsider to provide a fresh perspective. There's no magic bullet to fix this—it simply takes time. Use the same time, by the way, to finish the product and achieve sales, because not getting along is the flip side of poor sales. If sales were booming, you'd probably be getting along—if not euphoric.

One thing you don't do is lynch people because you want to (a) set a precedent; (b) show everyone you can make tough decisions; and (c) get it over with. You should give people a second chance. Maybe even a third chance. Focus on the positive: how people can help an organization, not how they are hurting it.

You have a moral obligation to give everyone a chance to change their ways and to succeed. If you don't fulfill this obligation, then the unintended message that you'll send through the organization is: "Anybody could be gone, so don't piss me off."

Problem: We are getting slammed by the press/analysts/blogosphere.

How you got here: Arrogance is the most likely cause: believing that your product is so great that you're going to make Google look like a lemonade stand. When you start believing this crap, you draw a nice target on your chest.

What to do now: The first thing you need to do is improve your reality. Ship your product. Fix it so that it's good. It makes no sense to seek press coverage if your product sucks.

The second thing you need to do is focus on customers, not the press. If you make customers happy, the press will always come around. They have no choice. For example, Apple currently gets great press because its customers are so happy. When Apple's customers are not happy, the press will turn on Apple like a pack of starving hyenas.

The third thing to do is to suck up to the press. I cover sucking up, sucking down, and general beguiling in the section called "The Reality of Beguiling" later in the book.

Problem: Venture capitalists are micromanaging us.

How you got here: First, let's set the record straight: Venture capitalists don't want to micromanage. We'd love to make an investment, show up for a brief monthly board meeting to hear how great things are going, help select an acquirer or investment bank for an IPO, and cash out. You're in this position because you either did something wrong or something out of your control went wrong. But it's not that a VC wants to be in your face.

What to do now: Ship. Sell. Achieve success. The venture capitalist will be more than happy to declare victory and move on to the next squeaky wheel. Until then, there's no simple, cosmetic fix for this. You dug yourself into a hole—now you have to dig yourself out.

Problem: Venture capitalists aren't helping very much.

How you got here: There are two likely reasons. First, you're gullible and believed the venture capitalist when she told you that she's a real "roll up the sleeves" investor who will be by your side. Second, you're not asking hard enough or often enough for her help.

What to do now: You can't do much about the first reason. What you got is what you got. However, whether it's the first reason or the second, you have to ask. Maybe you don't want to be a burden, but the only thing that's worse than asking for too much help from a person who's unwilling to give it is to ask for too little help from a person who is willing to give it. So ask. And keep asking.

Problem: Our PR/ad agency is not delivering.

How you got here: Let me guess: You were in a rush, so you interviewed a grand total of one or two agencies. You "really liked" Trixie and Biff because they gushed about how great your product is. You didn't check references because you've always been good at judging the quality of people based on a gut reaction. Plus, you've never worked with an agency before, but you insisted on selecting and managing it anyway.

You screwed up. What else can I say?

What to do now: I bet that whoever is working with the agency on a day-to-day basis (a) knows more about marketing than you do; (b) has a better understanding of the agency's capabilities than you do; and (c) knows how to get more out of the relationship than you do.

This is usually your vice president of marketing or director of marketing. Make it clear to the agency that this person is now running the show—including and especially the ability to change agencies.

Let's say that you don't have this person. Then you have to come up to grips with the fact that there are more lousy clients than lousy agencies. It's your job to understand how to be a good client. This is the subject of a later chapter in the book, "DIY PR." This chapter focuses on PR, but the concepts apply to advertising agencies as well.

Problem: We are going to run out of money before we can raise more.

How you got here: This is the perfect storm of entrepreneurship: The product is late, sales are less than hallucinated, and money is running out. You got here because your product delivery schedule was totally out of whack—a quality that it shared with your sales projections. To add fuel to the fire, you scaled up your infrastructure because you were afraid of too much sales swamping your systems.

What to do now: This is a tough question because each situation is different. However, here are actions to consider:

- Freeze all hiring—no matter how strategic a position may be. At the very least, you make a one-for-one trade: If you hire one, you fire or lay off one.

- Cut marketing expenditures. You're probably wasting money on stupid things, anyway.

- Get interns from local schools. They have something you want: free labor. You have something they want: real-world experience.

- Cut the pay of the management team. Merely symbolic? Too little too late? Then cut early and cut hard.

- Get the cofounders to put more money in the company as a bridge loan to the next round of financing.

- Do some nonrecurring consulting work to increase cash flow.

- Try to get some beta sites to pay for a pilot implementation.

Do you see any magic bullets in this list? I don't either. Here's the lesson:

> Don't get yourself into this position, because there is no easy way out.

Take whatever money you have and make it last as long as you can. I have never seen a company fail because it couldn't expand fast enough. I have seen many companies—I won't mention their names to protect the guilty—die because they "invested in the future" and "spent ahead" to avoid missing an opportunity. Once in my career, I'd like to invest in a company that can't scale fast enough for its orders. That's an easier problem to fix than lackluster sales and adoption.

CHAPTER 22

The Art of Bootstrapping

In early childhood you may lay the foundation of poverty or riches, industry or idleness, good or evil, by the habits to which you train your children. Teach them right habits then, and their future life is safe.

⁓ LYDIA SIGOURNEY

Too much money is worse than too little for most organizations—not that I wouldn't like to run a Super Bowl commercial someday. Until that day comes, the key to success for most organizations is bootstrapping. The term *bootstrapping* comes from the German legend of Baron von Münchhausen pulling himself out of the sea by pulling on his own bootstraps. That's essentially what you'll have to do, too.

- **Focus on cash flow, not profitability.** The theory is that profits are the key to survival. If you could pay the bills with theories, this would be fine. The reality is that you pay bills with cash, so focus on cash flow. If you know you are going to bootstrap, you should start a business with a small up-front capital requirement, short sales cycles, short payment terms, and recurring revenue. It means passing up the big sale that takes twelve months to close, deliver, and collect. Cash is not only king, it's queen and prince, too, for a bootstrapper.

- **Forecast from the bottom up.** Most entrepreneurs do a top-down forecast: "There are 150 million cars in America. It sure seems reasonable that we can get a mere 1 percent of car owners to install our satellite radio systems. That's 1.5 million systems in the first year." The bottom-up forecast goes like this: "We can open up ten installation facilities in the first year. On an average day, each can install ten systems. So our first year sales will be 10 facilities × 10 systems × 240 days = 24,000 satellite radio systems." That's a long way from the "conservative" 1.5 million systems in the top-down approach. Guess which number is more likely to happen.

- **Ship, then test.** "Perfect" is the enemy of "good enough." When your product or service is "good enough," get it out, because cash flows when you start shipping. Besides, unwanted features, not perfection, come with more time. By shipping, you'll also learn what your customers truly want you to fix. It's definitely a trade-off—your reputation versus cash flow—so you can't ship pure crap. But you can't wait for perfection either. (Nota bene: Life-science companies should ignore this recommendation.)

- **Forget the "proven" team.** Proven teams are overrated—especially when most people define proven teams as people who worked for a billion-dollar company for the past ten years. These folks are accustomed to a certain lifestyle, and it's not the bootstrapping lifestyle. Hire young, cheap, and hungry people—people with fast chips, but not necessarily a fully functional instruction set. Once you achieve significant cash flow, you can hire adult supervision. Until then, hire what you can afford and make them into great employees.

- **Start as a service business.** Let's say that you ultimately want to be a software company: People download your software or you send them CDs, and they pay you. That's a nice, clean business with a proven business model. However, until you finish the software, you could provide consulting and services based on your work-in-progress software. This has two advantages: immediate revenue and true customer testing of your software. Once the software is field tested and battle hardened, flip the switch and become a product company.

- **Focus on function, not form.** Mea culpa: I love good form. MacBooks, Audis, Graf skates, and Breitling watches—you name it. But bootstrappers focus on function, not form, when they are buying things. The function is computing, getting from point A to point B, skating, and knowing the time of day. These functions do not require the more expensive form. All the chair has to do is hold your butt. It doesn't have to look as though it belongs in the Museum of Modern Art. Design great stuff, but buy cheap stuff.

- **Pick a few battles.** Bootstrappers pick their battles. They don't fight on all fronts, because they cannot afford to. If you are starting a new church, do you really need a $100,000 multimedia audiovisual system? Or just a great message from the pulpit? If you're creating a content Web site based on the advertising model, do you have to write your own customer ad-serving software? I don't think so.

- **Understaff.** Many entrepreneurs staff up for what could happen, best case. "Our conservative (albeit top-down) forecast for first-year satellite radio sales is 1.5 million units. We'd better create a 24/7 customer support center to handle this." Guess what? You sell 15,000, but you do have 200 people hired, trained, and sitting in a 50,000-square-foot telemarketing center. Bootstrappers understaff knowing that all hell *might* break loose. But this would be, as we say in Silicon Valley, a "high quality problem."

- **Go direct.** The optimal number of mouths (or hands) between a bootstrapper and her customer is zero. Sure, stores provide great customer reach, and wholesalers provide distribution. But God invented e-commerce so that you could sell direct and reap greater margins. And God was doubly smart because She knew that by going direct, you'd also learn more about your customers' needs. Stores and wholesalers *fill* demand, they don't create it. If you create enough demand, you can always get other organizations to fill it later. If you don't create demand, all the distribution in the world will get you nothing.

- **Position against the leader.** Suppose that you don't have the money to explain your story starting from scratch. Then don't try. Instead, position against the leader. Toyota introduced the Lexus lines of cars by positioning them as being as good as a Mercedes but half the price. Toyota didn't have to explain what "as good as a Mercedes" meant. How much do you think that saved it? "Poor man's Bose noise-canceling headphones" would work, too.

As my friend Craig Johnson, the great Silicon Valley corporate finance lawyer, likes to say, "The leading cause of failure of startups is death, and death happens when you run out of money." As long as you have money, you're still in the game, and outlasting the competition is one of the hallmarks of bootstrapping.

CHAPTER 23

The Art of the Board Meeting

Meetings are an addictive, highly self-indulgent activity that corporations and other organizations habitually engage in only because they cannot actually masturbate.

~ ALAIN VAN DER HEIDE

I've been the entrepreneur (aka the "victim") and the board member (aka the "heavy"). These tips apply to startups, established companies, and—with very little modification—to school boards, church elders, and nonprofits.

Before we discuss board meetings, however, we need to discuss board composition. A board should contain five to seven members. Clueless entrepreneurs want rubber stampers with deep pockets, but in a perfect world, your board members would represent these archetypes:

- **The Customer.** This person is, or represents, the type of person or organization you hope will buy your product or service. You need this person as a reality check on features, pricing, and marketing practices.

- **The Geek.** This person provides a reality check on your technology, so that when your CTO tells you that he's going to rewrite the laws of physics, someone smacks some sense into you all. The downside to having the geek on your board, however, is that once in a blue moon your CTO may be right. Still, it's most likely that your CTO is too optimistic. Note: A benefit of having a geek on your board is that it will inspire your engineers who generally believe boards care only about financial issues.

- **Dad.** Or **Mom.** This is your mentor, buddy, and frequently pro bono psychiatrist. His or her role is to guide, comfort, and support you when things get tough. Think Marcus Welby, MD. One of these folks is plenty, because they tend to live in the past.

- **The Hardass.** This is the "adult" on the board who acts as the tough guy to tell you that your "conservative" sales forecast is off by 90 percent and that you cannot give your roommate the title of CTO just because she's a cofounder and the most technical person among the founders.

- **Jerry Maguire.** This person has the Rolodex that enables you to leap ahead of mere mortal startups by connecting you with customers, partners (I hate this word), vendors, and job candidates. Be forewarned, however; most of the time your perception of a board member's ability to open doors is overly optimistic.

- **The CEO.** This is someone you can "relate to" because he's in the middle of the fray, too. Unlike most board members, who have "been there and done that," this person "is there and is doing that." He acts as a reality check on the other board members who are victims of selective memory—for example, the attitude that "back when I was a CEO, we never missed a shipping date." This person can also provide firsthand information about what companies are paying engineers, which PR firms and advertising agencies are hot, etc.

- **Start in the morning.** I've been on boards that start in the morning, at midday, and in the afternoon. Without question, the most effective board meetings start at 8:00 A.M. or earlier. This is because people are fresh in the morning and not burdened by all the crises that pile up by the middle of the day. Plus, it makes you look better because you're an early bird that gets a jump on the day as opposed to the slug that gets in at noon.

- **Get the easy crap out of the way.** Most board meetings require the routine approval of administrative things like the minutes of the previous meeting and legal formalities. There are two reasons to get these done at the onset of the meeting: First, you will run out of time, and if some members have left early, you may not have a quorum; second, you want to set a tone for approving things before you start dropping the controversial bombshells.

- **Don't bullshiitake people.** The three most powerful words you can utter at a board meeting are, "We beat projections." The second most powerful three words are, "I don't know." When you don't know, admit it, and then follow up no later than the next board meeting. (A good board member will hate it when she asks for something and you ignore her and do not address the issue.) If you admit that you don't know the answer to a question, then when you say that you do know the answer to another question, board members will believe you.

- **Let the CEO run the show.** Maybe it's an American thing, but many teams want to show the board that the entire executive team is deeply involved and effective. However, a board meeting is not "share and tell," like elementary school, where participation counts as much as results. The CEO should handle 70 percent of the meeting. The CFO should handle 20 percent, and other employees (if any other employees are present) the last 10 percent.

- **Be brief.** The entrepreneur who pitches his company with sixty slides usually prepares sixty slides for a two-hour board meeting, too. The rule of brevity also applies to board meetings. You should be so lucky as to get ten topics covered in a board meeting. I guarantee you that you'll never get beyond the twenty-fifth slide in most board meetings. You may want to provide a "360 view" of your company, but most boards want only a 30-degree view:

  - What's going right?
  - What's going wrong?
  - What do you want the board to do?

If pressed, I could further boil these three issues into one: What is the level of revenues and how can we increase it? Truth be told, this is mostly what board members care about.

- **Don't surprise people.** This is the most important rule of board management. You should never, ever surprise your board. (Perhaps there is one exception: when sales are higher than expected.) If you have bad news, speak to each member before the meeting. Ideally, by the time the board meeting happens, (1) your board members will have calmed down; (2) you are on to the solution to the problem; and (3) they have thought of ways to help you with the problem, too.

  Incidentally, e-mailing a five-tab Excel spreadsheet and sixty-page PDF the night before the board meeting does not qualify as warning your board in advance. Most board members don't read these attachments before the meeting, so you'll walk into the meeting thinking that they've already heard the bad news when they haven't. Then you deserve to get blasted.

- **Presell as much as you can.** Along the lines of "no surprises," don't try to do any "hard selling" in a board meeting. For example, if you want to change your business model, hire that proven entrepreneurial superstar from Microsoft (this is a joke, guys), or buy a Super Bowl commercial, you should discuss your idea before the meeting. In this way, you'll learn what kind of support you'll have and what the issues are; you may decide not to try getting board approval for something that won't fly anyway.

- **Present solutions, not problems.** The reason why you're running the show is theoretically that you're the best person for the job. Therefore, you should present solutions. For example, take your best shot for the company logo, company mantra, product design, and introduction plan. Then solicit feedback and make the appropriate changes. This is very different from opening up cans of worms by asking, "How do you think we should introduce the product?" This question doesn't show flexibility and openness—it shows that the wrong person is running the company.

Board meetings need not be monthly torture sessions. If they are, you're probably at fault. Keep the meetings short and disciplined, and you'll find they are informative and maybe even enjoyable and creative.

CHAPTER 24

How I Built a Web 2.0, User-Generated-Content, Citizen-Journalism, Long-Tail, Social-Media Site for $12,107.09

Worst website ever discovered.

~ MARTIN VEITCH, describing Truemors

in the *Inquirer* (theinquirer.net)

It scares me when the author of a business book works for a highfalutin consulting company or is a full-time pundit. Neither of these qualifications is conducive to giving good advice about entrepreneurship. I'd much rather read what someone who is on the firing line, or at least was on the firing line until very recently, has to say.

You can accuse me of many things, but not hypocrisy. In 2007, I started a company called Nononina, and it launched a user-generated-content, citizen-journalism, long-tail, social-media site called Truemors. The way it works is this: People find interesting stories around the Web, write a synopsis, and post them to the site. Think of it as "NPR for your eyes" (as opposed to your ears).

As an example of bootstrapping and the new economics of startups circa 2008, this is how I spent $12,107.09 to launch it:

- **0.** I wrote zero business plans for it. The plan is simple: Get a site launched in a few months, see if people like it, and sell ads and sponsorships (or not).

- **0.** I pitched zero venture capitalists to fund it. Life is simple when you can launch a company with credit-card-level financing.

- **7.5.** Seven and a half weeks went by from the time I registered the domain truemors.com until the site went live. This time is so short because the Open Source community has created gobs of great, free software that companies can use.

- **$4,500.** The total software development cost was $4,500. Two factors were at work here: first, the goodness of Open Source stuff I just mentioned. Second, I lucked into hooking up with the great guys at Electric Pulp, a development company in South Dakota, through my blog. I wasn't a believer in remote teams trying to work together on version 1.0 of a product, but Electric Pulp changed my mind.

- **$4,824.14.** The total cost of the legal fees was $4,824.14. I could have used my uncle the divorce lawyer and saved a few bucks, but that will have been shortsighted if Truemors ever becomes worth something.

- **$399.** I paid LogoWorks $399 to design the logo. At this company's Web site, you write a creative brief and then designers submit their ideas for your perusal.

- **$1,115.05.** I spent $1,115.05 registering domains. I could have done this for less, but it still was only $1,100.

- **55.** I registered fifty-five domains (for example, Truemors.net, Truemors .de, Truemors.biz, Truemours, etc.). I had no idea that one had to buy so many domains to truly "surround" the one you use. Yes, I could have registered fewer and spent less, but who cares about saving a few hundred bucks compared to the cost of legal action to get a domain away from a squatter if Truemors is successful?

- **1.5.** At the time, there were 1.5 full-time-equivalent employees at Truemors. For us, Truemors was a labor of love—in other words, we didn't pay ourselves.

- **3.** TechCrunch, a technology news Web site, wrote about Truemors three times: the leak, the leak with a screen shot, and the opening. I wish I could tell you I was so sly as to plan this.

- **261,214.** There were 261,214 page views on the first day.

- **14,052.** There were 14,052 visitors on the first day.

- **$0.** I spent $0 on marketing to launch Truemors.

- **24.** However, I did spend twenty-four years of schmoozing and "paying it forward" to get to the point where I could spend $0 to launch a company. Many bloggers got bent out of shape: "The only reason Truemors is getting so much coverage is that it's Guy's site." To which my response is, "You have a firm grasp of the obvious."

- **405.** Because some people had nothing better to do, there were 405 posts on the first day.

- **218.** We deleted 218 of the 405 posts because they were junk, spam, inappropriate, or just plain stupid. Interestingly, half the bloggers complained the site was full of junk. The other half complained that I was deleting posts.

- **3.** A mere three hours went by before the site was hacked, and we had to shut it down temporarily. I was impressed. The hacker who did this might be the next Woz. Please contact me if you are the next Woz.

- **36.** A mere thirty-six hours went by before Yahoo! Small Business told us that we were inappropriate for this service because of our traffic.

- **$29.96.** Our monthly break-even point was $29.96, because that was our monthly fee from Yahoo! Small Business.

- **$150.** Because Yahoo! Small Business evicted Truemors, our monthly break-even point quintupled to $150.

- **2.** A mere two days went by before Truemors was called the "worst website ever" by the *Inquirer.*

- **246,210.** Thank you, God, for the *Inquirer,* because it caused 246,210 page views. Yes indeed, there's no such thing as bad PR.

- **150.** A week before we launched, if you typed "truemors" into Google, you would have gotten 150 hits.

- **315,000.** Eleven days after the launch, Googling "truemors" yielded 315,000 hits. I can't figure out how this can be, but I'm not arguing against it.

A year after we launched Truemors, we created another Web site. This one is called Alltop. It is an online magazine rack that contains "all the top" stories for more than one hundred topics, such as wine, food, sports, law, journalism, books, movies, and religion. It imports the feeds of approximately one hundred Web sites and blogs for each topic and then presents the most recent headlines from each source. As a reader of this book, you'll find smallbusiness.alltop.com, marketing.alltop.com, venturecapital.alltop.com, good.alltop.com, and nonprofit.alltop.com interesting.

I spent approximately $10,000 to launch Alltop: $3,000 to buy the domain Alltop.com, plus $6,000 for three MacBook Airs that I gave to the guys at Electric Pulp as gifts. Instead of paying Electric Pulp for development work, we're now "partners" (much as I hate that word) in Alltop, so we'll split the revenues and upside. Nota bene: This partnership is based on "spreadsheet reasons," because my costs and their revenue both changed.

Based on my Truemors and Alltop experience, no entrepreneur can tell me that she needs $1 million, four programmers, and six months to launch these kinds of Web sites. Open Source products like WordPress, MySQL, Ruby, and PHP make it possible to try ideas like these for credit-card money. If your idea takes off, hallelujah: There's no better time to raise money than after your prototype is scaling up. (Indeed, you may never need to raise money.) There is no worse time to raise money than when you have nothing but an idea. Actually, there *is* a worse time: when you've burned through the first million, and you haven't executed.

The Reality of Innovating

Many people think that innovation is easy: You sit around with your buddies and magical ideas pop into your head. Or your customers tell you what they need. Dream on. Innovation is a hard, messy process with no shortcuts. It starts with making something that you'd like to use that makes meaning, and it gets both easier and harder from there.

CHAPTER 25

The Art of Innovation

**Innovation is the specific instrument of
entrepreneurship . . . the act that endows
resources with a new capacity to create wealth.**

~ PETER DRUCKER

P eter Drucker was right: Innovation is what creates wealth. Innovation
had better create wealth because it's so damn hard to do. The purpose
of this chapter is to explain the principles of innovation that I learned
in the trenches of Apple, the three companies that I started, and the dozens of
companies that I've advised. I wish I could tell you that I did all these things
right. That would be a lie. Do as I say, not as I did.

1. **Build something that you want to use.** Many experts explain the creation of companies like Apple, Google, and Southwest Airlines as examples of visionary entrepreneurs who saw a large potential market whose
   needs were going unfulfilled. This is a crock of bull shiitake. My theory is
   that people start companies because they want to use the products or services that they were creating. So if you want to be innovative, create what
   you want to use.

2. **Make meaning.** A logical question quickly arises: What if you're the only
   person who wants your gizmo? The answer is that great innovations make
   meaning. They enable people to do old things better, do things they always
   wanted to do, and do things they never knew they wanted to do. The iPod
   is an example of this. For some, listening to music is an old thing that iPod

made much better than cassette-based Walkmans. iPod enabled others who refused to use Walkmans because of their size and the limits of cassettes to listen to music while on the move for the first time. And iPod enabled still others to listen to podcasts, a form of audio recording that did not exist before.

3. **Jump to the next curve.** Too many companies duke it out on the same curve. There was an ice-harvesting industry in the 1880s. During the winter, companies would cut blocks of ice. Ice factories put them out of business because they weren't limited to cold climates. Refrigerator companies, in turn, put ice factories out of business because of the added convenience of PCs (personal chillers). True innovation occurs when companies jump to the next curve—or better still, invent the next curve.

4. **Don't worry, be crappy.** Don't worry about shipping an innovative product with elements of crappiness. The first version of an innovation is seldom perfect—Macintosh, for example, didn't have software (thanks to me), a hard disk (it wouldn't matter with no software anyway), slots, or color. If a company waits until everything is perfect, it will never ship, and the market will pass it by.

5. **Churn, baby, churn.** I'm saying it's okay to *ship* with elements of crappiness—I'm not saying that it's okay to *stay* crappy. A company must improve version 1.0 and create version 1.1, 1.2, . . . 2.0. This is a difficult lesson to learn, because it's so hard to ship an innovation; therefore, the last thing employees want to deal with is complaints about their perfect baby. Innovation is not an event. It's a process.

6. **Don't be afraid to polarize people.** Most companies want to create the holy grail of products that appeals to every demographic, socioeconomic background, and geographic location. To attempt to do so guarantees mediocrity. Instead, create great products that make segments of people very happy. And fear not if these products make other segments unhappy. The worst case is to incite no passionate reactions at all, and that happens when companies try to make everyone happy.

7. **Break down the barriers.** The way life should work is that innovative products are easy to sell. Dream on. Life isn't fair. Indeed, the more innovative, the more barriers the status quo will erect in your way. Entrepreneurs should understand this up front and not get flustered when market acceptance comes slowly. I've found that the best way to break barriers is to enable people to test-drive your innovation by downloading your software, taking home your hardware, or using your Web site.

8. **"Let a hundred flowers blossom."** I stole this line from Chairman Mao. Innovators need to be flexible about how people use their products. Avon created Skin-So-Soft to soften skin, but when parents used it as an insect repellant, Avon went with the flow. Apple thought it created a spreadsheet/database/word-processing computer but came to find out that customers used it as a desktop-publishing machine. The lesson is to sow fields, not flower boxes, and let a hundred flowers blossom.

9. **Think digital, act analog.** Thinking digital means that companies should use all the digital tools at their disposal—computers, Web sites, instruments, whatever—to create great products. But companies should act analog—that is, they must remember that the purpose of innovation is not cool products and cool technologies but happy people. "Happy people" is a decidedly analog goal.

10. **Never ask people to do what you wouldn't do.** This is a great test for any company. Suppose you invent the world's greatest mousetrap. It murders mice better than anything in the history of mankind—in fact, it's nuclear powered. The problem is that the customer needs a PhD to set it, it costs $500,000, and the user has to drop off the dead, radioactive mouse 500 miles away in the middle of the desert. You wouldn't jump through those hoops, so don't expect customers to, either.

11. **Don't let the bozos grind you down.** The bozos will tell a company that what it's doing can't be done, shouldn't be done, and isn't necessary. Some bozos are clearly losers—they're the ones who are easy to ignore. The dangerous ones are rich, famous, and powerful: Because they are so

successful, innovators may think they are right. They're not right; they're just successful on the previous curve, so they cannot comprehend, much less embrace, the next curve.

These recommendations are so easy to read (or write) and yet so hard to do. These eleven points are the cornerstones of innovation, but I can boil down innovation to one challenge: Do not rest until you make meaning and jump curves.

CHAPTER 26

The Seven Sins of Solutions

**If the only tool you have is a hammer,
you tend to see every problem as a nail.**

~ ABRAHAM MASLOW

*T*raditional ways of thinking should not limit your creation of innova-
tive solutions. To help prevent this, here is an excerpt from "Mind of
the Innovator: Taming the Traps of Traditional Thinking" by Matt
May. Matt is the author of The Elegant Solution: Breakthrough Thinking the
Toyota Way (*Free Press, 2006*) and one of the world's leading authorities on
Toyota and innovation.

1. **Shortcutting.** Leaping to solutions in an instinctive or intuitive way—i.e.,
the "blink" method of problem solving—seldom leads to an elegant solution, because deeper, hidden causes don't get addressed. Watch *CSI* and
House: First they collect the evidence, then diagnose, and then solve. It's
never the guy or the disease you initially suspect.

2. **Blind spots.** Blind spots are the umbrella term for assumptions, biases,
and mind-sets that we cannot see through or around. Our brain does a lot
of "filling in" for us because it's a pattern maker and recognizer. Ths cn b
hrd fr ppl t cmprhnd hwvr, mst cn ndrstntd ths sntnc wth lttl prblm. But
clear thinking involves more than simply filling in spaces in words.

3. **Not Invented Here (NIH).** NIH means that you refuse to consider solutions that are from external sources. It means, "If we didn't come up with it, it won't work. It is of no use." Next time you're waiting for an elevator, watch someone walk up and hit the button even though it's already lit. We often don't trust others' solutions!

4. **Satisficing.** Ever wonder why some solutions lack inspiration, imagination, and originality? It's because by nature we satisfice (satisfy plus suffice). We glom on to what's easy and stop looking for the optimal solution. What's the least number of "sticks" you need to move to make this Roman numeral equation correct? XI + I = X. If you answered anything but zero, you satisficed. Look at it upside down.

5. **Downgrading.** Downgrading is the close cousin of satisficing but with a twist: a formal revision of the goal or situation. Reason? No one likes to fail. Result? We fall short of the killer app, so we pick the one that allows us to declare victory. Next time you're playing hockey or football, try winning the game by hitting the outside of the post or taking the ball down to the one-yard line.

6. **Complicating.** Why do we overthink, complicate, and add cost? And why do we *all* do it so intuitively, naturally, and (here's the killer) consistently? Answer: We're hardwired that way. Our brains are designed to drive hoarding, storing, accumulating, and collecting behavior. We are by nature "do more/add on" types. Don't believe it? Watch the customers at Costco or Sam's Club buy thirty-six rolls of toilet paper.

7. **Stifling.** We naturally do the "Yeah, but . . ." dance, in which we stifle, dismiss, and second-guess ideas. It's ideacide, pure and simple. And it's not just others' ideas we stifle; we often do it to our own and kick ourselves later when someone else "steals" our great idea. Remember how Decca Records rejected the Beatles? "Guitar bands are on the way out."

These sins should keep you awake at night, so you should ruthlessly eliminate them from your company. Incidentally, the last sin is the deadliest, because it can prevent you from trying at all. If you don't try, you will never know, and that's the worst outcome of all.

CHAPTER 27

The Myths of Innovation

The great enemy of the truth is very often not the lie—deliberate, contrived and dishonest—but the myth—persistent, persuasive, and unrealistic. Belief in myths allows the comfort of opinion without the discomfort of thought.

～ JOHN F. KENNEDY

Because of all the writing, speaking, and pontificating about innovation, you might believe that we truly understand it. This is wishful thinking. In the following interview, Scott Berkun explores (or, more accurately, explodes) the romantic notions of how innovation occurs. He is the author of a recently released book called *The Myths of Innovation* (O'Reilly Media, 2008). He also wrote the 2005 bestseller, *The Art of Project Management* (O'Reilly Media, 2005).

Q: How long does it take in the real world—as opposed to the world of retroactive journalism—for an epiphany to occur?

A: An epiphany is the tip of the creative iceberg, and all epiphanies are grounded in work. If you take any magic moment of discovery from history and wander backward in time, you'll find dozens of smaller observations, inquiries, mistakes, and comedies that occurred to make the epiphany possible. All the great inventors knew this—and typically they downplayed the magic moments. But we all love exciting stories—Newton getting hit by an apple or people with chocolate and peanut butter colliding in hallways are just more fun to think about. A movie called *Watch Einstein Stare at His Chalkboard for Ninety Minutes* wouldn't go over well with most people.

Q: Is progress toward innovation made in a straight line?—for example, transistor to chip to personal computer to Web to MySpace.

A: Most people want history to explain how we got here, not to teach them how to change the future. To serve that end, popular histories are told in heroic, logical narratives: They made a transistor, which led to the chip, which created the possibility for the PC, and on it goes forever. But of course, if you asked William Shockey (transistor) or Steve Wozniak (PC) how obvious their ideas and successes were, you'll hear very different stories about chaos, uncertainty, and feeling the odds were against them.

If we believe things are uncertain for innovators in the present, we have to remember things were just as uncertain for people in the past. That's a big goal of the book: to use amazing tales of innovation history as tools for those trying to do it now.

Q: Are innovators born or made?

A: Both. Take Mozart. Yes, he had an amazing capacity for musical composition, but he also was born in a country at the center of the music world, had a father who was a music teacher, and was forced to practice for hours every day before he started the equivalent of kindergarten. I researched the history of many geniuses and creators and always found a wide range of factors, some under their control and some not, that made their achievements possible.

Q: What are the toughest challenges that an innovator faces?

A: It's different for every innovator, but the one that crushed many is how bored the rest of the world was by their ideas. Finding support, whether emotional, financial, or intellectual, for a big new idea is very hard and depends on skills that have nothing to do with intellectual prowess or creative ability. That's a killer for many would-be geniuses: They have to spend way more time persuading and convincing others than they spend inventing, and they don't have the skills or emotional endurance for it.

Q: Where do inventors and innovators get their ideas?

A: I teach a creative-thinking course at the University of Washington, and the foundation is that ideas are combinations of other ideas. People who earn the label "creative" are really just people who come up with more combinations of ideas, find interesting ones faster, and are willing to try them out. The problem is that most schools and organizations train us out of these habits.

Q: Why do innovators face such rejection and negativity?

A: It's human nature—we protect ourselves from change. We like to think we're progressive, but every wave of innovation has been much slower than we're told. The telegraph, the telephone, the PC, and the Internet all took decades to develop from ideas into things ordinary people used. As a species, we're threatened by change, and it takes a long time to convince people to change their behavior, or part with their money.

Q: If you have a seemingly stupid idea, according to the "experts," how do you know if it will succeed or if it's truly stupid?

A: Don't shoot me, but the answer is, we can't know. Not for certain. That's where all the fun and misery come in. Many stupid ideas have been successful and many great ideas have died on the vine, and that's because success hinges on factors outside our control.

The best bet is to be an experimenter, a tinkerer—to learn to try out ideas cheaply and quickly and to get out there with people instead of fantasizing in ivory towers. Experience with real people trumps expert analysis much of the time. Innovation is a practice, a set of habits, and it involves making lots of mistakes and being willing to learn from them.

Q: If you were a venture capitalist, what would your investment thesis be?

A: Two parts: Neither is original, but they are borne out by history. One is portfolio. Invest knowing most ventures, even good ones, fail, so distribute risk on some spectrum (e.g., one-third very high risk, one-third high risk, one-third moderate risk). Sometimes seemingly small, low-risk/reward innovations have big impacts, and it's a mistake to only make big bets.

The other idea is people: I'd invest in people more than ideas or business plans—though those are important, of course. A great entrepreneur who won't give up and will keep growing and learning is gold. It's a tiny percentage of entrepreneurs who have any real success the first few times out—3M, Ford, Flickr were all second or third efforts. I'd also give millions of dollars to authors of recent books on innovation with the word *myth* in the title. The future is really in their hands.

Q: What are the primary determinants of the speed of adoption of innovation?

A: The classic research on the topic is *Diffusion of Innovation* (Free Press, 2003) by Everett Rogers, which defines factors that hold up well today. The surprise to us is that they're all sociological: based on people's perception of value and their fear of risks—which often has little to do with our view of how amazing a particular technology is. Smarter innovators know this and pay attention from day one to whom they are designing for and how to design the Web site or product in a way that supports their feelings and beliefs.

Q: What's more important: problem definition or problem solving?

A: Problem definition is definitely underrated, but they're both important. New ideas often come from asking new questions and being a creative question asker. We fixate on solutions, and popular literature focuses on creative people as being solvers, but often the creativity is in reformulating a problem so that it's easier to solve. Einstein and Edison were notorious problem definers: They defined the problem differently than everyone else, and that's what led to their success.

Q: Why don't the best ideas win?

A: One reason is because the best idea doesn't exist. Depending on your point of view, there's a different best idea or best choice for a particular problem. I'm certain that the guys who made telegraphs didn't think the telephone was all that good an idea, but it ended their livelihood. So many stories of progress gone wrong are about arrogance of perception: What some people thought was the right path—often the path most profitable to them—isn't what another, more influential group of people thought.

Q: Is innovation more likely to come from young people or old people? Or is age simply not a factor?

A: Innovation is difficult, risky work, and the older you are, the greater the odds you'll realize this is the case. That explanation works best. Beethoven didn't write his Ninth Symphony until late in his life, so we know many creatives stay creative no matter how old they are. But their willingness to endure all the stresses and challenges of bringing an idea to the world diminishes. They understand the costs better from the life experience. The young don't know what there is to fear, have stronger urges to prove themselves, and have fewer commitments—for example, children and mortgages. These factors make it easier to try crazy things.

CHAPTER 28

The Sticking Point

A complex system that works is invariably found to have evolved from a simple system that works.

~ JOHN GAULE

For entrepreneurs the most important real-world question is, "What makes an innovation stick?" Luck is a reasonable though not very useful answer. To figure this out, I interviewed Chip and Dan Heath, because they wrote *Made to Stick: Why Some Ideas Survive and Others Die* (Random House, 2007). Chip is a professor of organizational behavior in the Graduate School of Business at Stanford University. Dan is a consultant at Duke Corporate Education.

Q: Why didn't you name the book *The Sticking Point*?

A: It's genius . . . if only we'd thought of it earlier. . . . [Whose fault is that? Dan should have given me the draft earlier.]

Malcolm Gladwell is one of our heroes, and of course we borrowed the stickiness terminology from *The Tipping Point* (Back Bay Books, 2002). Gladwell's interest was in what makes certain trends likely to tip. In his chapter about stickiness, he talks a lot about the value of experimentation in educational shows, such as *Sesame Street* and *Blue's Clues*. He's absolutely right about the value of experimentation. But we think that you can know a lot, up front, about which ideas are more likely to succeed or fail, because successful ideas share common traits. Our book digs into those traits and how you can put them to use in communicating your own ideas.

Q: What separates ideas that stick from those that don't?

A: We spent lots of time researching sticky ideas—ideas that people understand and remember, and that change the way people think or behave. The ideas we studied ranged from the ludicrous to the profound, from urban legends (no, there is no kidney-theft ring) to great scientific theories (yes, the land we walk around on does ride on giant tectonic plates, and when they collide they cause mountain ranges and earthquakes). We found there were six principles (SUCCES) that link sticky ideas of all kinds. Sticky ideas won't always have all six, but the more, the merrier.

For example, JFK's idea to put a man on the moon in a decade had all six of them:

a. **Simple.** A single, clear mission.

b. **Unexpected.** A man on the moon? It seemed like science fiction at the time.

c. **Concrete.** Success was defined so clearly—no one could quibble about man, moon, or decade.

d. **Credible.** This was the president of the United States talking.

e. **Emotional.** It appealed to the aspirations and pioneering instincts of an entire nation.

f. **Story.** An astronaut overcomes great obstacles to achieve an amazing goal.

Q: Your principles sound pretty basic. If these six principles were all it took to make a sticky idea, why aren't there more sticky ideas in the world?

A: Basic, yes, but not natural. That's an important distinction. People tend to think that having a great idea is enough, and they think the communication part will come naturally. We are in deep denial about the difficulty of getting a thought out of our own heads and into the heads of others. It's just not true that "If you think it, it will stick."

And that brings us to the villain of our book: the Curse of Knowledge. Lots of research in economics and psychology shows that when we know something, it becomes hard for us to imagine not knowing it. As a result, we become lousy communicators. Think of a lawyer who can't give you a straight, comprehensible answer to a legal question. His vast knowledge and experience render him unable to fathom how little you know. So when he talks to you, he talks in abstractions that you can't follow. And we're all like the lawyer in our own domains of expertise.

Here's the great cruelty of the Curse of Knowledge: The better we get at generating great ideas—new insights and novel solutions—in our field of expertise, the more unnatural it becomes for us to communicate those ideas clearly. That's why knowledge is a curse. But notice we said "unnatural," not "impossible." Experts just need to devote a little time to applying the basic principles of stickiness.

JFK dodged the curse. If he'd been a modern-day politician or CEO, he'd probably have said, "Our mission is to become the international leader in the space industry, using our capacity for technological innovation to build a bridge toward humanity's future." That might have set a moon walk back fifteen years.

Q: Why has Windows stuck? It doesn't appear to be simple, unexpected, concrete, credible, emotional, or involve stories.

A: It's important to distinguish ideas and products. A fax is a product but not an idea. "Do unto others . . ." is an idea but not a product. We talk in our book about what makes ideas stick but we don't want to claim that our framework describes everything you need to know about why products stick—or pop stars or dance crazes. Everyone has a mailbox, but it's weird to say that mailboxes are an idea that has stuck.

Some parts of our idea framework may apply to Windows: In comparison to DOS, Windows was certainly simple and concrete, as had been the Macintosh and Xerox PARC graphical interfaces before it. Because of its association with IBM PCs, Windows also had more credibility—what are you going to trust for your business: an IBM PC or a Commodore 64? But let's face it, Windows lives closer to the fax side of the continuum than the idea side.

By 1985, when the first version of Windows came out, IBM had the largest market share in PCs. Even back then, people were starting to understand network effects: There was more software available for DOS and Windows machines, so people were more likely to be able to exchange files with coworkers, so they—and coworkers—tended to buy the same kind of computer. Network effects for products are powerful, but we don't want to claim credit for them as part of our framework for ideas.

Zooming out, there *are* things that live at the intersection of ideas and products—in almost any branding opportunity, there's a product and an idea. High-end vodkas, for example, would probably be indistinguishable in a blind taste test, so when people prefer one, they're preferring the idea promised by the brand. Our framework is more likely to apply to analyzing the ideas promised by different brands than the products that go along with them.

Q: Who's in the Heath Hall of Stickiness Fame?

A: JFK, of course, for his man-on-the-moon idea. But that example is somewhat misleading because JFK was a president and a hero. It's easy to think his idea was powerful because he was powerful. So in the book we discuss a lot of great ideas that come from relatively unknown heroes:

- An elementary school teacher who designed a shocking simulation that virtually cured prejudice in her students.
- A small-town publisher who created the most successful local newspaper in America by focusing on a simple mission for forty-plus years.
- The leader of the team that developed the PalmPilot, who kept his team obsessive about design simplicity.
- The Australian medical internist who figured out what caused stomach ulcers—and then faced the much larger challenge of convincing his colleagues that he was right. He was unknown at the time, but he isn't any longer, and he won the Nobel Prize in Medicine last year.

The important point is this: You don't need power or charm or resources to make a sticky idea. It's not solely a JFK thing.

Q: Time and again, you hammer on simplicity and core, and yet your jacket copy says, "This is a book written for anyone who strives to craft messages that are memorable and lasting: teachers, businesspeople, journalists, ministers, and nonprofit leaders." This sounds to me as though you want to be Malcolm Gladwell, Robert Cialdini, Rick Warren, and Peter Drucker. Isn't this a violation of your concepts?

A: Nope. Our book was written for a type of problem, not a type of person. The problem is this: When you have an important idea, how do you communicate it in a way that has impact? How do you construct a great idea? Teachers and businesspeople and ministers all have this problem in spades, so our book will help them—but only with this one problem! We've got absolutely nothing to say about long division or finance or salvation.

The cool thing, to us, is realizing that the idea playbook is similar for these diverse sets of people. Good science lessons and good Hollywood movies both raise mysteries that cause people to *want* to listen until the mystery is resolved. Aesop's *Fables* have survived over two thousand years because of their concrete examples, and if you want your business plan to survive more than fifteen minutes, you'd better be concrete as well.

Once you've got a great idea in your head—whether you're in engineering or business or teaching—there are a handful of principles that will help you communicate it. That's where our book comes in.

Q: Did Herb Kelleher "know" his core when the first Southwest Airlines flight took off?

A: We talk in the book about the importance of finding a simple message that expresses the core of your idea. Kelleher's core is that Southwest is *"the low-fare airline."* Most entrepreneurs struggle for years to find a core message, but Kelleher *started* with his.

In fact, the original core idea fit on a cocktail napkin: An entrepreneur named Rollin King, from San Antonio, Texas, owned a small commuter air service and had the idea of creating a larger commuter service with bigger planes. In a conversation with Kelleher in a bar, he sketched out his idea on a napkin. The original napkin is framed in the boardroom of Southwest. On it is a triangle with the vertices labeled Dallas, Houston, and San

Antonio. The idea was to launch a commuter airline flying big planes between those three cities. The driving distance between the cities is about three to three and a half hours. Rollins and Kelleher knew people might decide to fly instead of drive if the fares could be made cheap enough to present an attractive alternative.

Of course, it took a long time to put the napkin into practice. The other airlines tied up Southwest in court battles for four years. But the Southwest story has a nice lesson for potential entrepreneurs: the Cocktail Napkin Test. Lots of entrepreneurs can tell you a dozen reasons that their product or service will transform the world. A good challenge for them would be to sort through the dozen reasons and pick the single most important one. It's a worthy aspiration to paint a picture of the world that is simple enough and concrete enough to be sketched on a cocktail napkin.

Q: What is the relationship between stickiness and evangelism?

A: Evangelism has been one of your recurring themes over the years. As far back as *The Macintosh Way* (HarperCollins, 1990), you were arguing that the best partners are interested in the ideal of what you're doing, not just the potential for making money. The people in it for the money bail when times get tough; the people in it for the ideal stick with you.

We have a similar theme in our book. There are two basic approaches to creating an emotional idea that makes people care—you can appeal to consequences (e.g., money) or you can appeal to identity. Consequences are not as important as we sometimes think. Political scientists find that voters don't vote their personal pocketbook as much as they vote their identity—what's good for us as Americans or, more narrowly, for the other members of our religious or ethnic groups. Steve Jobs's 1984 commercial cleverly appealed to identity—Macintosh true believers were striking a blow for liberation in an oppressive world filled with IBM's big-box machines.

But though identity is powerful, we often ignore it. When we predict what motivates others, we all tend to assume that everyone else is motivated by consequences. We tend to think that we, personally, are motivated by learning and service and fulfillment, but others are motivated by bonuses. Research suggests that people tend to systematically neglect identity appeals. Bottom line, there's less evangelism than there probably should be.

Q: Is there a point in a market where it's impossible to make a new entrant stick? For example, how would you try to kick MySpace's butt?

A: In the beginning, MySpace started as a better idea. At the time the leading social-networking site was Friendster, founded by a former Netscape programmer, which assumed that being social was the ability to calculate the degrees of separation between you and someone else. On Friendster you couldn't see the profile of anyone who was separated from you by too many degrees.

By contrast, MySpace started as a place to bond with others over emerging bands and music, an important source of identity. You could see everyone's profile—you could easily meet strangers who shared your interest in Seaweed or the Bad Brains. Shared identity and hormones are a potent combination. Friendster, by contrast, tried to shut down "fakester" members that stood for shared interests or identities as opposed to real people.

At this point, MySpace is a sticky product because of network effects—just like the QWERTY keyboard or Windows—so the idea of MySpace may not matter as much as the product. You have to be there because that's where your friends are, just as you have to buy on eBay because that's where the sellers are. But if something can unseat MySpace, it might be a reverse of the basic identity appeal.

MySpace is getting so mainstream, it may be vulnerable to a rebellion strategy, just like fashion products that lose their cachet when knockoffs show up in Tulsa strip malls. MySpace has a serious problem: People in their forties have MySpace pages. That can't be good, and it might leave room for a hipper niche player.

Q: Can a slick marketer apply your principles and make a piece of crap stick, or does the intrinsic value ultimately decide stickiness?

A: Slick marketers are already using most of these principles. We wanted our book to serve as an equalizer. Because you're right—intrinsic value counts. The slick marketing recipe is: sticky communications about ideas with little intrinsic value. The social enterprise recipe is: ideas with huge intrinsic value communicated with little stickiness. We wanted to even the arms race.

The problem is that ideas with intrinsic value don't always win. It's not true that you use only 10 percent of your brain. Or that the Great Wall of China is the only man-made structure visible from space. And gum doesn't take seven years to digest in your stomach. The world of ideas is unfair. Teachers and public-health officials and legislators agonize over how to get their messages across, and meanwhile, dumb ideas, like urban legends, propagate with no advertising budgets and no authority figures supporting them.

We can bemoan the fact that dumb ideas win out. But we can also reverse engineer them. We can figure out the principles that make them stick and teach them to people who have worthwhile messages. Slick marketers know a lot of these principles already. Urban legends have them baked in. But no one teaches engineers or entrepreneurs or chemistry professors how to make their ideas stick.

Q: What's your advice to a product champion stuck in a large company who gets matrixed to death trying to implement your ideas?

A: Make people play on your turf by keeping things concrete. It is so much easier to bullshit with abstraction than with concrete examples. Don't say, "I think we should devote more resources to evangelism among mid-market IT decision makers." Say, "Here's a list of five hundred IT decision makers in the area around Salt Lake City. I want to invite them to a one-day conference on September 29. It will cost $60,000 to pull off. Who's in?" Even if they disagree, it will be productive disagreement, anchored in reality.

In the book, we tell about Melissa Studzinski, who joined General Mills as the brand manager of Hamburger Helper. She was twenty-eight years old. When she started, she was given three huge binders full of sales and volume data, ad briefs, and marketing surveys. The data was too abstract to provide much intuition. Then she ran a program called Fingertips, through which her team found Midwestern moms who would let General Mills employees barge into their homes and watch them cook. They wanted a concrete picture of their customer at their fingertips. What they found was that moms didn't care about variety of flavors. This was a shocking insight within the company: Previous generations of marketers and food scientists had created thirty flavors of Hamburger Helper!

On the other hand, the moms did care about being able to find the same predictable flavor that their kids would actually eat. Using this concrete information, Studzinski's team convinced people across General Mills to reduce the number of products. Costs went way down, and sales went up. Who's going to argue with Betty Jones in Wheaton, who says she stopped using Hamburger Helper because she could never find the spaghetti flavor? That's a very concrete example that convinced lots of people across a big bureaucracy to consider a different way of doing things.

Q: What does it mean if your book doesn't become a bestseller?

A: It means we should have been born the Grisham brothers.

Bestseller does have a nice ring, so please do buy some books, but remember that a sticky idea is one that people understand and remember, and causes some change in the way they think or behave. So our failure story has nothing to do with sales. Our failure story is that people who buy our book do nothing different the next time they pitch an idea and they've forgotten what they read three months later. Ergo, that would hurt.

We have a specific measure of success for our book. We want to get e-mails from people who used techniques from our book to make their ideas stick. If we get a lot of those e-mails, we're happy. If we don't, we'll keep studying ideas until we get it right.

SUCCES—I like that acronym, but it would stick better with one more S. However, six months after its introduction, *Made to Stick* is still in the top 500 sellers of Amazon, so it's clear that the Heaths' book is sticking. Will your product or service stick, too? Just ensure that it's simple, unexpected, concrete, credible, emotional, and tells a story.

CHAPTER 29

The Lies of Engineers

Programming today is a race between software engineers
striving to build bigger and better idiot-proof programs,
and the Universe trying to produce bigger and better idiots.
So far, the Universe is winning.

~ RICK COOK

Much as I put engineers on pedestals, they do frequently lie. Perhaps lying is necessary to create great innovation, because so many people tell you that what you want to do can't be done or isn't wanted by people. As long as you know when they are lying, you'll be fine.

1. **"I don't know anything about marketing."** This is a lie of false modesty. The engineer is thinking, "I don't know a thing about marketing, but how hard could it be compared to what I'm doing? I should run marketing and engineering. I just hope that the MBAs come up with something that is worthy of my code." However, don't worry too much about this lie, because it self-corrects as the engineer misses deadline after deadline and comes to realize that he has bigger issues.

2. **"We're about to go into beta testing."** This is a meaningless statement because it doesn't matter when you go into beta testing—what matters is when you come out of beta testing. (The only hard-and-fast deadline for coming out of a modern-day beta test is "before you run out of money.")

In the good old days, *alpha* used to mean, "All features are implemented though not necessarily working properly." *Beta* used to mean, "There are no more repeatable bugs." Nowadays beta means, "We've gone as long as possible past the shipping date that we promised our investors."

3. **"I'll comment the code, so that the next person can understand what I did."** This is a lie of good intentions. The engineer did intend to comment the code, but as the schedule slipped, priorities changed. The question put to management became: "Do you want me to comment the code or finish it sooner?" Guess what the answer was. Luckily, the lack of comments usually doesn't matter, because the code is so crappy that a total rewrite is necessary in a year.

4. **"Our architecture is scalable."** This is the lie that I enjoy hearing the most. Typically, an engineer who has never shipped a product says this after creating a prototype in Visual Basic. The whole lie goes like this: "Google's architecture isn't as scalable as mine. They can support 25 million simultaneous searches. We will be able to easily handle a billion." Luckily, in most cases, the adoption of the product is slower than the CEO's "conservative" forecast, so scalability never becomes an issue.

5. **"The code supports all the industry standards."** This is almost a truth, except for a short omission: "This code supports all the industry standards that I agree with." The engineer has made a personal decision to ignore standards he doesn't like—for example, those promulgated by Microsoft. To the engineer, it's no big deal because customers will never know.

6. **"We have an effective bug-reporting database and system."** However, the assumption behind the design of the bug-reporting database and system is that there are no bugs in the code, so there's not much to database and report. Generally speaking, if the largest number of documented bugs never exceeds 1,000, it means that the company isn't tracking bugs carefully.

7. **"We can do this faster, cheaper, and better with an offshore programming team in India."** Rank-and-file engineers usually don't tell

this lie; it's the CTO who does. Somehow people got it in their heads that every programmer in India is good, fast, and cheap, and every programmer in the United States is lousy, slow, and expensive. This simply isn't true.

8. **"Our beta sites love it."** In twenty-five years of working in technology, I've never heard a company report that its beta sites didn't like the product. There are three reasons for this: First, many beta sites are so honored to get prerelease software that they don't want to say anything negative. Second, most beta sites haven't used the software very much. Third, most beta sites don't want to seem cruel by criticizing a company's new product. Doing so is as socially unacceptable as telling someone that his baby is ugly.

9. **"This time we got it right."** The scary thing about this lie is that the engineer really believes it. Again. The problem is that "this time" occurs over and over. I have great faith in engineers and believe that in the long run, they do get it right. It's just that in the long run, we're all dead.

10. **"This code is so bad that it would be faster to write it all from scratch than debug and expand the current shipping code."** Every programmer says this about every other programmer's code. And someone will say this about the rewritten version, too.

11. **"I like thinking about architecture, but I can code."** This means that the programmer can't code. And probably can't design a good architecture, either.

12. **"It works on my machine."** And "my machine" is probably the only computer in the world that it does work on.

13. **"Of course I can let go of the code and run the business instead."** These are the famous last words of every engineer turned entrepreneur. It means that he (or she) can neither let go of the code nor run the business.

14. **"Even my mom can navigate the screens."** Of course, your mom has a PhD in computer science from MIT.

I love the lies that engineers tell for three reasons. First, their lies demonstrate the engineer's childlike ignorance of how companies really work. Second, engineers really believe the lies that they tell. You can't say this about entrepreneurs, venture capitalists, and lawyers. Third, most of the lies they tell aren't dishonest—they're just "early" and will eventually come true. If you're an engineer, now you know what you're unconsciously doing. If you work with engineers, now you know when engineers are lying to you.

CHAPTER 30

How to Kick Silicon Valley's Butt

They envy the distinction I have won; let them, therefore, envy my toils, my honesty, and the methods by which I gained it.

~ SALLUST

From the fjords of Norway to the sands of Israel to the ice of Alberta to the waves of Honolulu, many regions of the world have Silicon Valley envy. They look at the Valley as a place where innovative people start innovative companies that generate billions of dollars of wealth (and tax revenue), create thousands of jobs, and do not pollute the environment (at least compared to a smokestack).

The question I hear over and over is, "How can we be innovative and create our own Silicon Valley?" This chapter is for the leaders of places who want to learn the truth about re-creating Silicon Valley.

In reality, it's taken more than seventy years to create Silicon Valley. Any politician who thinks she can create another one in a term or two is overly optimistic. Also, to my knowledge, there was never a master plan for the creation of Silicon Valley. What stands before you is an amalgamation of hard work, luck, greed, and serendipity, but not planning. Indeed, Silicon Valley has probably worked because there was no plan.

Stuff You Can't Do Jack About

- **Beautiful, but not gorgeous, surroundings.** California is beautiful. The weather is good. It's fun to live here. No matter how great an entrepreneurial environment Cleveland creates, it's always going to have people wanting to move away. If a place is gorgeous, like Hawaii, then the distractions are sometimes too great. Someplace in the middle is what's ideal. At the very least, it would be good to have one lousy season so that the engineers are productive for part of the year.

- **High housing prices.** If houses are cheap, it means that young people can buy housing sooner and have kids. When they have kids, they can't take as much risk and don't have as much energy to start companies. (I have four kids—I barely have the time and energy to blog, much less start a company.) Also, if houses are cheap, it's easier to make it big, and you want it to be hard to make it big.

- **Cities and crowds but not overpopulation.** The pressure of these conditions makes people jealous of one another; this in turn makes them compete. Cities also bring people together to work. People can't telecommute to a startup. People need to get together to bounce ideas off one another, argue, and cajole. Also, crowded living conditions give people something to shoot for: that is, achieving success so they can get a bigger place to live.

- **Absence of multinational companies—especially from the finance industry.** If your companies have to compete with conglomerates or banks like Goldman Sachs throwing money at people, it's going to be hard to get anyone for a startup. Pity the startups in New York, London, and Singapore. Come to think of it, how many tech success stories have come from these cities? There is intense competition for employees in Silicon Valley, too, but we're using the same currency: the upside of equity, not high starting salaries.

- **Life-threatening enemies.** Israel is a speck of dust that has few natural resources, and it's surrounded by real enemies. And yet the country has produced some of the world's best technology companies. There's nothing like a life-threatening environment to get the entrepreneurial juices flowing. If a region has to do nothing more than stick a pipe in the ground, throw a net in the ocean, clean the beaches, or manage a natural seaport, it's going to be tough to be the next Silicon Valley.

Stuff You Can Do Jack About

- **Focus on educating engineers.** The most important action is to establish a world-class school of engineering. Engineering schools beget engineers. Engineers beget ideas. And ideas beget companies. End of discussion.

  If I had to point to the single biggest reason for Silicon Valley's existence, it would be the Stanford University School of Engineering. (Business schools are not as important, because MBAs seldom sit around discussing how to change the world with great products. Mostly they care about how to get interviews at multinationals and consulting firms.)

  On a tactical level, this means that aspiring regions should raid the best engineering schools. What do associate professors at Stanford, MIT, and Carnegie Mellon make? Whatever it is, offer them double the amount to move. Be clever: How hard could it be to recruit top-flight faculty to move to your beautiful (but not gorgeous) region if you conduct interviews at MIT in the winter? This is a trivial expense compared to the various incubator, tax treatment, and venture capital fund-formation schemes that are the usual solutions to the challenge.

- **Encourage immigration.** I am a third-generation Japanese American. My family moved here to drive a taxi and clean white people's homes. If I had a choice between funding someone from a family who moved here from Vietnam whose father and mother run a 7-Eleven versus a descendant of a Mayflower passenger with "IV" after his name, I'll give you half a guess as to my preference. You need to attract smart, hungry, and aggressive people from around the world. And to do that, you need good schools. To mix several metaphors, if you want to cover your ass, you need to open your kimono, because trust-fund kids don't make good entrepreneurs.

- **Send the best and brightest to Silicon Valley.** I can hear the complaints already: "This will lead to a brain drain, which is exactly what we are trying to prevent." This attitude misses the essence of entrepreneurship: It's not about preventing bad things, but fostering good things. Would it have been better for Hawaii if Steve Case had become a lawyer at his father's Hawaii law firm instead of moving to the mainland and creating AOL? I don't think so.

  The goal is to infect people with the disease called entrepreneurship and show them that there can be more to life than a job, that two guys/gals in a garage can change the world, and that a lot of money equals millions of dollars. Sure, some people will never return—like me. But those who do return come back with a much broader perspective on what life and a career can be. Maybe they will build another Silicon Valley because they've seen it done before.

- **Celebrate your heroes.** Every region needs its heroes. These folks take role modeling to an extreme; they have names like Steve Jobs, Bill Gates, Ted Turner, Steve Case, Anita Roddick, and Oprah Winfrey. Kids need heroes, so that they can say, "When I grow up, I am going to be the next Steve Jobs." In many places, a successful person is pulled back down because of jealousy. Sure, there's jealousy in Silicon Valley, but our way of dealing with it is to try to outdo the person, not pull her back down.

- **Forgive your failures.** There is no better place in the world to fail than Silicon Valley. Indeed, some people here have made a career of failing. Some of this is cultural—failing in Europe or Asia casts a cloud over one's family for generations. Not in Silicon Valley. Here, it doesn't matter (within reason) how many times you fail, as long as you eventually succeed. So many entrepreneurs who failed went on to create massive successes that we've learned that failure is a poor predictor of future results.

- **Be logical.** Make the challenge to create a Silicon Valley as easy as possible. Thus, a region should use its natural advantages—for example, aquaculture in Hawaii, security technology in Israel, alternative fuels in the Midwest, and solar power in the Sun Belt. There's a reason why the best woolen sweaters come from Norway and the best aloha shirts come from Hawaii. It's not because people tried to buck the trend.

- **Don't pat yourself on the back too soon.** Many regions declare victory because Microsoft, Sun, or Google opened a branch office. These branch offices don't hurt, but don't kid yourself into thinking that the existence of a branch office means that you are now a tech center. A region is truly a tech center when its companies open branch offices elsewhere, not when tax incentives and kowtowing got a company to open up a branch office in it.

- **Be patient.** There is nothing short-term in these recommendations. I estimate that creating something that begins to look like Silicon Valley is at least a twenty-year process. This is certainly longer than most politicians' reigns—hence the challenge of doing the right things for the long run.

Stuff You Shouldn't Do Jack About

The short recommendation is that government should not do much except provide more funding to the engineering schools. Unfortunately, that probably won't seem like enough to most people, so they may be tempted to implement other ideas.

- **Don't focus on "creating jobs."** When a region adds the second bottom line of creating jobs, things get wacky. Such a goal perverts the objective of a startup, because the primary, perhaps the sole, goal of a startup is to kick ass. If it also has to create jobs for the sake of creating jobs, then you defocus it. The thinking should be: "If this company kicks ass, then it will survive and grow. If it survives and grows, then it will create jobs." So let startups focus on kicking ass, and the jobs will come naturally—or not.

- **Don't pass a special tax exemption.** There's an assumption that tax benefits for investing in startups encourages entrepreneurship. I disagree; I think it mostly creates sloppy decisions by unsophisticated investors and crooked ones by others. Indeed, the unstated (and perhaps unrealized) goal of a sophisticated investor is to create, not avoid, tax liabilities. Nothing would make me happier than having to pay $100 million in income taxes. I would hand-deliver that income tax return to the White House.

• **Don't create a venture capital fund.** The thinking here is that a government-created venture capital fund would kick-start entrepreneurship because of the influx of money. However, if there's one thing you can depend on in venture capitalists, it's greed. If you show them good engineers with good ideas for good companies, they will appear by (private) plane, canoe, dogsled, and camel. Such a region doesn't need to create a fund.

(There is one notable exception to this: The government of Israel created a seed fund that launched its venture capital industry. However, my interpretation is that the fund was successful because there were already entrepreneurs there; the fund didn't cause entrepreneurs to suddenly appear out of the desert.)

There's one more thing you need to do: Aim higher than merely trying to re-create Silicon Valley. You should try to kick our butt instead. It's true entrepreneurship when Silicon Valley has to copy you.

CHAPTER 31

The Purest Form of Engineering: Woz

Never trust a computer you can't throw out a window.

~ STEVE WOZNIAK

What better way to end this section than by writing about Steve Wozniak, the cofounder of Apple. I didn't work directly with Woz in my tours of duty at Apple, so I loved reading Gina Smith's book, *iWoz: Computer Geek to Cult Icon—How I Invented the Personal Computer, Co-Founded Apple, and Had Fun Doing It* (Norton, 2007). In fact, I gave her this blurb for it:

Every engineer—and certainly every engineering student—should read this book. It is about the thrill of invention, the process of making the world a better place, and the purity of entrepreneurship. *iWoz* is the personal computer generation's version of *The Soul of a New Machine*. It is, in a nutshell, the engineer's manifesto. I hope that the so-called innovation experts and MBAs choke when they read it.

I loved the book because it isn't the typical theoretical tome written by an expert or consultant (i.e., someone who can't do but can write). Instead, the book takes you inside the mind of someone who was truly instrumental in one of the great revolutions of our time. After reading it, I was even prouder of having worked for Apple. Also, I swear that Woz doesn't use the word *strategic* once in the book—how many business books can you say that about? For your enjoyment, here's a list of the top ten things that I learned by reading *iWoz*.

1. In the sixth grade, Woz scammed gubernatorial candidate Richard Nixon with a certificate from the school's ham-radio club. The certificate was made with crayons just before the ceremony, and Woz was the only member of the club.

2. The Apple IPO made the most millionaires in one single day in history up to that point in time.

3. Woz and Jobs worked as Alice in Wonderland characters at a shopping mall in San Jose. (Steve Jobs doing this boggles my mind.)

4. Woz didn't return to the University of Colorado after his first year because he ran up too much computer time-sharing costs.

5. Woz tried to call the pope by impersonating Dr. Henry Kissinger. He almost got through, but the Vatican called the real Dr. Kissinger to verify the call.

6. A robber with a gun stole a blue box from Woz and Jobs in Sunnyvale.

7. Allen Baum alleviated Woz's concern about leaving Hewlett-Packard to start Apple by telling him, "You can be an engineer and become a manager and get rich, or you can be an engineer and stay an engineer and get rich."

8. Woz lost approximately $12 million in each of the two US Festivals that he put on.

9. Woz taught computer technology to elementary school students for ten years.

10. The book ends with Woz's thoughts on being a great engineer:

- Don't waver.
- See things in gray scale.
- Work alone.
- Trust your instincts.

When is the last time anyone told you to work like this?

The first time an "expert" tells you that you need to conduct market research, run your design past focus groups, and set up offshore development, just remember what Woz said, and you'll be fine.

The Reality of Marketing

Everybody wants to be the vice president of marketing, because you get to do the fun stuff: shuck and jive with the beautiful people, create fun marketing campaigns, drive German cars, and pierce parts of your body. If only this were the reality of marketing. More accurately, marketing is the process of convincing people they need your product or service. That's not so easy. This section explains the reality of marketing.

CHAPTER 32

Stupid Ways to Hinder Market Adoption

It's not the work which kills people, it's the worry. It's not the revolution that destroys machinery, it's the friction.

~ HENRY WARD BEECHER

I n a perfect world, you'd make a product that's so great that your marketing doesn't matter, and your marketing is so great that your product doesn't matter. This isn't a perfect world. The reality is that marketing does matter—although it can only do so much good (or damage). This section of the book provides ways to make your marketing better so that it accelerates your success.

This chapter is a compilation of silly and stupid ways companies hinder adoption of their products and services in the real world. I must admit that I've made these mistakes—in fact, that's why I know these mistakes are (a) silly, (b) stupid, and (c) inimical to adoption.

1. **Enforced, immediate registration.** Requiring a new user to register and provide a modicum of information is a reasonable request—just do it after you've sucked the person in. Most sites require registration as the first step, and this puts a barrier in front of adoption. At the very least, companies could ask for name and e-mail address but not require it until a later time.

2. **Impossibly long URLs.** When you want to send people a URL, the site generates one that's 70 characters long, or more! When you copy, paste,

and e-mail this URL, a line break is added, so people cannot click on it to go to the intended location. For example, the URL for a billiard table sold on the Costco site had 300 characters. Just how many billiard-table models could Costco be selling? As Steve Jobs said, "There must be a better way."

3. **Windows that don't generate URLs.** Have you ever wanted to point people to a page, but the page has no URL? You've got a window open that you want to tell someone about, but you'd have to write an essay to explain how to get that window open again. Did someone at the company decide that it didn't want referrals, links, and additional traffic? This is the best argument I can think of for not using frames.

4. **Lack of a search function.** Some sites don't allow people to search. This is OK for simple sites where a site map suffices, but that's seldom the case. If your site has a site map that goes deeper than one level, it probably needs a search box.

5. **Lack of ways to share an experience.** It's hard to make a product, service, or Web site that's so compelling that people want to share it. If you do, it's a shame when there's no easy way for people to spread the word about what they like. The next time you're visiting a Web site, look for buttons that say "Share this" or "E-mail this to a friend," and implement similar functionality.

6. **Limiting contact to e-mail.** Don't get me wrong: I live and die by e-mail, but there are times I want to call a company, or maybe even snail mail something to it. Many companies allow people to send only an e-mail via a Web form. Why don't companies call this page "Don't Contact Us" and at least be honest? Many companies don't even list a way to contact them at all, so I guess there are even dumber people out there.

7. **Lack of feeds and e-mail lists.** When people are interested in your company, they will want to receive information about your products and services. This should be as easy as possible—meaning that you provide both e-mail and RSS feeds for content and PR newsletters.

8. **Requirement to retype e-mail addresses.** How about the patent-pending, curve-jumping, venture capitalist–funded Internet company that wants to you to share content but requires you to retype the e-mail addresses of your friends?

   I have 8,000 e-mail addresses in Entourage. I am not going to retype them into the done-as-an-afterthought address book that companies build into their products. If nothing else, companies can use this cool tool from Plaxo or allow text imports into the aforementioned crappy address book. When do you suppose a standard format will emerge for transferring contacts?

9. **User names that cannot contain the @ character.** In other words, a user name cannot be your e-mail address. I am a member of hundreds of sites. I can't remember if my user name is kawasaki, gkawasaki, guy-kawasaki, or kawasaki3487. I do know what my e-mail address is, so just let me use that as my user name.

10. **Case-sensitive user names and passwords.** I know: User names and passwords that are case sensitive are more secure, but they also increase the likelihood of incorrectly typing them. In many a demo, a company's CEO can't sign into her own account because she didn't type the proper case of her user name or password. You'd think people would get a clue from that.

11. **Frictionful commenting.** "Moderated comments" is an oxymoron. If your company is trying to be a hip, myth-busting, hypocrisy-outing organization, then it should let anyone comment.

12. **Unreadable confirmation (CAPTCHA) codes.** Don't get me wrong: I don't support spam or account-creating robots. A confirmation system is a good thing, but many are too difficult to read: upper- versus lowercase, I versus 1, and 0 versus O. My theory is that technology is called CAPTCHA because it captures folks in an endless loop of trying to prove to a machine that you're a human.

13. **E-mails without signatures.** In e-mail lingo, a *signature* is text that is automatically included in every e-mail you send. Typically, it contains the

person's name, e-mail address, phone numbers, and Web site. This is very useful if someone wants to pick up the phone and call you or visit your Web site without having to ask for that information.

In Asia, people say, "Buddha is in the details." Adoption is in the details, too, so take this list and check it twice to ensure that finding, buying, and using your product or service is friction-free.

CHAPTER 33

The Name Game

The name we give to something shapes our attitude to it.

~ KATHERINE PATERSON

Did you know that *volvo* is a Latin word that means "I roll"? So the name of the manufacturer of the world's safest cars means "I roll." I'll never look at a Volvo without thinking about this irony again.

These are guidelines for naming a company or product. Most people's primary concern is whether a domain name is available. There are many other considerations to keep in mind.

- **Begin with letters early in the alphabet.** Here's the scenario: You bought a booth at a massive trade show like Comdex. The list of exhibitors in the show guide is alphabetized. Would you rather be listed in the front of the guide or at the back of the guide? Another scenario: A reviewer analyzes a dozen or so products. She lists them in alphabetical order in the review. Would you prefer that your product be at the beginning or end of the list?

- **Avoid names starting with X and Z.** This is somewhat repetitious, but it's a pet peeve of mine. The worst letters to start your company or product name with are X and Z. First, they are both late in the alphabet. Second, they're confusing to spell and to pronounce. "Please Zerox (or Xerox?) this form." "Let's check out the Zilinx (or Xilinx?) booth."

- **Embody verb potential.** A great name turns into a verb. Examples: Xerox (fortunately, they overcame the X), Google, Digg, and StuffIt. Words with verb potential are no more than three syllables and "active sounding." They need to work in phrases such as, "Why don't we just _____ it?" Or, "I'll just _____ it." (Did you know that "Kawasakied" is in the urban dictionary? Google "kawasakied" if you don't believe me.)

- **Sound different.** Quick: What do the following companies do? Claris. Clarin. Claria. Clarium. Clarins. Claritin. It's hard to remember whether they sell makeup, unplug your nose, or got killed by Apple. Great names sound different. They also spell different, for that matter.

- **Embody logic.** The absolute best example of naming things in a logical manner is the approach by the clever folks at Pokémon. You don't have to be a kid to figure out what Geodude and Lickitung look like. Can the same be said of names like Tenaris, Abaxis, and Ceradyne? Sounding different + spelling different + embodying logic = a memorable name. Here's a good test: If you told your company or product name to ten strangers, would at least half of them guess what business you're in?

- **Avoid the commonplace and generic.** If you name your product or company something commonplace and generic, people will never find it on Google, Download.com, and VersionTracker, Yahoo! For example, if you name your company Water and your product Word, people will have a difficult time using a search engine to find them when you need them to find it the easiest: when you first launch.

- **Avoid the trendy.** Mea culpa: We made a big mistake when we started what is now Garage Technology Ventures. We called it "garage.com." Yup, with a lower case G. It was a brief lapse into modesty and eBay envy. We had a great slogan, too: "We put the capital in you, not in our name." (Later, we considered an even better slogan: "We take the FU out of funding.") The .com was a mistake, too, because "dot-com" became synonymous with "no business model." If you think there's a cool trend in naming going on, my advice is that you avoid it.

It doesn't matter whether you check the domain first, then apply these recommendations, or vice versa. But please do both, because saddling a great company or great product with a crappy name is a real crime.

CHAPTER 34

The Art of Branding

Tell me what brand of whiskey that Grant drinks.
I would like to send a barrel of it to my other generals.

~ ABRAHAM LINCOLN

In the real world, you don't have infinite resources; you don't have a perfect product, and you don't sell to a growing market without competition. You're also not omnipotent, so you cannot enforce what people think your brand represents. Under these assumptions, most companies need all the help they can get with branding. Here are the keys to this mysterious process.

- **Seize the high ground.** Establish your brand on positive conditions like "making meaning," "doing good," "changing the world," and "making people happy"—not doing in your competition. Think about it: When is the last time you bought a product to hurt a company's competition? (Other than maybe Macintosh users.) If you want to beat your competition, establish an uplifting brand, but don't try to establish a brand based on your silly desire to beat your competition.

- **Create one message.** It's hard enough to create and communicate one branding message; however, many companies try to establish more than one, because they are afraid of being niched and want the entire market. "Our computer is for *Fortune* 500 companies. And, oh yes, it's also for consumers to use at home." Face it, Volvo can't equal safety *and* sexiness, and

Toyota can't equal economical *and* lexuriousness. You can pick one message, stick with it for at least a year if it appears promising, and then try another. But you can't try several at once or switch every few months.

- **Speak English.** Not necessarily English, but don't speak in jargon. If your positioning statement uses any acronyms, the odds are that (a) most people won't understand your branding, and (b) your branding won't last very long. For example, "best MP3 decoder" presumes that people understand what "MP3" and "decoder" mean. Ten years from now, who knows if MP3 will matter anymore. Not to be an ageist, but a good test is to ask your parents if they understand what your positioning means—assuming your parents aren't computer science professors.

- **Take the opposite test.** How many times have you read a product description like this: "Our software is scalable, secure, easy to use, and fast"? Companies use these adjectives as if no other company claims its product is scalable, secure, easy to use, and fast. See if your competition uses the antonyms of the adjectives that you use. If it doesn't, your description is useless. For example, I've never heard a company say that its product was limited, full of leaks, hard to use, and slow.

- **Cascade the message.** Let's say that you craft the perfect branding message. As the Japanese say, "Mazel tov." Now cascade your message up and down your organization. The marketing departments of many companies assume that once they've put out the press release or run the ad, the entire world understands the message. It's unlikely that even the entire company does. Start with your board of directors and work down to Trixie and Biff at the front desk, and make sure every employee understands the branding.

- **Examine the bounce-back.** You know what messages you send, but you really don't know what messages people receive. Here's a concept: You should ask them to bounce back the message that you sent so that you can learn how your message is truly interpreted. In the end, it's not so much what you say as much as what people hear.

- **Focus on PR, not advertising.** Many companies waste millions of dollars trying to establish brands with advertising. Too much money is worse than too little, because when you have a lot of money, you spend a lot of money on stupid things like Super Bowl commercials. Brands are built on what people are saying about you, not what you're saying about yourself. People say good things about you when (a) you have a great product and (b) you get people to spread the word about it.

- **Strive for humanness.** Great brands achieve a high level of humanness. They speak to you as an individual, not as part of a market. It's "my iPod," "my Macintosh," "my Harley-Davidson," "my bottle of Coke." By contrast, you never think "my Vista" or "my Microsoft Office," so I wouldn't call Microsoft a great brand—although kids think of "my Xbox." Unfortunately, Xbox and Microsoft are not closely linked.

Now step back and ask yourself the $64,000 question: "If we don't spend a dime on marketing, will people be aware of our brand and understand what it stands for?" Because the real world of marketing is this: You don't have a big marketing budget so you have to depend on people "creating" your brand for you. For decades Apple has tried to make the Macintosh brand stand for power with all its money. For decades consumers believed the Macintosh brand stood for ease of use. Ultimately, you flow with what's going, and you are thankful that anything is flowing at all.

CHAPTER 35

Frame or Be Framed

The more important the subject and the closer it cuts to the bone of our hopes and needs, the more we are likely to err in establishing a framework for analysis.

~ STEPHEN JAY GOULD

George Lakoff is a professor in the Linguistics Department of the University of California–Berkeley, and he's the author of a book called *Don't Think of an Elephant* (Chelsea Green, 2004). His interview in the *UC Berkeley News* (October 27, 2003) explains how Republicans are good "framers" and Democrats are lousy ones. Here are two questions from the interview:

Q: How does language influence the terms of political debate?

A: Language always comes with what is called "framing." Every word is defined relative to a conceptual framework. If you have something like "revolt," that implies a population that is being ruled unfairly, or assumes it is being ruled unfairly, and that they are throwing off their rulers, which would be considered a good thing. That's a frame.

If you then add the word "voter" in front of "revolt," you get a metaphorical meaning saying that the voters are the oppressed people, the governor is the oppressive ruler, that they have ousted him and this is a good thing and all things are good now. All of that comes up when you see a headline like "voter revolt"—something that most people read and never notice. But these things can be affected by reporters and, very often, by the campaign people themselves.

Q: Do any of the Democratic presidential candidates grasp the importance of framing?

A: None. They don't get it at all. But they're in a funny position. The framing changes that have to be made are long-term changes. The conservatives understood this in 1973. By 1980 they had a candidate, Ronald Reagan, who could take all this stuff and run with it. The progressives don't have a candidate now who understands these things and can talk about them. And in order for a candidate to be able to talk about them, the ideas have to be out there. You have to be able to reference them in a sound bite. Other people have to put these ideas into the public domain, not politicians. The question is, How do you get these ideas out there? There are all kinds of ways, and one of the things the Rockridge Institute is looking at is talking to advocacy groups, which could do this very well. They have more of a budget, they're spread all over the place, and they have access to the media.

Right now the Democratic Party is into marketing. They pick a number of issues like prescription drugs and Social Security and ask which ones sell best across the spectrum, and they run on those issues. They have no moral perspective, no general values, no identity. People vote their identity, they don't just vote on the issues, and Democrats don't understand that. Look at Schwarzenegger, who says nothing about the issues. The Democrats ask, How could anyone vote for this guy? They did because he put forth an identity. Voters knew who he is.

There's a good marketing lesson in Lakoff's work: You either frame your product or someone will frame it for you. And you are not in control if someone frames it for you. For example, an online music-sharing service is either "piracy" or "a music-listeners revolution." Using the word "revolution" implies that record companies are unfairly ruling people who listen to music. This beats the heck out of "piracy," and the company who provides relief from this oppression is logically a hero of the people. This is how to control the frame:

- **Be true to yourself.** A frame should represent what you stand for—as opposed to what market research might tell you to stand for. Which is to say, if you are nothing but music pirates, then don't think that calling yourselves revolutionaries will fix anything. If your product or service is crappy, then you need to fix the product or service and not alter your marketing and branding.

- **Avoid the frontal assault.** When framing the competition, the operative phrase is "damning with faint praise." The goal is to frame your competition in a way that isn't harshly critical, but clever and damning. For example, Microsoft framed Macintosh successfully for years by describing it as an easy-to-use but not powerful computer.

- **Align with core values.** When framing yourself, align with generally accepted core values. In America, circa 2008, this means concepts with positive connotations, like democratization, liberation, independence, efficacy, and freedom. For example, "democratizing video" sounds a lot better than "ripping off movie studios"—but only if that's what you truly do.

- **Draw first blood.** It's better to fire the first salvo that frames both your competition your own product or service. The second and later companies then have to react to what you've done—in a sense, they have to work within your framework and dig themselves out of a hole. Imagine if Mercedes had drawn first blood by framing Lexus as a "line of luxury cars from the maker of the Corolla." Toyota's frame of "as good as a Mercedes but half the price" would have been a lot less effective.

Framing is one of the most powerful and enjoyable marketing functions, so I hope that you'll try it. After a while, maybe you'll get bored with framing products and services, and you'll turn to politics. Then someday maybe Lakoff will write about you.

CHAPTER 36

Get a Clue: The Global Youth Market

> The error of youth is to believe that intelligence is a
> substitute for experience, while the error of age is to
> believe experience is a substitute for intelligence.
>
> ～ LYMAN BRYSON

Kathleen Gasperini is the cofounder and senior vice president of Label Networks. Her company helps leading brands, such as Apple Computer, Verizon Wireless, Pepsi, Vans, Levi Strauss, and Burton Snowboards understand the global youth culture. This interview will help you understand trends, marketing to young people, and how young people determine marketing, too.

Q: What is your methodology for studying trends?

A: Our methodology is unique in that we are mobile and go into their environments, i.e., shopping locations, cafés, malls, streets, sporting areas, and music festivals, and we talk with young people in face-to-face interviews. We created proprietary wireless research tools and methodologies that allow us to be mobile and go into such locations.

Because we are out there with them—in the heat, dust, and rain—we also gain their trust, and young people often tell us why they responded the way that they did. We capture this using images and in some cases video. Also, our field research teams come from these markets and understand the vernacular, music, fashion, and general vibe of the target demographic.

In youth culture markets, a guy with khaki slacks and a blue buttoned-down shirt and a clipboard simply scares off young people. Our field research teams are just as likely to have a tattoo as the person they're talking to, but they tend to be older than the target market and many have journalistic capabilities. We also use a traditional statistical analysis program for primary analysis of the data, but we add our own analysis based on the results, historic data, and our knowledge and intuition of youth markets.

Our representative sampling formula is based on a typical representative sampling model, as well as a country's census data as our control group. We figured out how to capture data remotely in multiple languages and have the data come back in English.

Q: Why do MySpace and Facebook appeal so much to young people?

A: The appeal is that they allow for creativity, communication, and discovery. Check out the Youtube.com video "MySpace: The Movie." It's brilliant, because it deals with the drama of being young and having to deal with updating your profile and "friends."

The popularity of these services has important marketing consequences. For example, MySpace is a great way to find out about new music, which is a major contributor to why young people are checking it out. It also is the epitome of grass roots. Consumer-generated content means that someone did it "just because." You can't get much more authentic and credible than that.

Brands that try to be this way don't always pull it off—although the video in the Sony Bravia commercial with colorful balls bouncing down the streets of San Francisco was good, because it makes you forget what the commercial is really for. This is similar to the impact of the early iPod commercials with the dancing dark figures.

For the small guys who use MySpace to promote their wares—CDs, T-shirts, stickers—it's got "cred," because it takes some effort to keep updating your profile and getting "friends." Look at what it did for Fall Out Boy from the Midwest and Arctic Monkeys in the UK: These bands came out of nowhere and are making it relatively big. Bands like My Chemical

Romance and Black-Eyed Peas are breaking new videos on MySpace rather than MTV. And it's going global.

Q: How long does a young-people fad last?

A: It depends on the country and age group, but generally young people do not think something is a fad. It's just what's happening right then. A fifteen-year-old's sense of history is about three years, which explains, for example, why they think they're creating punk rock, even though their parents may have listened to the Sex Pistols.

If something becomes "classic," then it's more long term and most likely has become a part of several aspects of youth lifestyle. Take Converse sneaks—most young people have no idea they were intended as basketball shoes. They represent quintessential punk. Timberlands have crossed over yet maintained their cred. Once used for utilitarian purposes, they are now the footwear of choice in various urban markets, particularly among the krumping scene in South-Central L.A., where they're a part of the tribal street-dance style, even if you're wearing a pleated Brazilian capoeira-inspired skirt with American Apparel–type tube socks and arm-sock sleeves.

A Japanese trend that's crossed over is BAPE—the Bathing Ape company—bringing colorful patent-leather sneaks, characters, urban vinyl dolls—an entire collection of cool, inspired by manga—to the States. I realize I just talked about a bunch of footwear examples, but hopefully they show concepts of fads, trends, and quintessential classics.

We asked a question across all our global studies about information overload: "Do you feel there's too much information coming at you to absorb?" The young people in the United States, Canada, and Japan said no. If anything, young people want more . . . they're hungry. You can see this in our China study, too.

But the European results are much different. In the UK, they feel overloaded, saturated, can't handle it; and in Germany, there's a similar feeling. It's like they don't want change as much. Whereas in Spain, they're far more into information in general and don't feel that overwhelmed. Italy's like Spain in that sense. Here's a generalization: China and Japan are futuristic and optimistic; Western Europe is stuck in their history; and America has no past and no future—we're now.

Q: How different is a young person in Shanghai from one in Palo Alto, Los Angeles, London, Munich, Addis Ababa, or Seoul?

A: First, a fifteen-year-old today in North America, for example, is much different than a fifteen-year-old was five years ago. It used to be "I want my MTV," but those people are now the parents of the fifteen-year-olds who want their MP3s. And it's not just about having an MP3 or cell phone, but personalizing it with mashup ring tones, which they download for free from 3Gforfree.com, and a personal, only-friends-understand texting language, for example. They don't just expect control of their entertainment, they create it themselves. Very DIY culture. Not so much in Japan and China, where it's still more "I'm an individual but as a group" thinking.

The Shanghai girl is far more imaginative than the guy, whose life is still very structured by parents because of the draconian one-child rule. She is incredibly happy about living in the time of now and seeing the changes all around. She embraces things and feels lucky. She is part of the growing Pan-Asianism taking place. She is proud of China.

The Los Angeles kid is the most entrepreneurial, the most culturally diverse, and creates her world by utilitarian means—that which inspires and surrounds her. One thing about this generation of thirteen- to twenty-five-year-olds is that it's more genderless. There's more assimilation across boundaries, across sports, music, fashion, technology, and genders. For example, one of the top sports girls want to learn—other than skateboarding—is football, and guys are really getting into dance—mostly street and martial arts–inspired.

The London kid right now isn't as hopeful but thinks he's trendsetting in his own head. The Munich kid is more philosophical, but socially "younger" than the fifteen-year-old in L.A. or Palo Alto, mainly because he's not online as much and this isn't encouraged by parents. For the Addis Ababa kid, it depends on socioeconomic level, but like the others, this kid is heavily influenced by music. Music is the common thread, because it's emotional and personal and taps into that mammalian cortex.

The Addis Ababa kid is probably the "oldest" of all. Not necessarily in terms of social skills, but knowing life, because they've seen extremes—child soldiers who can see things the L.A. kid cannot. There is a great desire to learn—they are more hopeful than you may believe. There is fortune at the bottom of the pyramid, as C. K. Prahalad said in his book about the subject.

Q: Are companies deluding themselves if they think they can create trends for young people from the top down?

A: Yes, it's rather laughable. Or sad. Millions of dollars are wasted only to result in brand backlash, which takes millions more to undo. Many large brands or agencies can't see beyond the thirty-second TV pitch. "But how do I reach them?" they ask. There are so many ways. You can walk right past a big idea if you have your cultural blinders on.

These top-down companies are running with blinders on into a future that has a huge cliff. Grass roots and bottom-up is the most authentic way to go, and you can do this much faster than in the past, given the speed of communication and viral marketing. But you can't try to be cool and grassroots if it's not true and real. Grass roots takes being out in the marketplace—being there, in their lives, and relevant.

Young people don't care if they're sweating and being hot, say, at an outdoor festival. Older people do. Success can truly smell! And young people can smell anything that smacks of insincerity a mile away. To them, some companies just stink. They are so removed from their reality. The reason so many companies try to do top-down trending is because they don't know how to do bottom-up marketing or are afraid of change. Or of getting sweaty.

Q: Generally speaking, how does a company build cred with young people?

A: There's no silver-bullet solution, because each market has specific threads of influence. Generally, it's very important to be a part of the lifestyle of young people and be more than one thing for one aspect of their lives—this also gives a company greater longevity. If you follow the threads of influence, then you can build cred more easily. I'll give you two ideas: First, get associated with music and artists; sponsor up-and-coming bands; and know what's going on in various new music subcultures.

Second, there's a unique opportunity to actually do some good and build cred at the same time. The North American youth culture marketplace of thirteen- to fifteen-year-olds is among the most philanthropic and environmentally conscious demographic in the world. Young people tend to support brands that give back, and they have far greater respect for celebrity activists. What this means is that there's a great opportunity for reaching young people in an authentic and grassroots level by appealing to their sense of "good causes."

Q: How will young people shop during the next two years?
A: Online—more so because there are limitations to getting to stores that carry what young people want. They are also very cost-conscious and will look for the best deals, which is easier to do online. eBay is the new thrift store/vintage "find."

But smaller cool brands, i.e., T-shirt upstarts and things like that, are not only going to be places to shop, but the destinations to hang out, virtually. Discount is moving into the direction of being OK. Shopping at Target is OK because they offer decent styles and have great ads.

Disposable fashion trends are moving in, especially with the launches of H&M in North America, which are already all over New York and L.A., and a huge one in San Francisco. This trend is coming from Europe, though it originally came from Japan. "Disposable" means being able to buy stylish looks at inexpensive prices that make the piece almost disposable.

The flip side of disposable is that there will be special "investment" shopping trends for that coveted piece of glamour: Look to footwear, denim, special T-shirts, and accessories being key shopping pieces/experiences. I'd also say that "pop-up" retail is in the future and will change shopping patterns—it will be more like an event than a retail experience, and you'll have to find out where the store is before it moves on and goes away. But pop-up retail is more like five years out. You already have this in various places like Tokyo and New York, but it's going to happen in other areas, too.

Q: What is your analysis of the following segments for young people?

A: Cell phone: Trends are moving toward pushing multiple platforms into one unit. It's a mobile generation. The brand that can create a high-end cell phone that also has hybrid capabilities of texting, images, video, Internet access, games, and an MP3-type device is the way things are headed. The hype is on Apple to do this. If so, then not only are they in the industry of computers and music technology, but also competing in the phone marketplace. And it will change that industry dramatically.

Music: This is a progressively moving niche. There's a blending of styles that young people completely identify with, like indie rock right now and punk-indie. Look for recontextualized grunge on the radar. I'm not talking full-on Nirvana or Pearl Jam, but a mashup of this with indie. Hip-hop has plateaued, but there will be a reinvention, but it will be different, like what's going on in the hyphy scene coming out of San Francisco. And like reggaeton and dancehall coming out of cities such as Miami, Houston, and Atlanta.

Fashion: Fashion follows music and street culture—from the bottom up. It's not like couture, which is very much more "top-down."

Sports: The sport of the world is soccer, but Americans obviously don't embrace this sport that much. There's a lot of turmoil right now in sports, and therefore the influence of sports is affected. There are "hooligans" from the UK not being able to go to matches, basketball players getting into various trouble, and baseball players and doping issues.

Action sports, such as surfing, skateboarding, and snowboarding, were the hottest thing for youth culture, but this has plateaued. Just two years ago, everyone was looking like a skater. A shining star is snowboarder Shaun White. It'll be interesting to see what happens with him and snowboarding because of the incredible coverage the sport received from the Olympics in February and the high percentages of young people who watched snowboarding on TV and online. He could be the next Tony Hawk or Michael Jordan in the future. So brands associated with White, such as Burton and those associated with the lifestyle surrounding the sport, may be new drivers of trends.

Q: Knowing all that you know, what kind of company would you start in the young-people market?

A: There's opportunity for true lifestyle brands that cross over into every aspect of a young person's life, such as a T-shirt company. People may laugh, but look at Volcom. Of young people in America, 57.3 percent buy ten to fifteen T-shirts per year, making T-shirts one of the highest-grossing markets within the youth fashion industry. This new T-shirt company would be online, but only the pinnacle of much more underneath.

I would also get it into special boutiques in Japan first. Even as a U.S.-based company, I would do pop-up retail. This T-shirt brand could sponsor up-and-coming artists, perhaps spin off a record label and an entertainment division (which works on getting sponsored artists and athletes into video games), then quickly move into the $13 billion denim market by getting the tightly woven high-end denim from Japan, with Italian stitching and dyes, and selling clothes in the United States.

From there, the T-shirt brand would do footwear. Keep the accessories coming—not just jewelry, but cell-phone and iPod cases. The brand would also have graffiti and street artists involved in many aspects, including exhibitions and various elements of design, which of course will get picked up by the Mountain Dews, Motorolas, and Toyotas. From the start, this T-shirt brand will also have a unique nonprofit collaboration, to which a percentage of profits will be delivered.

Gasperini taught me that trends are funny things: Chase them, and they move away faster. Create them, and they defy you. But study them, and they just might reveal their lessons so that you can ride them to success.

CHAPTER 37

The Lesson of Tam's Art Gallery

**If you want to be truly successful invest in yourself to get the
knowledge you need to find your unique factor. When you find
it and focus on it and persevere your success will blossom.**

~ SIDNEY MADWED

During a trip to Hong Kong, I visited Stanley Market, a large bazaar (nothing to do with the Stanley Cup). Mind you, it's a kiosk compared to the Grand Bazaar in Istanbul, but it's jammed with stores. Most of the stores carry a little bit of everything: T-shirts, shoes, consumer electronics, leather goods—you name it.

After spending an hour there, I bought something from only one store: Tam's Art Gallery. This store specializes in making "chops" (a stamp with Chinese characters that's used to prove one's identity). You provide the English word, and the employee makes a chop with the Chinese characters. I relearned a marketing lesson at Tam's that serves as the most important lesson of branding:

Do one thing well.

The other stores offered too much and made decisions more difficult. Granted, it may take you a while to figure out what the one thing is (for all I know, Tam's started off selling a bunch of stuff, too), but strive to stand for just one thing. This is probably one more thing than your competition.

The Reality of Selling
and Evangelizing

Though many people disagree me, my theory is that "sales fix everything." This is because as long as you have sales, cash will flow, and as long as cash is flowing, (a) you have the time to fix your team, your technology, and your marketing; (b) the press won't say much, because customers are paying you; and (c) your investors leave you alone, because they don't want to jinx your success. This section examines selling and evangelism. I grouped evangelism with sales because it is the purest form of selling—that is, getting people to buy into your product or service as much as you do.

CHAPTER 38

The Art of Selling

Pretend that every single person you meet has a sign around his or her neck that says, "Make me feel important." Not only will you succeed in sales, you will succeed in life.

~ MARY KAY ASH

H ave you heard the acronym ABC? It stands for Always Be Closing. That is, you should always be trying to make a sale. You can overdo this—or more accurately, you can lack subtlety and make people resent your efforts. Indeed, the best sale is a long-lasting and repeating one, but don't kid yourself: You either make a sale or you don't. This chapter explains the art of selling.

- **See the gorilla.** Daniel J. Simons of the University of Illinois and Christopher E. Chabris of Harvard University ran an experiment (Google "Gorillas in Our Midst") in which they asked students to watch two teams of players throwing basketballs. The students were told to count how many times one team passed the basketball to their own teammates. Thirty-five seconds into the video, an actor dressed as a gorilla entered the room, thumped on his chest, and remained in the room for another nine seconds. Fifty percent of the students did not notice the gorilla! If you want to make it rain, you have to see the gorilla markets in the mist, so to speak. Decades ago, Univac was a leader in computers, but it believed that the market for computers was scientists; it did not see that the gorilla market for computers was businesspeople. That's why everyone knows who IBM is and few people remember Univac.

- **Sell, don't enable buying.** An iPod is bought because people walk into the Apple store intending to buy it. They've already made the decision. However, the products and services of most organizations are sold, not bought. If you don't have an iPod-like product, you need face-to-face, personalized, and intense contact. Advertising can't do this, so for most organizations the best lead-generation methods are seminars, presentations by company executives, and schmoozing.

- **Find the key influencers.** The higher you go in most organizations, the thinner the air. The thinner the air, the more difficult it is to find intelligent life. Thus, if you focus your rainmaking efforts on CXO-level people, you will deal with the dumbest people in the organization. The biggest titles do not have the biggest brains, so don't go after the biggest titles. Instead, go after the key influencers. They have humbler titles like secretary, administrative aide, database administrator, or customer service manager. They usually do the real work, so they know what products and services are needed, and the CXOs ask them for their recommendations. The logical question now is, How do you find the key influencers? The answer is that you ask people at the company to answer this simple question, "When there are problems, who does everyone go to at this organization?"

- **Give customers less information.** Here's a counterintuitive thought: Shoppers with less information about a product are happier than those with more information. Researchers at the Tippie College of Business came to this conclusion after conducting a study in which people were asked their opinions of chocolate and hand lotion. One group was given extensive information and the other much less. For each product, the group given less information was more optimistic about the product, because it was easier to engage in wishful thinking. Perhaps if people are given more information, it's harder for them to kid themselves. When it comes to product information, more might not be more—especially when you have a crappy product.

- **Make prospects talk.** If prospects are open to buying your product or service, they will usually tell you what it will take to close them. All you have to do is (a) get them talking about their needs, (b) shut up, (c) listen, and then (d) explain how your product or service fills their needs (if it indeed does). Most salespeople can't do this, because (a) they're not prepared to ask good questions, (b) they're too stupid to shut up, and (c) they don't know their product or service well enough to know whether it can in fact fill these needs. When it comes to rainmaking, there's clearly a reason why God gave us two ears but only one mouth.

- **Disrupt, then reframe.** The theory of "disrupt, then reframe" is that if you introduce a non sequitur or unexpected element into your conversation and then immediately inject a call to action, the customer is more likely to agree to your proposition. The disruption theoretically neutralizes critical thinking and makes a person more likely to agree. This concept is the result of a study by Barbara Davis and Professor Eric Knowles in which they sold note cards door-to-door for a charity. When they told people that the cards were eight for $3.00, they had a 40 percent success rate. When they told people that the price was eight for 300 pennies and then said, "which is a bargain," 80 percent of the people bought cards.

- **Cut the hype.** Assistant professor Vanessa Patrick at the University of Georgia, along with Debbie MacInnis and C. Whan Park of the University of Southern California, found that "people take notice when they feel worse than they thought they would, but—oddly—not when they feel better than expected." The team coined the term "affective misforecasting" to describe the gap between anticipated and actual feelings. This supports the old adage that people tell five others about a bad experience but only one about a good experience (negative evangelism?). Thus, "underpromising and over-delivering" is the way to go.

- **Don't use sex.** Ellie Parker and Adrian Furnham of the Department of Psychology of the University College, London, claim that advertising during television programs with sexy content is less effective than during programs with no sexy content. "The fact that recall of adverts was hindered by sexual content in the programmes suggests that there is something particularly involving or disturbing about sexual programmes. . . ." Maybe online advertising is less effective on sites with sexy content. The eyeballs are there, but are they distracted?

- **Enable test-drives.** People are inherently smart. If you provide them with the right information, they are the best judges of the suitability of your product or service. You should not try to bludgeon them into becoming a customer. My recommendation is that you enable people to test-drive your product or service in order to make their own decision. Essentially, you are saying, "I think you're smart. Because I think you're smart, I'm going to enable you to try my product to see if it works for you. I hope that it does and that we can do business." Therefore, do whatever it takes to enable people to download a trial version of your software, use your Web site, drive your car, eat at your restaurant, or attend your church service.

- **Provide a safe, easy first step.** Unsuccessful rainmakers make it hard for prospective customers to adopt their products or services. I've been guilty of it myself—for example, asking Fortune 500 companies to throw out all their MS-DOS machines in favor of a new IT infrastructure based on Macintoshes. The technique is to make the adoption of your product or service as safe and easy as possible, so customers can slide into a sale. One powerful method is to offer a subscription service, so that customers don't have to make a major purchase but can pay on a monthly basis.

When it comes to the importance of sales, you can believe me now or you can believe me later, but "sales fixes everything." This is one lesson that most repeat entrepreneurs and small-business owners have learned—often the hard way and at the expense of their investors. If you'll just believe me and master the art of making it rain, you can learn the easy way.

CHAPTER 39

The Art of Distribution

**Neither was there any among them that lacked: for as
many as were possessors of lands or houses sold them,
and brought the prices of the things that were sold, and
laid them down at the apostles' feet: and distribution
was made unto every man according as he had need.**

— ACTS 4:35

In the digital economy that we live in, distribution isn't about logistics,
supply-chain management, and the transfer of physical goods. Today
companies focus on "virality" and "eyeballs" and have made it necessary
to redefine *distribution* as: "Convincing companies with a lot to lose to help
companies with a lot to gain."

For example, the telephone carrier Verizon distributes the games of software companies on its phones. The underlying and important assumption in
modern-day distribution is the asymmetry of the arrangement. For most
entrepreneurs, distribution involves piggybacking on another organization
with much greater momentum. This reality affects many decisions and
actions, so come to grips with it.

- **Separate distribution from virality.** Distribution is not the same as virality. *Viral* describes to a product that is so compelling that people are involuntary users of it. For example, if someone sent you a PDF, for a time you
had no choice but to install Acrobat Reader.

   Distribution, by contrast, involves companies making your product
available to potential users. It may or may not cause involuntary use. A viral
product could have no distribution, and a distributed product might not be

viral. To use a medical example, a person with hepatitis who is alone in the middle of the ocean won't spread the virus, and someone with a noncontagious disease won't spread it even if she is in the middle of Mumbai during the morning commute.

- **Allocate responsibility.** The ultimate goal is a viral product that is well distributed. Understand the roles here: Engineering's task is to make a viral product. Sales, marketing, or business development's task is to find the right distribution partner and cut a deal. Then it's engineering's task to integrate the products. Then it's sales, marketing, or business development's task to ensure that the world knows about the distribution partnership. A clear delineation of responsibilities and fulfillment of those responsibilities by all parties is necessary, because there's a difference between a viral product and a viral-marketing campaign.

- **Obey the law of big numbers.** The most important characteristic of a good distribution partner is that it is has millions of customers, Web site visitors, or whatever can help you. Yes, its customers and traffic might not be perfect customers for you; yes, you'll only get a tiny fraction to try your wares, but a small percentage of a big number is a big number, so don't think too much.

  For example, if your target market is mommy bloggers, you might conclude that MySpace wouldn't be a good distribution partner because its customers are Trixie and Biff, sixteen-year-old kids. There are two things wrong with this reasoning: First, when you're introducing a product (which is when you need distribution the most), you don't know who will use it or what they'll do with it.

  Second, there's the "you never know" phenomenon, which goes like this: "You never know. Maybe Trixie and Biff will use your mommy-blogger-intended product in their MySpace profile and even end up telling their mommies about it." You will never know unless you try, so don't be closed-minded.

- **Look for adjacency.** My buddy Bryan Starbuck suggested this. The most logical distribution partners have "adjacent" businesses that truly need each other to function well—for example:

- eBay and PayPal. Big eBay needed a payment system for sellers who couldn't take credit cards.
- LinkedIn and SimplyHired. Is there a better reason to use LinkedIn than to find a job?
- FeedBurner and TypePad. Once you figure out that many people prefer RSS feeds, TypePad's FeedBurner widget becomes a no-brainer.

Nota bene: "Truly need" is different from "same customer base." For example, a hearing-aid manufacturer might like a deal with the American Association of Retired Persons (AARP), but call it what it is: advertising, not distribution. The AARP doesn't need a hearing-aid manufacturer to function.

- **Focus on revenue.** Money talks, and bull shiitake walks. No matter what either party says, a good distribution deal always comes down to making money. If you hear or use the words *strategic* and *brand awareness* more than the word *revenue*, then your distribution deal is probably doomed. But if your partner will make money, then the deal will probably happen.

- **Look out for the other guy.** The right perspective for distribution partners is: Let's both make money. For sure, it's not: "How can we make a ton of money and stick it to our partner?" I have never seen a case in which only one partner makes money. Either everyone makes money, or no one does.

- **Bake a bigger pie—don't slice up the same pie differently.** The best reason to do a distribution deal is to enlarge the size of the market for both of you as quickly as possible. For example, Pixar made great movies, and Disney provided great distribution. Together, they made the pie much bigger for both organizations.

- **Skim the cream, sometimes.** There are cases in which the pie isn't going to get bigger, but you're leaving money on the table that a partnership can harvest—monetizing traffic on a popular Web site, for example. Skimming can work, too, but such a deal is seldom essential.

Distribution deals are very seductive: An 800-pound gorilla of a company seems interested in helping you. You can understand why it needs minuscule old you. In fact, you think that the deal has many reasons why it will work, but the reality is different:

Reason	Reality
"We can easily integrate our technology into the gorilla's technology."	The gorilla's technology is held together with gum and duct tape. So is yours, for that matter. When you touch either of them, everything blows up.
"Its marketing department is primed to help us make this a success."	The gorilla's marketing department is already at wit's end, and they deeply resent having another marketing "opportunity."
"We truly understand what our partner wants and how we can deliver this."	You truly understand what your wishful thinking is for how this deal will work.
"We can cut a fair deal with the gorilla because our board member knows someone there."	Your board member's contact leaves before the deal is done, and you have to start all over.
"Luckily, the only challenge that we foresee is expanding fast enough."	Expanding fast enough is seldom the problem. Getting anyone to use the fruits of the deal is usually the problem.

If you find yourself thinking these reasons are why the deal makes sense, step back and take a careful look about the distribution you're getting into. Don't say that I didn't warn you. Distribution deals take a long time and usually don't pan out.

CHAPTER 40

The Art of Evangelism

**Give me one hundred preachers who fear nothing but sin,
and desire nothing but God, and I care not a straw whether
they be clergymen or laymen; such alone will shake the
gates of hell and set up the kingdom of heaven on earth.**

~ JOHN WESLEY

Another reality is that you can't do everything by yourself, so it's great when your customers become evangelists and help you spread the good news. You can blow all the smoke that you like about partnerships, brand awareness, and corporate image, but you either attract believers or you don't.

If I could get paid a dollar every time someone asks me, "How do I get people to evangelize my product?" I would be able to stop working and play hockey every day. The short answer is called "Guy's Golden Touch." You might think this means, "Whatever Guy touches turns to gold." If only this were true. The real definition is, "Whatever is gold, Guy touches."

Memorize this: The key to great evangelism is great innovation. It is easy—almost unavoidable—to catalyze evangelism for a great product. It is hard, almost impossible, to catalyze evangelism for crap. (Evangelism, after all, comes from the Greek word for "bringing the good news," not "the crappy news.") The important question is, "What are the characteristics of an innovative product or service?" The answer is to think DICEE:

- **Deep.** A great product is deep. It doesn't run out of features and functionality after a few weeks of use. Its creators have anticipated what you'll need once you come up to speed. As your demands get more sophisticated, you discover that you don't need a different product.

- **Intelligent.** A great product screams that someone was thinking when she created it. Panasonic, for example, makes a flashlight that takes three battery sizes. This triples the probability that you have a battery that will work. The product's benefits may be obvious when you see it, but someone had an insight to create it.

- **Complete.** A great product is more than a physical thing. Documentation counts. Customer service counts. Tech support counts. Consultants and third-party developers count. Online communities count. A great product provides a great total user experience—sometimes despite the company that produces it.

- **Elegant.** A great product has an elegant user interface. Things work the way you'd think they would. A great product doesn't fight you—it enhances you. Metaphorically, you take it home, plug it in, and it works. The first step is to use it, not search for a manual online to teach you how to use it.

- **Emotive.** A great product incites you to action. It is so deep, indulgent, complete, and elegant that it compels people to tell others about it. They're not necessarily an employee or shareholder of the company that produces it. They're bringing the good news to help others, not themselves.

If you've created a DICEE product, that hard part of evangelism is done. Upon this foundation, you can build an evangelistic approach for your product, service, or company by following these recommendations.

- **Love the cause.** *Evangelist* isn't simply a job title; it's a way of life. It means that the evangelist totally loves the product and sees it as a way to bring the "good news." A love of the cause is the second-most important determinant of the success of an evangelist—second only to the quality of the cause itself. No matter how great the person, if he doesn't love the cause, he cannot be a good evangelist for it.

- **Look for agnostics, ignore atheists.** Most of the time, people understand and like a product in ten minutes, or they never understand it and like it at all. If they don't see the light in the ten minutes, cut your losses and avoid them, because it's very hard to convert someone to a new religion when he believes in another one. It's much easier to convert a person who has no religion at all.

- **Localize the pain.** No matter how revolutionary your product, don't describe it using lofty, flowery terms like "revolutionary," "paradigm shifting," and "curve jumping." Macintosh wasn't positioned as the third paradigm in personal computing; instead, it increased the productivity and creativity of one person with one computer. People don't buy "revolutions." They buy "aspirins" to fix the pain or "vitamins" to supplement their lives.

- **Learn to give a demo.** An evangelist who cannot give a great demo is an oxymoron. A person simply cannot be an evangelist if she cannot demo the product. If a person cannot give a demo that quickens the pulse of everyone in the audience, he should stay in sales or in marketing.

- **Ignore pedigrees.** Good evangelists aren't proud. They don't focus on the people with big titles and big reputations. Frankly, they'll meet with, and help, anyone who gets it and is willing to help them. This is much more likely to be the database administrator or secretary than the CIO.

- **Don't lie.** Very simply, lying is morally and ethically wrong. It also takes more energy, because if one lies, then it is necessary to keep track of the lies. If one always tells the truth, then there's nothing to keep track of. Evangelists know their stuff, so they never have to tell a lie to cover their ignorance.

- **Remember your friends.** Be nice to the people on the way up because one is likely to see them again on the way down. Once an evangelist has achieved success, he shouldn't think that he'll never need those folks again. One of the most likely people to buy a Macintosh was an Apple II owner. One of the most likely people to buy an iPod was a Macintosh owner. One of the most likely people to buy an iPhone is an iPod owner. And so it goes.

- **Give them schwag.** I don't advocate paying evangelists, as you'll read below. However, I recommend kind and frequent gifts of "premiums," or stuff with your logo on it, including T-shirts, bags, mugs, pens, stickers, and other gifts. Their monetary value is usually under $100, but these gifts go a long way with believers.

A final thought: Many companies try to find ways to financially reward their evangelists. Before you do this, consider a study by Professor Kathleen Vohs of the University of Minnesota in Minneapolis. She and her colleagues subtly prompted half the test subjects to think of money—by having them read an essay that mentioned money, for example, or seating them facing a poster depicting different types of currency—before putting them in a social situation.

In one experiment, the researchers gave volunteers a difficult puzzle and told them to ask for help at any time. People who had been reminded of money waited nearly 70 percent longer to seek help than those who hadn't. People cued to think of money also spent only half as much time, on average, assisting another person who asked for their help with a word problem and picked up fewer pencils for people who'd dropped them.

This may be my own twisted logic, but I believe this study has important, counterintuitive, and even puzzling implications for evangelism. If a company brings money into an evangelistic relationship with its customers—for example, if Apple, Harley-Davidson, and TiVo paid their customers to spread the word—it could create barriers instead of incentives.

Remember that evangelism is the process of getting people to believe in what you do, and that should not require compensation. Indeed, compensation makes it looks like you have to pay people to use your product, and the people whom you paid look like sellouts.

CHAPTER 41

DIY PR

If I was down to my last dollar, I'd spend it on public relations.

~ BILL GATES

More Glenn Kelman wisdom: He believes that most companies are too dependent on their PR agency. He felt so strongly that he penned this alternate solution to using an agency. His advice, explained in his own words below, is "Don't hire an agency; do it yourself."

Nobody knows if Charlemagne could read, because an adviser always read aloud for him. It was considered humbling for the king to do anything himself. The same fears drive the most captivating, articulate entrepreneurs to hire publicists. Who wants to risk looking like a fool? As a result, hardly anyone in technology ever tries to talk to a journalist by herself.

That's too bad. Just the other day, a newspaper's technology editor told me, "It's just so hard to meet entrepreneurs these days. You always get their PR people." A dozen entrepreneurs sprang to mind who would kill to tell their stories. All have agencies. So what I am recommending is not how to manage an agency, but something more radical: not hiring an agency at all. Here are ten reasons why.

1. **The truth will set you free.** Over and over, publicists tell their clients to stick to the agreed-upon message to avoid mistakes, but this guarantees you'll never say anything thoughtful or spontaneous. Maybe your company has two and a half customers. So what? If you're reading this book, you're probably not dumping toxins into a river or selling cigarettes to teenagers. Let GE and Philip Morris retain agencies. If you were stripped absolutely naked for the world to see, a few warts might show up, but more people would do business with you. Once you get comfortable with that, you're ready to deal with the press on your own.

2. **The Rolodex is already online.** Almost every journalist publishes his e-mail address, and many have a blog. You can also use LinkedIn and Jigsaw. The point is that you can communicate with journalists without a PR person. Usually a sincere note from an entrepreneur is enough to start a conversation. Pick out something good that the journalist wrote and say what you really think. Make a top-five list of what your company has learned in its first six months. Suggest an idea for a story. Keep it short; ask for nothing. It'll mean a lot more coming from you rather than a publicist. Odds are you'll hear back.

3. **You don't have to seem all grown-up and boring.** Every entrepreneur feels vaguely disreputable. Maybe you drive a crappy car. Maybe you never went to the prom. There are enough stuffed suits in this world to fill fifteen *Wall Street Journals* a day. As anyone who watches *American Idol* will tell you, what this spun-out, overhyped world is absolutely famished for is a little genuine personality. And, outside of your technology, it's probably the only thing you have. So stop trying to be like IBM and just be yourself.

Ideas are the precious things. Most entrepreneurs are bursting with unconventional ideas: Maybe you think an ad-crazy Silicon Valley has lost its nerve; maybe you're a grown woman delivering pizzas to diffident recruits in Stanford's computer science lab; maybe you've always wanted to meet the hairy guy living in a trailer park who sends you the inspired spam about mail-order pheromones. These are the kinds of ideas that journalists love.

Imagine how you would finish this sentence if you were having two beers with your best friend: "You know, the strangest thing about what we're going through is . . ." What comes next is your best story idea. Even if the story isn't about your company, you'll be a part of the conversation. The rest will come naturally.

4. **Let the fur fly.** When proposing a story, consider Michael Jordan's response when asked how much to bet on golf: "Whatever makes you nervous." If there's no drama, there's no story. Most publicists are terrified of a genuine story with real characters and an unpredictable outcome, so no journalists are allowed into your data center on launch day, nor can they mingle with customers at your user conference. As an entrepreneur, you're going to be more comfortable with risk than a publicist. And you won't win as a startup without taking risks, over and over again.

5. **Nerd-to-nerd networks are where it all happens—and value speed in everything you do.** Most publicists feel threatened by the systems of attribution, glorification, and punishment on the Internet, where Digg can make an obscure posting more important than the evening news. Agencies don't have the street credibility, the technical chops, the instinct for candor, the distinct voice, and, above all, the commitment to speed to engage in a meaningful conversation with the blogosphere. In the thick of things, you don't want to have to coordinate with consultants or get permission from anybody. Just ask John Kerry.

6. **Even bad coverage isn't so bad.** I was once profiled in a national business magazine doing odd things in my underwear. It was terrible; I lay facedown on a couch for an hour after reading it. And you know what? It wasn't that bad. Never whine to the journalist about coverage, avoid narcissistic story lines, and don't worry if you make a few mistakes.

7. **Go in alone.** It's hard to make a move when your dad drives you on a date, or to sound contrite about the neighbor's begonias with your mom standing behind you. It's just as hard to connect with a journalist when a publicist is always at your side. You often need a candid space in which

you can say what you really think. Just bring a notebook so you can jot down any follow-up items, and you'll be fine.

Passion + expertise = credibility. A publicist will never have your passion for your project, and she'll never have as many colorful customer stories as you do. A friend of mine once told me about "the greatest idea in the history of capitalism," which turned out to be a massive, semi-pornographic, multiplayer video game. A publicist would never have pitched it as well as he did.

8. **Make time.** Most entrepreneurs say they don't have time for DIY PR. Sure, it takes a while to spam a hundred journalists with every press release. But that doesn't work, anyway. Focus on a few big ideas, and you can tell them yourself. Use a feed-reader and Google alerts to track industry news and company mentions. Conveying your company's story in a personable, compelling way is one of your most important jobs.

9. **Hire an employee, not an agency.** When you need help, hire a person, not an agency. This is especially important if you're not interested in journalism. And if you can afford it at all, it's worth hiring an employee rather than a contractor. You want someone who can dive into what you're doing whole hog because he believes in it, without all the staff churn and management overhead of an agency.

What should you look for in this employee? The worst PR person has contempt for journalists, because he either believes journalists can be easily spun or becomes aggravated when they can't. The three best questions to ask when interviewing a publicist are "Who are your favorite writers in journalism?" "Why are they your favorites?"—so you can find someone who actually cares about the craft of journalism—and "What is an example of a feature story that you've pitched?"—so you can find someone excited about ideas.

Also, ask for a writing sample. As with any other position, value brains, drive, and a soft touch over looks. Most of all, don't hire anyone fake. Of course, you'll need to make it clear that the PR person won't be managing an agency.

Thanks to Kelman, you have the information to do your own PR. You may elect to hire an agency or employee, but Glenn's advice is still applicable, because the more you give an agency to work with, the better the results you'll achieve.

CHAPTER 42

Straight from the Press's Mouth

Fortune sides with him who dares.

～ VIRGIL

Adam Lashinsky covers high tech in Silicon Valley for *Fortune*. He works with some of the best-known companies and PR firms in the world. His perspective on working with the press provides a final reality check for marketing people.

Q: How do you pick what to cover?

A: I have two basic kinds of assignments: what I want to cover and what they want me to cover—"they" being my editors. I follow what's going on in the tech world, think about what interests me, and follow my nose. Then, of course, when New York wants something, I hop to it. What I really like is variety. I also like to connect the dots. My Murdoch story last year led to my Facebook story that led to my craigslist story. That was fun continuity.

Q: When—if ever—does it make sense for a company to hold a press conference?

A: It makes sense for a significant product launch, some major embarrassing news, or the introduction of a new CEO. If it's important to show something or someone, a group grope helps. Otherwise, don't bother, because most journalists don't like showing up for press conferences that are just staged events with no real news.

Q: How many companies or their PR firms pitch you per day?

A: Two or three.

Q: What's the most common mistake that companies and their PR firms make when they pitch you?

A: The most common mistake is not having a knowledge of *Fortune*. You've got to know what I'm interested in, and cold-calling to ask me isn't the way to find out. You would think that these companies and PR firms would at least read my last few articles. Is that too much to ask?

Q: By contrast, how would you describe the perfect pitch?

A: The perfect pitch would involve a major corporation with a great, tension-filled story with the offer of an exclusive opportunity to interview all the relevant people at the corporation. Short of this, a pitch that would work would involve high-level access and a story line that is relevant to my readers, not just the PR firm's client.

Q: Do gifts and suck-ups (cookies, T-shirts, flowers, invites to swanky parties) matter at all to you?

A: I throw nearly everything away. If I'm not being good about my diet, I sometimes eat the food, and I often take home the T-shirts for running or rags. That's about it. I go to parties based more on who'll be there than the quality of the venue. (Note: In the "Art of Evangelism" chapter, I recommend giving gifts to evangelists. The reason why it works for evangelists and not people like Adam is that Adam gets gifts all the time for things he doesn't care about.)

Q: What is the dumbest thing a company or its PR firm has ever done to get your attention?

A: Outcast PR on behalf of Salesforce.com stands out for sending every imaginable piece of crap under the stars. It's become a joke in the journalism world. You can walk around the offices of *Fortune* and see footballs and other paraphernalia, and you say, "Yeah, I got that, too."

Q: Has the growth of online readership made you change your reporting style?

A: No, not really. It has changed the notion of instant gratification. I know that companies will see what I write almost as soon as I write it.

Q: If a company receives negative press, what should it do?

A. Stay focused, be a good company, and don't stop talking to the press. Bad press doesn't make for bad products. It's the other way around.

Q: How would you rank the PR expertise (from best to worst) of the following organizations: Apple, Microsoft, Google, Yahoo!, the Bush administration, and the PLO?

A: I'm not going to touch that one. I have to work with these people all the time—well, except the Bush administration and the PLO. Sometimes people tell me things that are not for publication. It's the same thing here: I'd be happy to share this with you but not your readers!

If you've used a PR agency, you'd recognize that much of what Adam says contradicts what companies and their agencies do. I know many members of the press—and I might argue that I *am* a member of the press—and I can tell that Adam speaks the truth. Combining the wisdom of Kelman and Lashinsky yields a simple formula: Figure out if you have a real story, figure out which members of the press the story is relevant to, and make your executives directly accessible. This isn't rocket science.

{ CHAPTER 43 }

Forget the Influencers After All?

You have the Midas touch.
Everything you touch turns to a muffler.

~ UNKNOWN

I n an article called "Is the Tipping Point Toast?" (*FastCompany,* February 2008), Duncan Watts of Yahoo! Research refutes the theory that a few high-status, influential people lead others to adopt a product or service. The key to marketing according to this theory is to attract these influentials, and the rest of the market will fall like dominoes. In my days at Apple, this meant convincing a handful of experts and reporters to like Macintosh. Watts differs with this theory:

> It [achieving marketing success through influentials] just doesn't work. A rare bunch of cool people just don't have that power. And when you test the way marketers say the world works, it falls apart. There's no there there.

Watts believes the key factor is the readiness of the market: "If society is ready to embrace a trend, almost anyone can start one—and if it isn't, then almost no one can." There will be first movers, but almost anyone can be this first mover—and therefore what Watts calls an "accidental influential."

Several additional studies support this line of thinking. First, a study reported in the December 2007 issue of the *Journal of Advertising Research* says that common word-of-mouth advertising by regular folks is more power-ful than "key influencers." According to James Coyle, one of the coauthors of the study:

> We find that trying to track down key influencers, people who have extremely large social networks, is typically unnecessary and, more importantly, can actually limit a campaign or adver-tisement's viral potential. Instead, marketers need to realize that the majority of their audience, not just the well-connected few, is eager and willing to pass along well-designed and rele-vant messages.

Finally, CNET Networks conducted a three-part study called "The Influ-encer Study from CNET Networks: Challenging Perceptions." It explored the structure of social networks, the motivations for giving advice, and methods of acquiring information. The conclusion:

> The flow of information isn't coming just from a small group of connected individuals at the top. It flows between networks, regardless of the size of the network. Instead of a pyramid, the model of influence is more accurately shown as a diamond, emphasizing the importance of the large number of moderately connected influencers.

I added these three studies together, extracted their core messages, and came up with these recommendations:

- **Don't focus exclusively on the top of the pyramid.** Marketing doesn't flow downhill. It spreads in unpredictable and perhaps random ways. Spend more time and effort pressing the flesh of any customers. (Typically, you won't meet too many customers at a conference at the Ritz-Carlton.)

- **Use mass marketing, because you never know who will be your "accidental influential."** Admittedly, the challenge is to find a cost-effective way to do mass marketing, but mass marketing is the only way to diffuse your product or service and get to broadcast your message.

- **Don't worry too much about what the A-list is saying.** Lousy reviews by them cannot kill your product. Great reviews cannot make it successful. Treat the long tail of millions of bloggers as a channel to reach people. If enough people like your product, the A-list bloggers will have to write about you.

- **Ensure that your marketing information is comprehensible and credible to moderately connected people.** Most companies tailor their information to industry experts and leaders. Moderately connected people who aren't working full-time as gurus have different informational and emotional needs.

- **Enable these folks to easily take action for you.** The *Wall Street Journal* will publish the story of its top-o'-the-pyramid reporter. How can you help a moderately connected person spread the good news? The answer is simple things like "Forward to a Friend" links on your site or at least a URL that doesn't contain 500 characters. Refer back to the "Stupid Ways to Hinder Market Adoption" chapter for similar information.

How do these recommendations square with selling, evangelism, and public relations? There isn't as big a conflict as you might think, because I don't recommend sucking up only to people who are famous and important. Few Fortune 500 CIOs helped make Macintosh successful. It was unknown artists, designers, hobbyists, and user-group members who got Macintoshes through the bottoms and sides of companies, but never through the tops.

The Reality of Communicating

Entrepreneurship is an outward-focused activity. It requires that you communicate with others using e-mails, presentations, speeches, panels, and blogs. Every one of these modes of communication is a skill that entrepreneurs need to master. When consultants tell you that you need special training to master these skills, don't believe them. All it takes is reading this section and practicing for twenty years.

CHAPTER 44

The Effective E-mailer

The very existence of flamethrowers proves that sometime, somewhere, someone said to himself, "You know, I want to set those people over there on fire, but I'm just not close enough to get the job done."

~ GEORGE CARLIN

We begin with a discussion of e-mail because it is the most commonly used form of business communication. It's also the bane of my existence. This chapter explains how to make e-mail more effective and efficient.

- **Craft a subject line.** The subject line is the window into your message's soul. First, it must get your message past the spam filters, so take out anything about sex and money-saving special offers. Second, it must communicate that your message is highly personalized. For example, "Love your blog," "Love your book," and "You skate well for an old man," always work on me. Third, it must titillate, but not overpromise, just enough to get the message read.

- **Limit your recipients.** As a rule of thumb, the more people you send an e-mail to, the less likely any single person will respond to it, much less perform any action that you requested. This is similar to the Genovese syndrome (or the "bystander effect"): In 1964, the press reported that thirty-eight people stood by while Kitty Genovese was murdered. If you are going to ask a large group of people to do something, then at least use blind carbon copies; not only will the recipients think they are important, you won't burden the whole list with everyone's e-mail address. Nor will you reveal everyone's e-mail address inadvertently.

- **Don't use ALL CAPS.** Everyone probably knows this by now, but just in case: Text in all caps is interpreted as YELLING in e-mail. Even if you're not yelling, it's more difficult to read text that's in all caps, so do your recipients a favor and use standard capitalization practices.

- **Keep it short.** The ideal length for an e-mail is five sentences. The ideal content level is one idea. If you're asking something reasonable of a reasonable recipient, simply explain who you are in one or two sentences and get to the "ask." If it's not reasonable, don't ask at all. My theory is that people who tell their life story suspect that their request is on shaky ground so they try build up a case to soften up the recipient. Another very good reason to keep it short is that you never know where your e-mail will end up—anywhere from your minister to an attorney general.

- **Refrain from attaching files.** How often do you get an e-mail that says, "Please read the attached letter"? Then you open the attachment, and it's a Word document with a three-paragraph message that could have easily been copied and pasted into the e-mail. Or, even worse, someone believes that because of his curve-jumping, paradigm-shifting, patent-pending way to sell dog food online, you'll want to receive his ten-megabyte pitch. Now that lots of people are opening messages with smart phones, sending files when you don't have to is a sure sign of cluelessness.

- **Don't FUQ (Fabricate Unanswerable Questions) up.** Many people ask questions that are unanswerable. For example, "What do you think of the R.I.A.A. lawsuits?" "What kind of person is Steve Jobs?" "Do you think it's a good time to start a company?" My favorite ones begin like this: "I haven't given this much thought, but what do you think about . . . ?" In other words, the sender hasn't done much thinking and wants to shift responsibility to the recipient. Dream on.

If your question is only appropriate for your psychiatrist, mother, or spouse, then ask them, no one else. When I get this type of message, I go into a deep funk: Should I just not answer? But then the person will think

I'm an arrogant schmuck. Should I just give a cursory answer and explain that the question is not answerable? Should I carefully craft a heartfelt message probing for more information so that I can get into the deep recesses of the sender's mind and begin a long tail of a message thread that lasts two weeks? Usually, I pick the middle way.

- **Ask permission.** If you must ask unanswerable questions or attach a file, then first seek permission. The initial e-mail should be something like, "May I tell you my background to explain why I'm contacting you?" Or, "May I send you my pitch to explain what our company is doing?"

- **Quote back.** Even if e-mails are flying back and forth within hours, be sure to quote back the text that you're answering. You can assume that the person you're corresponding with has fifty e-mail conversations going at once. If you answer with a simple, "Yes, I agree," most of the time you will force the recipient to dig through his deleted mail folder to figure out what you're agreeing to. However, don't "fisk" either. Fisking is quoting back the entire message and responding line by line, often in an argumentative way. This is anal if not downright childish, so don't feel you have to respond to every issue.

- **Use plain text.** I hate HTML e-mail. I tried it for a while, but it's not worth the trouble of sending or receiving it. All those pretty colors and fancy typefaces and styles make me want to puke. Cut to the chase: Say what you have to say in as brief and plain a manner as possible. If you can't say it in plain text, you don't have anything worth saying.

- **Control your URLs.** I don't know what's gotten into some companies, but the URLs that they generate have dozens of letters and numbers. It seems to me that these thirty-two-character URLs have almost as many possible combinations as the number of atoms in the universe. If you're forwarding a URL and it wraps to the next line, clicking on it probably won't work. If you really want someone to click through successfully, go to the trouble of using an online utility like SnipURL to shorten it.

- **Chill out.** This is a rule that I've broken many times, and each time that I did, I regretted it. When someone writes you a flaming e-mail, the temptation is to retaliate. You will make the situation worse by doing this. A good practice is to wait twenty-four hours before you respond. A better practice is to never say in e-mail what you wouldn't say in person. The best practice is to not answer and let the sender wonder if his e-mail got caught in a spam filter or didn't matter enough to merit a response. If you still want to flame back, then refer to Matthew 7:3: "Why do you look at the speck that is in your brother's eye, but do not notice the log that is in your own eye." Generally, flames require logs if you know what I mean.

- **Add a good signature.** A signature is the block of text that's automatically added to all your outgoing messages by your e-mail client. It should include your name, title, organization, e-mail address, Web site, and phone. This is especially true if you're asking people to do something. Why make it hard for them to verify your credibility or to pick up the phone and call you? Also, I often copy and paste people's signatures to put them into the notes field of an appointment.

- **Never forward something that you think is funny.** The odds are that by the time you've received it, your recipient already has, too, so what is intended as funny is now tedious. However, I do have the Neiman Marcus recipe for cookies.

This takes care of e-mail. These recommendations should make you more efficient and effective at this most common form of business communication. Even more important, done right, these recommendations should make your e-mail recipients more efficient and effective, too.

CHAPTER 45

The Zen of Presentations

Shariputra,

Form does not differ from emptiness;

Emptiness does not differ from form.

Form itself is emptiness;

Emptiness itself is form.

So too are feeling, cognition, formation, and consciousness.

~ HEART SUTRA

All hail Garr Reynolds! He has written the definitive book for people who want to make great presentations: *Presentation Zen: Simple Ideas on Presentation Design and Delivery* (*Voices That Matter*) (New Riders Press, 2008). I asked him to spill his guts in this interview with me so that you can master the art of presentations.

Q: What is the Presentation Zen approach?

A: Presentation Zen is indeed an approach, not a method. There are many paths and many methods to presenting insanely well today. At its heart, Presentation Zen is about restraint, simplicity, and a natural approach to presentations that is appropriate for an age in which design thinking, story-telling, and right-brain thinking are crucial complements to analysis, logic, and argument.

Q: How did we get to this place where most presentations suck?

A: PowerPoint and Keynote are both pretty simple tools, but there has been too much focus on the tools themselves. If people want to learn how to make better slides, they should study good books on graphic design and visual communication to improve their visual literacy. When it comes to designing appropriate visuals, there is a hole in our education. Concerning quantitative displays, for example, very few people have had proper training in how to design graphs and charts, etc. The great master Edward Tufte has written many useful books on this subject.

There are many reasons. First of all, presenting exceptionally well isn't easy. In fact, it's hard. That's why we find great presenters—and great communicators in general—so remarkable. They are all too rare. Many professionals simply don't practice enough and just follow conventional wisdom and do it "like everyone else" instead of doing it effectively.

Q: Are PowerPoint and Keynote now part of the problem or part of the solution?

A: There is no question that PowerPoint has been at least a part of the problem, because it has affected a generation. It should have come with a warning label and a good set of design instructions back in the 1990s. But it is also a cop-out to blame PowerPoint—it's just software, not a method. True, the templates and wizards of the past probably took most of us—who didn't know any better anyway—down a road to "really bad PowerPoint," as Seth Godin calls it. But today we know better, and we can make effective presentations even with older versions of PowerPoint—often by ignoring most of the features.

Ultimately it comes down to us and our skills and our content. Each case is different, and some of the best presentations include not a single slide. In the end, it is about knowing your material deeply and designing visuals that augment and amplify your spoken message.

Q: In a nutshell, what makes a good presentation stick?

A: If you want to know how to make better presentations, read *Made to Stick* (Random House, 2007) by Chip Heath and Dan Heath. (Also see the chapter called "The Sticking Point.") The Heath brothers found that sticky, compelling, memorable messages and ideas share six common attributes: simplicity, unexpectedness, concreteness, credibility, emotions, and stories. Ask yourself how your presentations rate for these elements, and you are on your way to crafting presentations that stick.

Q: Specifically, what makes Steve Jobs's presentations so great?

A: Steve Jobs makes it look easy. He's comfortable and relaxed. This in turn makes the audience feel relaxed. His keynotes usually rate very high on the Heath brothers' "sticky scale." Steve also speaks in a manner that is conversational, and even though he practices a lot before the event, his words never sound scripted. Steve uses the slides to help him tell a story, and he interacts with them in a natural way, rarely turning his back on the audience, because monitors in front show the same on-screen image, as well as the next slide. Steve uses visuals, his own words, and a natural presence to tell his story. His visuals do not overpower him, but they are an important component of the talk. Steve also demos his own software. How many CEOs can do that? This is much harder than giving a presentation, but he pulls it off well.

Q: Do you think that Bill Gates knows his presentations are lousy and doesn't care, or doesn't know they are lousy at all?

A: Who knows? Historically, Bill has been a good contrast in style to Steve Jobs. In the past, we said, "Do it more like Steve and less like Bill." The thing is, one-on-one, Bill seems very engaging and very likable, but he has always struggled with the keynote address. The awful slides behind him usually do not help. I wish Microsoft would call Bert Decker for some coaching and hire Duarte Design for the visuals. If Duarte can make Al Gore an extraordinary presenter, think what they could do for Bill. Bill is a remarkable man, not for his software so much as for his philanthropy and his work with his foundation. So it would be nice for a remarkable man like Bill to be a remarkable presenter, too. His CES keynote was better—not great, but an improvement. Perhaps Bill will abandon the all-too-common "death by PowerPoint" method in future.

Q: What's your recommendation for the optimal number of slides, length of presentation in minutes, and font size?

A: It really depends on a great many things, but I'd probably recommend your 10/20/30 method. I especially like the twenty-minute limitation of this method. There are a myriad types of presentation situations, and the actual number of slides and the time may vary greatly, depending on the specific circumstances and method. However, the audience should have no idea how many slides you have. Once they start counting slides, all is lost. As far as text goes, I say as little as possible on slides, but when text does appear, it should be large and serve to complement your words. People did not come to read; they came to hear. Any speaker can read bullet points. The audience wants to *hear* your story, not read it.

Q: How many slide-transition effects should a presentation contain?

A: It's good that PowerPoint and Keynote have many transition options, but people need to exercise restraint and use very few effects. I suggest using no more than two or three different types of transition effects per presentation and not using transition effects for every slide.

I use a fade to black between the major sections of a talk to communicate closure of one section and the opening of the next one. I often use a smooth dissolve to gently move from one visual to the next as I continue speaking. Using no transition effects is also often appropriate. When you watch a film or a TV show, you are usually not aware of the transition effects from one scene to another—that would be distracting. Audiences should not notice the effects we employ between slides, either.

Q: Why do you think 2-D graphs are better than 3-D graphs?

A: 3-D charts and graphs are very popular with consumers, but in almost every case it is preferable to use 2-D graphics to display 2-D data. Charts with 3-D depth and distortion usually make things harder to see, not easier. Some of the precision is lost. There is beauty in the simple display of the data itself; there is no need to decorate with distorted perspectives. If the graphic is just for showing the roughest of general trends, then there is nothing really wrong with a 3-D chart, I suppose, but when you are trying to show a true visual representation of the data in the clearest way possible, a simple chart without 3-D adornment is usually better.

Q: How many times do you think a person should rehearse a presentation?

A: You should rehearse at least three or four times all the way through and rehearse the first three minutes at least ten times, or more. You also need to do a formal dress rehearsal in front of a real audience, such as co-workers, who can give you constructive criticism. In some ways, good presenting is like good writing; you've got to pare it down and dump the superfluous and the nonessential. But since we are so close to the material, it is hard for us to see what works and what does not, or what is repetitive, etc.

This is why you cannot rehearse only alone. You've got to rehearse in front of others so that you can experience the nerves, the blank stares, etc. The more you rehearse, the more the fear of the unknown is removed. The more the fear is removed, the more confident you will become. As you become more confident, you will feel more relaxed, and your confidence will shine through. The thing about confidence is that it's impossible to fake, but with practice you will indeed become a confident speaker. And it is possible to rehearse too much. You want it to sound natural and fresh, not mechanical and memorized. Usually three to four full rehearsals will get you there.

Q: What is the single most important thing people could do to enhance their presentations?

A: Turn off the computer, grab some paper and a pencil, and find someplace quiet. Think of the audience. What is it they need? What is it you want to say that they need to hear? Identify what's important and what is not. You can't say everything in a twenty-minute talk—or even a two-hour talk. The problem with most presentations is that people try to include too much. You can go deep or you can go wide, but you can't really do both. What is the core message?

This time "off the grid" with paper and pencil or a whiteboard is when you can clarify your ideas and then get them on paper visually. After your ideas and basic structure are clear, then you can open up the software and start laying out the story in the slide-sorter view.

If the computer ever freezes in your live talk, you need to move on. The work you did in the preparation stage "off the grid" and away from the computer will help make things concrete in your own mind, so that you can move forward sans your Macintosh in the event of a technical glitch. If you ask the audience to bear with you as you try to make the computer work, you might as well stick a fork in it, because you are done. Keep moving forward in the unlikely event of a technical glitch.

Q: Who are the ten best presenters?

A: I have pointed to many on my site over the years, such as Seth Godin, Steve Jobs, you, Al Gore, Lawrence Lessig, Tom Peters, Hans Rosling, and many more. Recently I have come to think that Barack Obama is an amazing speech maker as well. But more than anything, I point people to TED. [TED stands for Technology, Entertainment, Design, a prestigious conference where the likes of Al Gore speak.] There they can see some really good presentations and speeches by some very smart and creative people who are all trying to change the world in their own way. Each case is different, but really, if you're not trying to change the world, what is the point of making a presentation?

Q: By the way, who indexed your book? I know I'm in it, but I'm not in the index. Of course, it does say something about me that I would look for my name in the index.

A: I was horrified when I saw that! A thousand apologies. I since learned a good piece of advice for new authors: Always do your own indexing or at least be very involved in it. The indexer did a very good and quick job, so it was my fault for not checking and adding a few names and page numbers to subjects. The index was designed to be light to save space, but not that light. Live and learn.

To align with the spirit of *Presentation Zen*, I end this chapter with only three words: Less is more.

CHAPTER 46

How to Get a Standing Ovation

Don't speak unless you can improve on the silence.

~ SPANISH PROVERB

Pitching and presenting are scary, but they are less scary than speaking to large audiences. When I started public speaking in about 1986, I was deathly afraid of it. For one thing, working for the division run by Steve Jobs was hugely intimidating: How could you possibly compete with Steve? It's taken me twenty years to get comfortable with public speaking, and this chapter explains what I've learned. I am not content that you merely survive a speech. I want you to get a standing ovation.

- **Have something interesting to say.** This is 80 percent of the battle. If you have something interesting to say, then it's much easier to give a great speech. If you have nothing to say, you should not speak. End of discussion. It's better to decline the opportunity so that no one knows you don't have anything to say than it is to make the speech and prove it.

- **Remove the sales pitch.** The purpose of most keynotes is to entertain and inform the audience. It is seldom to provide you with an opportunity to pitch your product, service, or company. For example, if you're invited to speak about the future of digital music, you shouldn't talk about the latest MP3 player that your company is selling.

- **Customize.** In the first five minutes, show your audience that you know who they are, and you'll be set for the rest of the speech. All that's required is a little research beforehand to grasp the trends, competition, and key issues that the audience faces. I push the edge of customization far more than most speakers. When I spoke for Hewlett-Packard, I showed pictures of the HP printers and fax machines in my home and office. When I spoke for S. C. Johnson, I showed them pictures of the household cleaners and containers that I own from the company. When I travel to a foreign country, I typically get to the location the day before and do a little sightseeing. Then I show my pictures of the sites that I visited.

- **Focus on entertaining.** Many speech coaches will disagree with this, but the goal of a speech is to entertain the audience. If people are entertained, you can slip in a few nuggets of information. But if your speech is deathly dull, no amount of information will make it a great speech. If I had to pick between entertaining and informing an audience, I would pick entertaining—knowing that informing will probably happen, too.

- **Overdress.** My father was a politician in Hawaii. He was a very good speaker. When I started speaking he gave me a piece of advice: Never dress beneath the level of the audience. That is, if they're wearing suits, then you should wear a suit. To underdress is to communicate this message: "I'm smarter/richer/more powerful than you. I can insult you and not take you seriously, and there's nothing you can do about it." This is hardly the way to get an audience to like you.

- **Don't denigrate the competition.** Never cut down your competition in a speech, because it indicates that you are taking undue advantage of the privilege of the audience's attention. You are not doing the audience a favor. The audience is doing you a favor, so do not stoop so low as to use this opportunity to slander your competition.

- **Tell stories.** The best way to relax when giving a speech is to tell stories. Any stories. Stories about your youth. Stories about your kids. Stories about your customers. Stories about things that you read about. When you tell a story, you lose yourself in the storytelling. You're not "making a speech" anymore. You're simply making conversation. Good speakers are good storytellers; great speakers tell stories that support their message.

- **Precirculate with the audience.** True or false: The audience wants your speech to go well. The answer is: true. Audiences don't want to see you fail—why would people want to waste their time listening to you fail? The way to heighten your audience's concern for your success is to circulate with the audience before the speech. Meet people. Talk to them. Let them make contact with you, especially the ones in the first few rows. Then, when you're on the podium, you'll see these friendly faces. Your confidence will soar. You will relax. And you will be great.

- **Speak at the start of an event.** If you have the choice, get in the beginning part of the agenda. The audience is fresher then. They're more apt to listen to you, laugh at your jokes, and follow along with your stories. On the third day of a three-day conference, the audience is tired, and all they're thinking about is going home. It's hard enough to give a great speech—why increase the challenge by having to lift the audience out of the doldrums?

- **Ask for a small room.** If you have a choice, get the smallest room possible for your speech. If it's a large room, ask that it be set classroom style—i.e., with tables and chairs—instead of theater-style. A packed room is a more emotional room. It is better to have 200 people in a 200-person room than 500 people in a 1,000-person room. You want people to remember, "It was standing room only."

- **Practice and speak all the time.** This is a duh-ism, but nonetheless relevant. My theory is that it takes giving a speech at least twenty times to get decent at it. You can give it nineteen times to your dog if you like, but it takes practice and repetition. There is no shortcut to Carnegie Hall. As Jascha Heifetz said, "If I don't practice one day, I know it. If I don't practice two days, my critics know it. If I don't practice three days, everyone knows it."

It's taken me twenty years to get to this point. I hope it takes you less. Part of the reason why it took me so long is that no one explained the art of giving a speech to me, and I was too dumb to do the research. Now my goal, every time I get up to the podium, is to get a standing ovation. More important, I hope that I'm standing and clapping in the audience for your speech soon.

CHAPTER 47

As Good As Steve Jobs

My passions were all gathered together like fingers that made a fist.
Drive is considered aggression today; I knew it then as purpose.

~ BETTE DAVIS

Majora Carter won a MacArthur Award (the so-called Genius Award) in 2005 for her work as the executive director of Sustainable South Bronx. She gave a presentation at the 2005 TED conference that was as good as a Steve Jobs performance. She is the rare speaker who makes meaning, personifies passion, and exemplifies Garr Reynolds's Zen of presentations. She also proves a point: You don't need to be the CEO of a powerful company who has a private jet and an entourage of handlers to be a good speaker.

Google "Majora Carter + TED" to find this speech online at the TED Web site, and then watch what she does by following the time codes that I've provided.

- She wastes no time and immediately sucks you in to her speech by arousing your curiosity with a story about her dog. (:59) One wonders, "What's a dog got to do with urban renewal?"

- She immediately provides a clear problem statement. (1:00–2:00)

- She personalizes her story all the way through the speech. Sure, there's all the heart-wrenching stuff, but I loved how she discussed her engagement

(2:45) and caps off this story with a great use of humor and double entendre: "pressing my buttons . . ." (2:47)

- She uses very little text, and her pictures and graphics are highly effective and emotive. For example, she uses a stunning picture of a kid when she discusses obesity in her neighborhood. (3:49)

- She uses vanity in a charming way: "incredibly good-looking." (4:44) She does this in a way that no rich white man could ever hope to.

- She shows raw emotions and unveils a piece of her soul when she breaks into tears when talking about her brother being gunned down. (5:10)

- She capitalizes on alliteration, "pimps and pushers and prostitutes" (6:50), and repetition, "economic degradation begets environmental degradation which begets social degradation" (7:24), in Martin Luther King–like fashion.

- She flouts a conference rule against pitching for money and then immediately begs for forgiveness (10:39). How can you not like a person who has the ovaries to do this?

- She exhibits excellent coordination with the person who is advancing her slides. I assume this is her fiancé doing this. If I find out that they didn't rehearse this at least twenty-five times, I'll switch to Windows.

- She is brilliant and buff. Her presence exudes power and confidence without a trace of arrogance, fear, or condescension. (You'd be amazed at how often this ironical combination exhibits itself in most speakers.) She has great teeth (public speakers should get their teeth whitened—I did a few years ago) and shows them by smiling a lot. She animates and emphasizes her points with powerful hand movements while walking around the stage.

- She used a Countryman E6i wireless mike (the world's best mike, in my opinion). The conference folks probably provided these mikes to all the speakers, but you can't do her level of animation with a handheld mike or standing behind a podium. Here's a subtle piece of irony: She's using a "white" flesh-tone Countryman. It is available in "black," too. When I bought my Countryman, I was asked if I wanted a "yellow" one.

- She speaks rapidly—bordering on too rapidly, but she is articulate at all times. And she slows her cadence for her most important points. You can tell that she's trying to observe her time limit—communicating that she respects the audience's time.

- She ends with an insanely great call to action: "Please don't waste me" (17:57). How can you top this?

Yes, she reads from notes a few times. But she slices and dices Al Gore in such a wonderful, nonthreatening way (16:45) that I forgive her for using them. The scene is a priceless juxtaposition of an old, rich, and powerful white man and a black woman from the Bronx. It reminds me of samurai movies where a master swordsman decapitates his opponent, but it takes a few seconds for the victim to realize what's happened.

I would love it if my daughter would grow up to be a warrior like Majora. Heck, I would love if my sons grew up to be a warrior like Majora. At the very least, anyone with a daughter should watch this video.

CHAPTER 48

Speaking as a Performing Art

What comprises good performance?
The ability through singing or playing to make the ear
conscious of the true content and affect of a composition.

⁓ CARL PHILIPP EMANUEL BACH

inging and speaking have much in common: The main goal of each is to engage the audience and make it listen to you. Doug Lawrence is a professional singer, music director, and speech coach. He has, literally, gotten to Carnegie Hall. Because of his professional performance career, I asked him to come up with speaking tips, and this is what he provided me:

- **Warm up with a towel.** Singers often have to get their chops "up" in their hotel rooms before leaving for rehearsals or performances. They do this by screaming and yelling into a towel.

- **Just say "Whoooo!"** One of the best ways to get a voice ready is to make a siren sound on "whoooo" from the lowest pitch you can make to the highest and back again. Repeat it several times. This obnoxious sound thins your vocal cords and makes them more supple for easy speaking or singing.

- **Flutter your lips.** Blowing a pitch—any pitch—through your lips to make them flutter will loosen up your articulators: the tongue, lips, and throat muscles. When your voice is tired and husky, and you're afraid you can't go on, give this a shot. It will work wonders.

- **Eat light, eat protein.** If you have to eat before a big presentation (singers prefer going in lean and mean), eat stuff that gives you energy, not a cheap high like carbohydrates. Singers always party after the show!

- **Allocate three hours to wake up.** Singers often take a nap in the afternoon before they perform, but they always allow at least three hours to get their brain and voice back. Getting to a wakeful state takes a lot longer than just putting your clothes on.

- **Skip the tea.** Tea is an astringent and will close your voice down. Drink hot water instead—it keeps your voice supple as a baby's cheeks (either set).

- **Leave your jaw out of it.** If you use your jaw to speak, you will exhaust your voice. Jaws don't sing, and they don't speak. Don't try to overform your words by chewing them, because you'll be outrageously tired within a few minutes. Use your articulators (tongue and teeth) and leave your jaw for a nice meal after you speak.

- **Circulate with your audience.** Before every concert, speech, and seminar, I try to mingle with the crowd, ask questions, and let them know I'm glad they came. This isn't always possible in the real world, but it is a way to create a bond with the people and undo some of the jitters that are a natural part of being "on."

- **Command attention.** The breastbone (sternum) has to be out front and facing your audience if you want to project authority. You might want to pretend you're a rooster showing off, or you're trying to scare a bear. Relaxed sternum = loser, high sternum = winner!

- **Snarl.** If people can't hear you, they won't listen to you. Add some nasal resonance to your voice, but keep smiling. *Snarl* is that nasal sound you get when you speak partially from your nose instead of your mouth. It generates overtones above 2,800 cycles per second that make a room "sing."

Pretend you're trying to yell to warn a child who's about to run out in front of a bus—like yelling, "STOP!"

- **Bite your tongue.** If your mouth gets dry in the middle of your presentation, try gently biting your tongue. Opera singers use this all the time to release saliva that moistens your mouth.

- **Perform a sound check before you speak.** A good sound person will adjust the equipment to your voice and its idiosyncrasies. If you're comfortable using a hand mike, do so. Work close to the mike and you'll have a better chance of being heard. If you turn your head, make sure you turn the mike with your head. Lapel mikes usually work fine, but for softer speakers they're very frustrating. Wraparound mikes that fit over your ear are the best for intelligibility. If you speak often and you know your venues will support this technology, buy a really good one and take it with you.

- **Use your eyes all the time.** Hand gestures and pacing around the platform can be useful tools in presentation, but the eyes . . . the eyes have it! If you can't engage people with your eyes, you will eventually lose your audience's attention. Your eyes always tell people whether or not you believe in what you're saying! Scan the room, select a person to make a point to, and look right at them. It's a little intimidating for them, but it keeps you focused on the individuals who make up your audience. Keep moving to new people—right, left, middle. If all else fails, look at each person as though you've loved him or her all your life—like your mom or your child.

- **Move away from center to make your point.** When you come to a place in your presentation where you really want people's attention, move to the left or right of your primary speaking position. This will always make people look up at you. If you are a constant mover or shaker, stand still for a few moments—it will have the same effect.

- **Get quiet.** If you really want to get people's attention, get quiet suddenly. It will scare the sound guy to death, but I guarantee the audience will pay attention. Singers use this trick all the time. That's the "you could hear a pin drop" effect.

- **"Underline" certain words with a pause or repetition.** If you really want to make a point, slow down, pause, and say the word or phrase that you most want people to hear with a calculated emphasis on each word. The sudden switch in style gets attention. Also, repeat a word or phrase before you make your big point. For example: "You know (pause) you know (pause) you know, the thing I want you to remember is . . ." Songs are full of repeated text, a device that locks down meaning!

- **Take a risk and be vulnerable.** Say or do something that's totally out of character for you. Use a "pretend" voice like Mickey Mouse or Barry White for effect while you're telling a joke or saying something shocking or humorous. Whether your persona is reserved or funny, it's endearing to have a little fun. This trick humanizes the most serious topics.

- **Tee it higher.** Raising the overall pitch of your voice for a few seconds will create urgency. It shows your passion for the subject matter and also relaxes your exhausted larynx. Low-pitched voices relax the room; high-pitched voices increase the adrenaline flow of the audience.

- **Know when it's time to go.** You don't have to be a genius to know you've overstayed your welcome. Check your "presentation barometer" often to see if everyone is still with you. Change something—anything—if you're starting to lose the crowd. If all else fails, stop talking, start thanking, and get off the platform. People will love you more for knowing when to stop than for all the wonderful content you brought to your topic!

- **Use Q&A as an encore.** Singers usually prepare an encore, because this practice makes the audience feel special and makes them think you like them more than other audiences you've encountered. Q&A functions something like an encore. You may think you told them stuff they needed to know, but questions often reveal the important things you left out of your content. Where this opportunity exists, use it as a tool for picking up the pieces you left dangling in your talk, and warm the crowd to your candor and self-effacing graciousness.

- **Don't overwhelm the audience.** Be entertaining, but use moments of silence, soft speech, and slow cadence. Any performer will tell you the trick to a really great performance is to make the audience come to you. The more you go after them, the more you push them away. When people watch Steve Jobs, they think they know what he's going to do, but he titillates them until they can barely stand it and makes the audience come crawling to him.

- **Rehearse, rehearse, rehearse.** That's how I got to Carnegie Hall! Where possible, memorize your material the way singers memorize their songs. Remember, the more you rehearse, the freer you will be to make your talk fresh and engaging.

- **Perform for a hero.** Several years ago I was asked to sing a command performance for the queen of Spain. I worked harder on that concert than any I have ever sung. It was very successful and I was proud of my preparation. From that time on, I imagined I was about to sing for the queen, and it made me twice the performer I had been previously. Pick a hero, and give her your best shot!

No pun intended, but I'd like to amplify one of Doug's points: using a good microphone. A few years ago I bought a Countryman E6i. It's one of those wraparound mikes that hangs over your ear. There are two benefits of bringing your own Countryman. First, it's a great mike. Second, the audiovisual team knows that you know what the hell you're doing and takes better care of you.

CHAPTER 49

How to Be a DEMO God

Acting is standing up naked and turning around very slowly.

~ ROSALIND RUSSELL

Twice a year, executives from seventy companies do a six-minute demo of their products to an audience of venture capitalists, analysts, and journalists. This event is called, logically, DEMO. It's a great event—especially if you understand the dance that's going on: entrepreneurs acting as though they don't need capital, and venture capitalists acting as though they don't need entrepreneurs. (This dance is akin to acting prudish in a brothel.)

This chapter is ostensibly for the 70 souls who will do the demo plus another 140 vice presidents of marketing and PR account execs who will go to DEMO. Let's call it 300 or so people. But it's also for anyone who has to give a good demo, because the reality is that this skill is essential in order to raise capital, make a sale, garner press, and recruit employees.

- **Create something worth demoing.** If you want to be a DEMO god, create a great product to demo. If you create mediocrity, and you somehow slipped past the gatekeepers of DEMO, you will be outed there. I know DEMO is a great PR opportunity, but if you don't do a demo, only you will know you have created mediocrity. If you do the demo, the whole world will.

- **Bring two of everything.** There is one place for duplication: equipment. Expect everything to break the night before you're onstage, so bring two, maybe even three, computers, phones, thumb drives, whatever you'll use in your demo. There is zero slack for equipment failures at DEMO other than the projector and audio, which are the responsibility of the DEMO folks.

- **Get organized in advance.** You should never futz around in a demo—for example, looking for folders and files on your hard disk. You have weeks to prepare for these six minutes; you're absolutely clueless if you haven't set everything up in advance.

- **Reduce the factors you can't control.** Should you assume that you'll have Internet access during your demo? Yes, but have a backup anyway. Sure, the hotel has a T1 line, but several hundred people in the audience are accessing it. Better yet, simulate Internet access to your server by using a local server. You don't have to show the real system. This is, after all, the demo.

- **Get to it.** You have only six minutes, so within thirty seconds, stop jawboning and start demoing. Nobody cares about the genesis of your company or that you have a PhD in cognitive science from Stanford. They came to see a demo, not hear your life story. Believe me, if your demo is good, they'll hunt you down to get your whole story later. If your demo sucks, it won't matter if you've won a Nobel Prize.

- **Cut the jokes and skit.** If you're wondering if your jokes are funny, they aren't. Very few people are funny enough to pull off jokes at DEMO. Most audiences want the speaker to succeed, so they will laugh at all but the worst jokes. However, the DEMO audience wants you to fail, because it's full of insecure egomaniacs, and it's online or using BlackBerrys. Thus you have an audience that isn't empathetic and isn't paying attention. That's too tough a crowd for jokes and skits.

- **Do it alone.** A DEMO god works alone. You may think it will be interesting if the two cofounders do the demo together. And you think it will show the world how they're getting along so well. It's hard enough for one person to do a demo. Trying to get two people to do an interactive demo is four times harder. If you want to be a duet, go to a karaoke bar.

- **"Do the last thing first."** I stole this from my buddy Peter Cohan, who teaches people how to do a great demo. What he means, and I second, is that you have about one minute to captivate your audience, so don't try building to a crescendo. Start with "shock and awe"—the absolute coolest stuff that your product can do. The goal is to blow people's minds.

  Once you've blown their minds, then you work backward and show them the "how." This is the knockout punch: Not only is the "what" fantastic, but the "how" makes it possible for mere mortals to do this, too. True or false: What's coming out of your mouth should impress the audience. The answer is: false; what the audiences sees, not hears, should do the impressing.

- **Cut the jargon.** The DEMO attendee thinks that she is very sophisticated and tech savvy. She may well be, but jargon seldom impresses people. The ability to speak simply and succinctly is the best way to go. You may have the world's greatest enterprise software product, but the consumer device partner of your dream venture capital firm is in the audience. If she can't understand your demo, she's not going to be telling her counterparts about it back in the office.

- **Don't take any questions until the end.** There are no questions during a demo at DEMO because of the six-minute limit. However, in other circumstances, you may be tempted to field questions as you go. Don't do it. It's too risky. You never know what the audience will ask. Doing so could take you down a rat hole so deep that you'll never come back up. The upside of showing that you can answer any question in real time is an ego trip that doesn't justify the downside of getting derailed.

- **End with an exclamation point.** You want to start on a high. You also want to end on a high. (If I had to choose, though, I'd rather start with a higher high than end with a higher high.) This is Steve Jobs's keynote trick; he always has one more great announcement in his bag of tricks. Scary but true: The goal is to end like the Ginsu knife commercial: "But wait, there's more. . . ." And when you do end on this exclamation point, leave the screen alone. Give the audience plenty of time to let the exclamation point sink in.

I've given this advice to many companies. I also know that thousands of people have read it online. And still most people's demos suck. This is because they think this advice applies to only the great unwashed masses who don't have a curve-jumping, paradigm-shifting, patent-pending product and are not naturally funny presenters. You're probably thinking the same thing. You're wrong. And you're going to learn the hard way.

CHAPTER 50

How to Kick Butt on a Panel

Man clamors for the freedom to express himself and
for knowing that he counts. But once offered these
conditions, he becomes frightened.

~ ROBERT C. MURPHY

At any given conference, there are usually three keynote speakers and twenty-five panelists, so the odds are much higher that you'll be a panelist than a keynote speaker. Superficially, a panel looks easy. There are four or five other people on it—all of whom you think you're smarter than—and it only lasts sixty minutes. How hard could it be? Herein lies the problem: Everyone thinks a panel is easy, so they don't take it seriously. This is what you should do if you want to be the person everyone comes up to talk to after a panel.

- **Know the subject.** If you're invited to a panel on wireless security, and you don't know much about the subject, then you should decline. I don't care how wonderful the opportunity seems to be. If you can help it, never provide an audience the opportunity to know that you're clueless.

- **Control your introduction.** The first mistake that most panelists make is that they assume the moderator has an up-to-date and accurate bio. Odds are that the moderator either knows nothing about you or has done a Google search and printed a bio that is inaccurate. Before the panel starts, hand the moderator a three-sentence description of who you are and tell her to read it verbatim.

- **Speak up.** The optimal distance between your lips and the microphone is one inch. You're sitting down. You're hunched over. You're not projecting. So get close to the mike and speak up. Assume there's a fifty-one-year-old geezer in the back with a hearing aid, like me.

- **Entertain, don't just inform.** As in keynotes, your goal is to entertain, not only inform. The funnier you are, the more people will think you're smart, because it takes great intelligence to be funny. I'd go so far as to pick a friendly fight with the moderator or another panelist. Let it rip. Have fun. Think of a panel as friendly, though emotional, conversation in front of 500 of your closest friends.

- **Tell the truth, especially when the truth is obvious.** If you're lucky, and there's a good moderator, that moderator will try to pin you to the wall with tough, embarrassing questions. This is a good thing because it provides an opportunity to (a) be funny and (b) show that you're a straight shooter. "The truth will get you glee." If everybody knows the truth, don't even try to fudge. It would be far better to say, "I take the Fifth Amendment." That will get a laugh.

- **Answer the question that's posed, but don't limit yourself to it.** When asked a question, answer the question (unless you have to take the Fifth). Answer it as fast as possible, but then feel free to take the conversation in a direction that you want. For example, let's say that the moderator asks, "Do you think cell phones will get viruses soon?" It's perfectly OK to answer, "Yes, I think this is an issue, but the real issue is the lack of good cell phone coverage," if that's what you really want to talk about.

- **Be plain, simple, and short.** Let's assume you are on a panel of experts. Let's further assume the moderator is an expert. The moderator asks a question. You think that you're answering her and the other panelists—all experts, so you launch into alphabet soup, acronym du jour. Big mistake. The audience is, well, the audience. Not the moderator, nor the panelists. Reduce the most complex and technical issues to something plain, simple, and short, and you'll position yourself as (a) unselfish and (b) a star.

- **Fake interest.** This may be one of the hardest aspects of a panel. Let's say another panelist launches into a long, boring, jargon-filled response. The temptation is to whip out a BlackBerry at worst or to look bored at best. Don't do it. Fake rapt interest, because the moment you look bored, a photographer is going to snap a picture or the cameraman is going to put your face on the ten-foot screen. You've got it made if you can fake sincerity.

- **Never look at the moderator.** The moderator is asking the questions, but he is merely a proxy for the audience. When you answer, don't look at the moderator. Look at the audience, because the audience doesn't want to see the side of your head. (FYI, a good moderator will not make eye contact with you—forcing you to look away from him and look at the audience.)

- **Never say, "I agree with the previous panelist."** A moderator will often ask everyone to answer the same question. If you're not the first one to answer, there's the temptation to say, "I agree with what my colleague just said." That's a dumb-ass response. Come up with something different, and if you're not quick enough on your feet to do this, don't go on the panel. At the very least say, "I think that question has been answered. For the audience's sake, let's move on."

A panel is a good opportunity to stand out from your competition, because you are juxtaposed to four or five people at the same time. Take these recommendations to heart, and you'll do just fine—especially if the panel has a great moderator, the kind I describe in the next chapter.

CHAPTER 51

How to Be a Great Moderator

Be sincere; be brief; be seated.

～ FRANKLIN D. ROOSEVELT

How many times have you watched an entertaining and informative panel? Your answer is probably a small number, and it's the moderator's fault. Moderating a panel is harder, in fact, than keynoting, because the quality of the clowns on the panel is beyond your control. This is what it takes to moderate a panel.

- **Represent the audience.** First and foremost, the moderator's responsibility is to make sure the panelists are entertaining and informing the audience. The moderator is called the moderator because her role is to ensure that there is only a moderate level of bull shiitake and sales pitches. A good moderator is the audience's advocate for truth, insight, and brevity—any two will do. When a panelist makes a sales pitch or tells lies, you are morally obligated to smack him around in front of the audience.

- **Make everyone else look smart.** The second most important responsibility of the moderator is to make the panelists look smart. It is not to make himself look smart or grab the most attention. Moderators can make panelists look smart in two ways: First, give them questions that they can knock out of the park. Second, extract nuggets of gold by rephrasing, summarizing, or clarifying what the panelists said. A good moderator accounts for only 10 percent of the speaking time of a panel—she is the "invisible hand," not the star.

- **Don't overprepare the panelists.** The more the panelists prepare in advance, the more likely they will be boring. If you provide all the questions in advance, many panelists will prepare carefully crafted, devoid-of-content responses—in the worst case, even tapping PR people for help. The most you should provide is the first two or three questions to make panelists feel comfortable and "prepared," whether you ask these questions or not.

- **Do prepare yourself in advance.** Moderators need to prepare more than panelists because they need to be able to pepper the panelists with questions about the latest industry controversies and hot issues. It's hard to do this in real time, so prepare the questions in advance using multiple research resources. If you don't have enough industry knowledge to stir up the pot, then decline the invitation to moderate the panel.

- **Never let panelists use PowerPoint (or Keynote).** Even if the panelists are CEOs and Nobel Prize winners, never let them give a "brief" Power-Point presentation. If one panelist uses PowerPoint, everyone else will want to. Then the session will encounter the technical difficulty of making multiple laptops work with the projector or the challenge of integrating many presentations into one. Even if you solve the technical issues, the presentations are still likely to suck, so forget them.

- **Never let panelists use props.** Suppose everyone accepts the no-Power-Point rule, but a panelist comes up with the clever idea of showing a "brief" corporate video. Again, the answer is, "No can do." Frankly, if a panelist needs a PowerPoint presentation or a video, he's probably not articulate enough to be on the panel, so get rid of him if you can.

- **Make them introduce themselves in thirty seconds.** The moderator shouldn't read each panelist's bio, because he will inevitably (a) mispronounce something (I didn't know I was Polish until I was introduced as "Guy Kawolski"); (b) get some fact wrong: "Oh, you didn't graduate from Harvard Business School, you just attended a one-week executive boondoggle there"; or (c) fail to highlight some crucial part of the panelist's background.

- **Break eye contact with the panelists.** Look at the panel, ask a question, and then look at the audience. Do not continue eye contact with the panelists, because you want them to speak directly to the audience, not to the moderator. Also, don't hesitate to tell panelists to speak louder or get closer to the microphone.

- **Involve the audience.** Moderators should allocate approximately 30 percent of the duration of the panel to questions from the audience. Any more, and the audience will run out of high-quality questions. Any less, and the audience will feel that it did not participate. However, don't feel obligated to accept stupid questions from the audience any more than you accept stupid answers from the panelists. Always have a few good questions in your hip pocket just in case no one in the audience has a question. Or, even better, you could "seed" the audience in advance.

- **Seize the day.** A moderator gets an A+ if she can nail a panelist "in the act." For example, many venture capitalists cop the attitude "We knew that the dot-com bubble would burst, so we were very careful about what we invested in." The moderator should win a prize if he can come back with, "Then why did you invest in discountdogfood.com?" I realize this conflicts with "make everyone else look smart," but moderating is a complex task.

I hope that you get the chance to moderate some panels during your career. You'll find moderating as rewarding as keynoting, but the challenges are different. Keynotes are about what you can do. Panels are about what you can get the panelists to do. Just remember that your goal is to entertain and inform the audience. Most panels don't come close to accomplishing this.

CHAPTER 52

The Art of Blogging

blogger *n.* **Someone with nothing to say
writing for people with nothing to do.**

〜 GUY KAWASAKI

I was late to blogging because I thought it was arrogant: "My thoughts are so important that you'll want to know what I think every day about everything." It's taken three years, but now I'm a believer, and I'll tell you why. On a personal level, blogs are an outlet for expression and creativity. Truly, if no one but your dog reads your blog, it's still worth doing.

On a business level, blogs are a marketing and communications weapon. They're fast, free, and under your control. You can use a blog to reach potential customers, establish a brand, provide support, and build a community. You can also use it to do favors for people by promoting their books and products, so that they'll do favors for you.

As in other arts, there are techniques and practices that make you more effective. These are the principles that guide my blogging.

• **Think "book," not "diary."** First, a bit of philosophy: Think of your blog as a product. A good analogy is the difference between a diary and a book. When you write a diary, it contains your spontaneous thoughts and feelings. You have no plans for others to read it. By contrast, if you write a book, from day one you should be thinking about spreading the word about it.

- **Answer the little man.** Now that you're thinking of your blog as a product, ask yourself if it's a good product. A useful test is to imagine that there's a little man sitting on your shoulder reading what you're writing. Every time you write a blog entry, he asks, "So what? Who gives a shiitake?" If you can't answer the little man, then you don't have a good blog/product. Take it from someone who's tried: It's tough to market crap, so make sure you have something worth saying. Or write a diary and keep it to yourself.

- **Collect links for blog rolling.** This is something I wish I had done on day one, but I was totally ignorant of this linking thing. If I had to do it over again, I would look for all the interesting blogs that cover similar topics. Then, I would blog-roll them all and ensure that Technorati pings my blog, so that the bloggers might find out that I exist.

- **Scoop stuff.** There's a very interesting honor system in blogging. Suppose blogger A finds an obscure article and posts it to his blog. Blogger B reads about it on blogger A's blog and links to it. However, blogger B doesn't link only to the article; she also links to blogger A to give him credit for finding the article. This means that if you hustle and scoop stuff, other bloggers will link to you.

- **Supplement other bloggers with follow-up entries.** Read the blogs of the top fifty or so bloggers and see if you have in-depth knowledge about their topics. Then instead of leaving useless drivel, craft a real comment that complements the blogger's entry.

  When someone does this for my entries, I want to get down on my knees and thank God, because it's less stuff that I have to write. I don't know about other bloggers, but one of the biggest challenges that I face is feeding the content beast. If you can help me feed it, I'll gladly link to you and give you publicity.

- **Acknowledge and respond to commenters.** Only good things can happen when you read all the comments in your blog and respond to them. It makes commenters return to your blog. This, in turn, makes commenters feel they are part of a community, and that encourages them to tell more people to read your blog.

- **Ask for help.** If you are providing value in your blog, don't hesitate to ask your readers to help. In a perfect world, you provide something valuable in your blog and your readership will want to pay you back by helping you spread the word.

- **Be bold.** I'm not saying you should intentionally piss other bloggers off, but if you can't speak your mind on your own blog, you might as well give up and stay on the porch. This is a fascinating thing about blogging: Even when people torch you, they link to your site.

- **Make it easy to join up.** Enable people to get to your blog in multiple ways like RSS feeds and e-mail subscriptions. This is no different from distributing physical products through multiple channels.

Two years ago, my wife saw me typing away on my Macintosh late at night. She asked me what I was doing, and I answered, "Changing the world, 10,000 readers at a time." Without missing a beat, she deadpanned back, "Oh, you're blogging." If you do it properly, she's absolutely right.

The Reality of Beguiling

The word *beguile* has a bum rap. Most people think of it as using trickery, flattery, or deception to get what you want. A better and more positive take on the term is "getting the job done by creating win-win situations." I'm not sure that nice guys finish first, but the beguiling ones sure do. This section explains the reality of what it takes to get what you want by giving people what *they* want.

CHAPTER 53

The Psychology of Influencing People

Life is made up, not of great sacrifices or duties,
but of little things, in which smiles, and kindnesses,
and small obligations, given habitually, are what win
and preserve the heart and secure comfort.

~ HUMPHREY DAVY

The best place to start learning to beguile people is the work of Dr. Robert Cialdini, a psychology professor at Arizona State University. His book, *Influence: Science and Practice* (Allyn & Bacon, 2000), is a must-read for anyone who wants to succeed. I would be astounded if reading this book doesn't make you a better (business) person. This interview of Dr. Cialdini provides an overview of his concepts and research.

Q: What is your definition of influence?

A: Influence means creating change in some way. Change can be in an attitude; it can be in a perception, or a behavior. But in all instances, we can't lay claim to influence until we can demonstrate that we've changed someone.

Q: Who has influence?

A: We all have the potential to be influential, although some of us make more use of it than others.

Q: How do we do that?

A: The ability to influence is not simply inborn. We can learn to become dramatically more successful at it. For centuries, the ability to be influential and persuasive has been thought of as an art, but there's also a science to it. And if it's scientific, it can be taught. It can be learned. So we all have the potential to become more influential.

Q: Are there any ethical concerns surrounding the use of influence to get people to say yes?

A: Because the principles of influence can be so powerful in causing change in others, we have to consider our ethical responsibilities in the process. Fortunately, the way to be ethical in the use of these principles is the same as the way to be profitable in using them. Always be sure to influence another in a way that ensures that you haven't damaged your ability to influence this person again in the future. In other words, the other person must benefit from the change you've created. We can do this by harnessing one or more of the six universal principles of influence:

- **Reciprocation.** People give back to you the kind of treatment that they have received from you.

- **Scarcity.** People will try to seize the opportunities that you offer them that are rare or dwindling in availability.

- **Authority.** People will be most persuaded by you when they see you as having knowledge and credibility on the topic.

- **Commitment.** People will feel a need to comply with your request if it is consistent with what they have publicly committed themselves to in your presence.

- **Liking.** People prefer to say yes to your request to the degree that they know and like you. No surprise there.

- **Consensus.** People will be likely to say yes to your request if you give them evidence that people just like them have been saying yes to it.

Just because there are six optimal approaches to influence doesn't mean that everyone uses them optimally. In fact, in my own research, I was able to detect three kinds of influence practitioners. There are bunglers of influence; there are smugglers of influence; and then there are sleuths of influence—the detectives of influence.

Bunglers are the people who fumble away their chances to use the principles in a beneficial way, either because they don't know what the principles are or because they don't know how to engage them properly. These people are always dropping the ball when it comes to the influence process.

Smugglers, on the other hand, do know—quite well—what the principles are and how they work. But they import these principles into situations where they don't naturally exist. An example would be a salesperson who pretended to be an authority on a particular computer system in order to get a customer to buy it. Although the smuggler's approach often works in the short run, it's deadly in the long run because only one person wins. The customer, who gets fooled into buying the wrong system, will be unhappy with it and will be unlikely to ever return to that salesperson or dealer for future business.

Sleuths are more knowledgeable than bunglers, more ethical than smugglers, and overall more successful than either. They approach each influence opportunity as a detective, looking to uncover and use only those principles that are truly part of the situation and that therefore will steer people correctly when to say yes.

For instance, if our computer salesperson genuinely was an expert in a particular type of system that a customer was interested in, it would be foolish not to share this information with the customer right at the outset. And if the salesperson had been good enough as a detective to find out that that one particular system had a unique feature that no other system had, he or she would be a bungler not to say so and make use of this scarcity principle that was a natural part of that situation. It's not sufficient to know what the most powerful principles of influence are. We have to train ourselves to search every influence situation for the principles that reside there naturally, and to use only those principles. That way, we ensure an exchange in which both parties profit.

Q: What's the most important thing in making a request?

A: Oddly enough, often the most important thing in making a request is not in the request itself. It's what you do before you make that request. This is a little secret that's understood very well by the most accomplished, influential professionals, the people whom I call the influence aces. I've found that those who were most successful at getting what they asked for work very hard at first arranging a favorable psychological environment for their request. After all, even if you've got a perfectly wonderful idea to offer, many people won't bother so much as to listen to your offer unless you've first done something to make them like you, to see you as an authority on the topic, or to feel a commitment to your idea. So by first establishing an environment of liking or authority or commitment or obligation or scarcity or consensus, you give your request the benefit of falling on fertile, rather than stony, ground.

Q: Please give an example of how to apply one of these principles of influence in a way that is effective, ethical, and enduring.

A: Let's take the first principle I listed: reciprocation. People want to give back to you the kind of treatment that they've received from you. For a manager, this rule is simply a gold mine. We all know the value of having positive attitudes and personal relationships in the workplace. Now think of the advantages to a manager of understanding the rule of reciprocation in the achievement of those goals. Because people give back what they've received, it means that you can increase the level of whatever you want from your coworkers and employees by giving it first. If you want more information, you provide it to them. If you want to create a feeling of trust, you offer it first. If you want to foster a cooperative attitude, you show it first. By acting first, you get to set the tone for the type of workplace relationships you want.

Now let's take information sharing as an example. It's undeniably true that in any business, a manager will be able to plan, execute, and complete tasks more successfully to the degree that he or she has access to the necessary information.

By providing to others the amount, the level, and the quality of information that he or she wants, the manager will get the amount, the level, and the quality of desired information in return. And it will flow naturally. No need for any arm-twisting or surveillance, because as the research clearly shows, disclosure is a reciprocal thing.

I did some research in the airports of our country to see how one particular organization, the Hare Krishnas, use this principle to get people to give them money when the people don't know anything about this organization or don't especially like it. The Hare Krishnas have hit upon a strategy that works remarkably well. Before they ask you for a contribution, they give you something. It can be a book; it can be a flower. In the most cost-effective version, they walk up and hand you a flower or they pin a flower on your lapel, and you say, "I didn't ask for that. Here, take this flower back." And they say, "Oh no, no, no. That's our gift to you. However, if you'd like to give a few dollars for the good works of this society, that would be greatly appreciated."

I saw them work for an entire day in the O'Hare Airport. And what I saw was a remarkable testimony to the power of this rule: People feel that if they have received, they can't just walk away without giving something in return. It goes against all our upbringing. Remember our teachers told us, our parents told us, "You must not take without giving in return." We have very nasty names for people who take without giving in return. We call them moochers or takers, or, as somebody at a conference where I was speaking said, teenagers. Nobody wants to be thought of as immature or a moocher or a taker. What the Krishnas learned was that if they could get somebody to accept something, then that person would feel an obligation to give something back.

What the Krishnas are doing is giving people something that they don't want, that has no value for them, in exchange for something that does have value: their money. And that has created an immediate success for the Krishnas and a long-term disaster. Did you know that they declared bankruptcy in the United States?

Q: Why?

A: Because once people have encountered this kind of ploy—this exploitation of the influence principles, they don't want to deal with this person again. If people believe that they received something of value, then they feel that you're entitled to get something in return. You've established a relationship with them—a relationship that leads to referrals, repeat business, good word-of-mouth advertising, and so on. And that relationship is a very positive lever for future profit.

Q: What is your definition of ethical influence?

A: The ethical approach to influence is to find one or more of these six principles that we talked about. Find something that people would value, give it to them, and they will want to give you something of value in return. They will want to return that business. If they've seen that you've done a good job, then they will want to have a relationship with you—a continuing relationship.

Identify what it is about what you can offer that your competitors can't give them. It may not be any one single thing. It may be a bundle of opportunities or benefits or services that you can provide—especially maybe customer service. Tell them what it is that they can't get anyplace else. If you can find this and show that to them, they'll want to move in that direction because that will be beneficial to them.

Let me give you one quick example that should finish our discussion of reciprocity. Something that we've already alluded to: People feel indebted to those who give to them, and information is one of those things you can give to people.

Let's say a customer owns a trucking business or a dry-cleaning store. You read an article in a newspaper or in a magazine about how the trucking industry is working or the dry-cleaning industry is working in another city, like Cleveland. You need to cut that out and send it to your past customer. That's a way of saying, "Here, I thought you'd be interested in it. Here's some information for you."

Now, he's going to know two things about you as a consequence. First, you care about him. Second, you are interested in improving his business. So what does the rule of reciprocity say? I have to be interested in improving his business.

Q: What are some ways to recognize and construct elusive moments of influence during which people are particularly receptive to requests?

A: It's what you do beforehand. So, for example, there is a moment of power that you are afforded immediately after someone has said thank you. You need to fill the moment with a request for a testimonial or a referral, or some sort of written commitment that doesn't allow that honest recognition of your good work to evaporate into the air. You deserve it.

In that moment, you should say, "Well, I really appreciate that. If I have other customers in your situation who have the same kind of housing floor plan or same kind of situation, I would love to be able to demonstrate to them that we do a good job in these kinds of situations. Would you mind writing me a note to that effect or sending me an e-mail?" Or, "Would you be willing to receive a phone call from a customer who is kind of wondering, and tell them what you think?" And at that moment after they've said thank you, they just can't say no, after they've just told you that you did a wonderful job.

It's more than just recognizing that moment. It's getting a commitment for that thank-you. There's something that you need that's more than a verbal acknowledgment that you've done well. You need it in writing. People live up to what they have written down. And that's the key. That's the key to leveraging that thank-you into the future, getting a commitment to it.

And the more public that commitment is, the better. There was a study done on college students who as freshmen were having trouble. They weren't doing very well in their classes, and they went into a program that was set up to help them with their study habits. They all made a commitment to study at regular and specific times in a systematic way every night. One group kept that commitment in their heads. Another group wrote it down and kept it private. Another group wrote it down and showed it to everybody else in the room, and said, "Here's what I promise that I'm going to do."

The first two groups didn't improve at all on their next test. But in the group that showed their public commitment to everybody else in the room, 86 percent got one full grade better, moving from a C to a B or a D to a C on the next exam. Eighty-six percent versus virtually nothing from the other groups because they made those commitments public—that's one of the advantages of written commitments.

We should call Cialdini's six principles of influence the Beguiling 6 because they are so powerful and so effective. Look at how these principles work as a checklist for sales training:

- **Reciprocation.** If you take care of your customer, your customer will take care of you.

- **Scarcity.** It's easier to sell something that people perceive as popular and in short supply.

- **Authority.** The customer will believe in you if you're knowledgeable.

- **Commitment.** If your customer publicly commits to an order or request, he's likely to go through with the sale.

- **Liking.** Ever bought something from someone you disliked? Ever turned down someone you liked?

- **Consensus.** It's easier to close a sale if everyone around is also buying your product.

I love Cialdini's material. I hope that I've persuaded you to read *Influence* and his current book, *Yes! 50 Scientifically Proven Ways to Be Persuasive*.

CHAPTER 54

The Art of Creating a Community

**Never doubt that a small group of thoughtful, committed citizens
can change the world. Indeed, it is the only thing that ever has.**

~ MARGARET MEAD

C reating a community is the fad these days, but it wasn't always so.
Many companies considered—and some still consider—their customers and fans a bunch of pains in the ass. This perspective is so
wrong—it's completely contrary to the Cialdini concept of reciprocation. If
nothing else, it fails to capitalize on a resource that can help a company with
sales, support, and evangelism. The purpose of this chapter is to explain how
to create a community.

- **Create something worth building a community around.** This is a
  repeated theme in my writing: The key to evangelism, sales, demoing, and
  building a community is a great product. Indeed, if you create a great product or service, you may not be able to stop a community from forming even
  if you tried. By contrast, it's hard to build a community around mundane
  and mediocre crap no matter how hard you try. Power tip: Once you have
  the community, let them tell you how to improve your product by exposing
  your engineers to the cheers and jeers. This type of feedback is one of the
  greatest values of a community.

- **Identify and recruit your thunder lizards immediately.** Most companies are stupid: They go for months and then are surprised—"Never heard

of them. You mean there are groups of people forming around our products?" If you have a great product, then proact: Find the thunder lizards and ask them to build a community. Indeed, if you cannot find self-appointed evangelists for your product, you may not have created a great product. If it is a great product, however, just the act of asking these customers to help you is so astoundingly flattering that they'll help you.

- **Assign one "champion" the task of building a community.** Sure, many employees would like to build a community, but who wakes up every day with this task at the top of her list of priorities? Another way to look at this is, "Who's going to get fired if she doesn't build a community?" A community needs a champion—an identifiable hero and inspiration—from within the company to carry the flag for the community. Therefore, hire one less MBA and allocate this slot to a community champion. This is a twofer: one less MBA and one great community.

- **Give people something to chew on.** Communities can't just sit around composing love letters to your CEO about how great she is. This means your product has to be customizable, extensible, and malleable. Think about Adobe Photoshop: If it weren't for the company's plug-in architecture, do you think its community would have developed so quickly? However, giving people something to chew on requires killing corporate hubris and admitting that your engineers did not create the perfect product. Nevertheless, the payoff is huge, because once you get people chewing on a product, it's hard to wrest it away from them.

- **Create an open system.** No company has a monopoly on ways to add value to its products, and many communities form to fill these holes. All a company has to do is provide the needed tools and information. For example, Adobe did this with Photoshop and Apple with Macintosh, and eventually iPhone. The more people creating add-ons, plug-ins, and complementary products, the better—for both customers and the company.

- **Welcome criticism.** Most companies feel warm and fuzzy toward their communities as long as these communities toe the line by continuing to say nice things, buy their products, and never complain. The minute that the community says anything negative, however, companies freak out and pull back their community efforts. This is a dumb-ass thing to do. A company cannot control its community. Indeed, the more a company welcomes—even celebrates—criticism, the stronger its bonds to its community.

- **Foster discourse.** The definition of "discourse" is a verbal exchange. The key word here is "exchange." Any company that fosters community building should also participate in the exchange of ideas and opinions. At the basic level of community building, your Web site should provide a forum where customers can engage in discourse with one another as well as with the company's employees. At the bleeding edge of community building, your CEO participates in community events, too. This doesn't mean that you let the community run your company, but you should listen to what they have to say.

- **Publicize the existence of the community.** If you're going to all the trouble of catalyzing a community, don't hide it under a bushel. Your community should be an integral part of your sales and marketing efforts. Check, for example, what Harley-Davidson is doing by Googling "Harley Owners Group."

A community is a beautiful thing. It protects you from the heat and cold of a marketplace. It energizes your employees and resellers. It provides a talent pool and free sales, marketing, and support. Implement these recommendations, and you'll see what I mean.

CHAPTER 55

The Art of Customer Service

**To care for anyone else enough to make their problems one's own,
is ever the beginning of one's real ethical development.**

⁓ FELIX ADLER

Two recommendations in the previous chapter were to welcome criticism and foster discourse. These two concepts are the core of great customer service. The purpose of this chapter is to provide more information about the art of fantastic customer service.

1. **Start at the top.** The CEO's attitude toward customer service determines the quality of service that a company delivers. If the CEO thinks that customers are a pain in the ass, her company will provide lousy service. If the CEO thinks customers are treasured assets, it will provide great service. If you're not the CEO, either change her mind, quit, or learn to live with mediocrity—in that order.

2. **Put the customer in control.** The best customer service happens when management enables employees to put the customer in control. This requires two leaps of faith: first, trusting customers to not take advantage of the situation; second, trusting employees to make sound decisions. If you can make these leaps, then the quality of your customer service will zoom; if not . . . well, there is nothing more frustrating than working for a firm that cops the attitude that something is "against company policy."

3. **Take responsibility for your shortcomings.** Companies that take responsibility for their shortcomings garner good customer-service reputations because they have acknowledged that the problem is their fault and their responsibility to fix. Most people understand that "shiitake happens," but it's aggravating when companies deny that the problem is their fault and responsibility. That's when you hear people say, "It's the principle."

4. **Don't point the finger.** This is the flip side of taking responsibility. For example, when a computer program doesn't work, vendors resort to finger pointing: "It's Apple's system software." "It's Microsoft's application." "It's Adobe's PDF format." A great customer-service company doesn't point the finger; it figures out what the solution is, regardless of whose fault the problem is, and makes the customer happy. As my mother used to say, quoting Eldrige Cleaver, "You're either part of the solution or you're part of the problem." (By the way, as a rule of thumb, the company with the largest market capitalization is the one at fault.)

5. **Don't finger the pointer.** Great customer service companies don't shoot the messenger. It could be a customer, an employee, a vendor, or a consultant who's doing the pointing. The goal is not to silence the messenger, but to fix the problem so that the messenger never has to bring that message again.

6. **Don't be paranoid.** One of the most common justifications for lousy service is "What if everyone did this?" For example, to cite the often-told, perhaps apocryphal, story of a customer returning a tire to Nordstrom even though Nordstrom doesn't sell tires: What if everyone started returning tires to Nordstrom? However, the worst case is seldom the common case. There will be abusers, but generally people are reasonable.

7. **Hire the right kind of people.** To put it mildly, customer service is not a job for everyone. The ideal customer-service person derives great satisfaction by helping people and solving problems. This cannot be said of every job candidate. It's the company's responsibility to hire the right kind of people for this job, because it is a bad experience for the employee and the customer when you hire folks without a service orientation.

8. **Underpromise and overdeliver.** The goal is to delight a customer. For example, the signs in the lines at Disneyland that tell you how long you'll have to wait from each point are purposely overstated. When you get to the ride in less time, you're delighted. Imagine if the signs were understated—you'd be angry because Disneyland lied to you.

9. **Integrate customer service into the mainstream.** Let's see: Salespeople make the big bucks. Marketers do the fun stuff. Engineers: You leave them alone in their dark caves. Accounting cuts the paychecks. And customer service? They handle angry people when something isn't working, and something isn't working all the time. Customer service largely determines the company's reputation, so do not consider it a profit-sucking necessary evil.

10. **Don't give them a sales pitch.** Never give customers a sales pitch unless they're calling your sales department. When customers call for customer service or technical support, they are hardly in a mood for a sales pitch. If you sell anything, you're in danger of losing the customer, so you certainly should not ask customers to shell out more money to fix problems that they perceive as the company's fault. And don't even think about offering more free defective products as a token of your appreciation for their business.

11. **Use operating procedures, not scripts.** You've probably called at least a few companies and been sure the representative is reading a script—it's annoying and certainly not personal. Have standard operating procedures for common things, like cancellations and product returns, to ensure the job is done properly, but never ask or train your representatives to read from a script.

12. **Use operators.** Use people, not PBX systems (the push 1 for sales, 2 for billing). Make it so the operator can answer basic questions (like How do I sign up?), collect information about problems, assign a ticket number or reference ID, and find an available representative to take the call. If you must use a PBX system, keep it to one level with three or four options, as well as an option to be connected immediately to an operator.

13. **Use a callback system.** A few companies have a callback system by which they offer the option of calling you back at a set time rather than making you wait on hold. The first time I encountered one of these systems, I hesitated, thinking I might lose my place in the queue, but it really worked, and I've been a believer ever since.

14. **Keep customers in the loop.** Customers should never have to ask what you are doing. Let them know what's happening as you're doing things like looking up their account or researching an issue. Extending this concept, you can post information about outages right on your Web site, so people don't have to call to figure out what's happening. Be honest: Tell them if there's a problem and what's causing it, when service will be restored, and what you're doing to prevent it from happening again.

15. **Make customers feel important.** Train your employees to make customers feel important. If a customer makes a suggestion, the representative should note it and let the customer know he's noted it. Don't hesitate to do things like give credits or say things like "because you're a valued customer, we can do this for you." Customers are usually frustrated when they call customer service or support, so try to make them feel good.

16. **Follow up.** The biggest difference between acceptable and great customer service is how often and how well the customer-service department follows up on requests. Give customers a call or send them an e-mail with the result of their complaint or request. If a customer calls with a problem and you believe it's resolved, call or send an e-mail to ask if the issue has been resolved to their satisfaction.

The irony of customer service is that at an intuitive level, most people know that it largely determines a company's reputation, but companies spend less money on it than sales and marketing. The double irony of customer service is that nothing I've listed is particularly expensive. Now you know what to do, how to do it, and how cheap it is to do, so you have absolutely no excuses for poor customer service.

CHAPTER 56

Power 3.0: Kinder, Gentler, and Better

I suppose leadership at one time meant muscles;
but today it means getting along with people.

~ GANDHI

hoose your form of strength: Power 1.0 = muscle and weapons. Power 2.0 = money, market share, or brain power.

Given these choices, most people and companies choose both. However, both Power 1.0 and 2.0 reflect Machiavelli's thinking that it's better to be feared than loved. Dacher Keltner, a professor at the University of California–Berkeley, has defined what I would call Power 3.0 in an article called "The Power Paradox" (*Greater Good* magazine, Winter 2007–2008).

In a nutshell, his concept is that power is the ability to influence people using skills in responsible ways to fulfill their needs and interests. Note: *their* needs and interests—not those of the person or organization exerting power. The paradox is that these skills are likely to deteriorate once you have power. Truly, beguiling requires a different perspective on power. According to Keltner there are three myths of power:

1. **"Power equals cash, votes, and muscle."** Not true. In psychological terms, power is defined as "one's capacity to alter another person's condition or state of mind by providing or withholding resources, such as food, money, knowledge, and affection, or by administering punishments, such as physical harm, job termination, or social ostracism." Thus, a child can exert power over her parents—as every parent knows. This means that you don't need to possess cash, votes, or brute force to exert power.

2. **"Machiavellians win in the game of power."** Not true, according to Keltner. " . . . one's ability to get or maintain power, even in small group situations, depends on one's ability to understand and advance the goals of other group members. When it comes to power, social intelligence— reconciling conflicts, negotiating, smoothing over group tensions—prevails over social Darwinism."

3. **"Power is strategically acquired, not given."** Not true. The truth is that people without power can band together and "constrain the actions of those in power." According to Keltner's research: "We've found that Machiavellians quickly acquire reputations as individuals who act in ways that are inimical to the interests of others, and these reputations act like a glass ceiling, preventing their rise in power."

Keltner concludes that "Power tends to corrupt and absolute power corrupts absolutely," quoting British historian Lord Acton, and power frequently makes people act in three dysfunctional ways:

1. Relying on stereotypes of people and less sophisticated reasoning.

2. Acting on one's own "whims, desires, and impulses."

3. Acting like a sociopath.

Keltner concludes with this penetrating thought:

Social behaviors are dictated by social expectations. As we debunk longstanding myths and misconceptions about power, we can better identify the qualities powerful people should have, and better understand how they should wield their power. As a result, we'll have much less tolerance for people who lead by deception, coercion, or undue force.

Here's to zero tolerance and using Power 3.0 to beguile people. Remember: Don't coerce or dominate, reconcile conflicts, and give power to get power. That's how to influence people.

CHAPTER 57

The Art of Schmoozing

**Flattery is telling the other person precisely
what he thinks about himself.**

~ DALE CARNEGIE

Guy's Tips

According to Susan RoAne, the queen of schmoozing, "It's not what
you know or who you know, but who knows you." I love this distinction. She should know, because she wrote the book on schmoozing:
How to Work a Room: Your Essential Guide to Savvy Socializing (Collins,
revised 2007). Schmoozing, networking, or whatever you want to call it is an
essential skill for beguiling people. First, my tips, then Susan's.

1. **Understand the goal.** Darcy Rezac in his book, *The Frog and the Prince*
   (Frog and Prince Networking Company, 2003), wrote the best definition
   of schmoozing: "Discovering what you can do for someone else." Herein
   lies 80 percent of the battle: Great schmoozers want to know what they
   can do for you, not what you can do for them. If you understand this, the
   rest is mechanical.

2. **Get out.** Schmoozing is an analog, contact sport. You can't do it alone
   from your office on the phone or via a computer. You may hate them but
   force yourself to go to trade shows, conventions, and seminars.

3. **Ask good questions, then shut up.** The mark of a good conversationalist is not that you can talk a lot. The mark is that you can get others to talk a lot. Thus, good schmoozers are good listeners, not good talkers. Ask softball questions like, "What do you do?" "Where are you from?" "What brings you to this event?" Then listen. Ironically, you'll be remembered as an interesting person.

4. **Unveil your passions.** Talking only about business is boring. Good schmoozers unveil their passions. Great schmoozers lead off with their passions. Your passions make you an interesting person—you'll stick out because you'll be the only person not talking about 802.11 chipsets at the wireless conference. In case you ever meet me, my passions are children, Macintoshes, Breitling watches, digital photography, and hockey.

5. **Read voraciously.** In order to be a good schmoozer, you need to read voraciously—and not just the *EE Times, PC Magazine,* and the *Wall Street Journal.* You need a broad base of knowledge so that you can access a vast array of information during conversations. Even if you are a pathetic, passionless person, you can at least be a well-read one who can talk about a variety of topics.

6. **Follow up.** When asked, I've given my business cards to thousands of people over the course of my career. I noticed something: One out of a hundred people uses the information to get in touch. Great schmoozers follow up and do so within twenty-four hours. A short e-mail will do: "Nice to meet you. I hope we can do something together. Hope your blog is doing well. I loved your Breitling watch. I have two tickets to the Stanley Cup finals if you want to attend." Include at least one item to show the recipient that she isn't getting a canned e-mail.

7. **Make it easy to get in touch.** Many people who want to be great schmoozers, ironically, don't make it easy to get in touch with them. They don't carry business cards, or their business cards don't have phone numbers and e-mail addresses. Even if they provide this information, it's in gray 6-point type. This is great if you're schmoozing teenagers, but if you

want old, rich, famous, and powerful people to call or e-mail, you'd better use a big font so they can read your business card.

8. **Give favors.** One of my great pleasures in life is helping other people; I believe there's a big karmic scoreboard in the sky. God is keeping track of the good that you do, and She is particularly pleased when you give favors without the expectation of return from the recipient. The scoreboard always pays back. You can also guess that I strongly believe in returning favors for people who have helped you.

9. **Ask for the return of favors.** Good schmoozers give favors. Great schmoozers also return favors. Fantastic schmoozers ask for the return of favors. You may find this puzzling: Isn't it better to keep someone indebted to you? The answer is no; this is because keeping someone indebted to you puts undue pressure on your relationship. Any decent person feels guilty when indebted. By asking for, and receiving, a return favor, you clear the decks, relieve the pressure, and set up for a whole new round of give-and-take.

Susan's Tips

Susan, bless her heart, was kind enough to send me her power-schmooze tips. I accepted. And I am gladly awaiting the chance to return the favor.

1. **Think analog, not digital.** We still have to interact with people, although the digital world has afforded us many ways to stay in touch using technology. We must know how to meet, mingle, make small talk, and connect with others in the analog world in both our professional and our personal lives. You can IM, text, ping, or Twitter, and yet you will still get invited to an office party or a cousin's wedding and have to do the face-to-face.

2. **Prepare for every event.** We now have many online sources to find out about the event, association, company, or organization. Take note of the news on the site, the people highlighted, and the news that is noted. Find

out whom you need to meet and whom you want to meet. Ask your network or the event host to make the introduction.

3. **Determine what you have in common with the other people at that event.** When you find that common point, you both will be more comfortable. If you alter your focus and think about making others comfortable with you, they will be.

4. **Prepare a self-introduction.** Be ready to introduce yourself if there is no greeting committee. It's a seven-to-nine-second pleasantry, not a thirty-second elevator speech, and key it to the event, so others know why you are attending. That will help them figure out what to say to you.

5. **Read voraciously.** This means blogs, online newspapers, and even the good old analog print newspaper. Every page of the paper provides news, information, scores, reviews, and even gossip (the newsy kind of schmooze) that is fodder for conversation. Jot down three to five items so you have something to add in case there is a lull. Don't forget to read industry journals and national magazines. Other people may have read that interesting article in *Fast Company, Forbes,* or *O.* If they haven't, you can highlight it and get the conversation rolling. It's OK to watch TV; I often quote Jon Stewart of *The Daily Show!*

Also, read Truemors.com every day. This will make you a better schmoozer, because you'll be on top of the latest news in a broad selection of areas. This will make you the king or queen of small talk.

6. **Approach the person standing alone.** He or she will welcome your company. No one, not even CEOs, want to stand by themselves in a room full of people. It just feels dorky.

7. **Just smile and say hi or hello.** According to research, those are the best opening lines. While we wait for the utterly brilliant icebreaker to pop into our brains and then to come out of our mouths, the person we want to meet may already have moved to the opposite side of the room. Depending on your age or crowd, the word "hey" may be the greeting du jour.

8. **Make small talk.** Too many of us think that we must be talking the important, deep stuff and consider small talk to be trivial. Wrong. Author Michael Korda's uncle, movie producer Sir Alexander Korda, said, "A bore is someone who has no small talk." Small talk is how we learn about our common interests, experiences, and connections.

9. **Listen, listen, listen.** People tell us about their interests. If we listen and stop planning what to say next, drafting our grocery lists or personals ad, we'll all be better conversationalists. I would be remiss if I didn't mention that we are not paying attention if our iPods are in our ears, our Black-Berrys or Treos are in our hands, or we are waiting for our Bluetooth cell phones to ring. In fact, doing any of the aforementioned behaviors does send a message to others, and it might not serve you in the long run.

10. **Go everywhere with the intention of having fun.** People want to be around the upbeat, fun, interesting, and interested person.

Between my tips and Susan's, you can achieve world-class schmooze status. It is a skill that comes in handy for all functions of starting and building an organization, from finding employees to raising money to making sales.

CHAPTER 58

The Art of Sucking Down

Flattery is the infantry of negotiation.

~ LORD CHANDOS

One of the great misconceptions of selling, pitching, and partnering—basically, any time you want to get someone to do something for you—is that you should suck up to the people with the big titles. Sometimes you need to, and we'll come to that soon, but the ability to suck down to the folks who don't have big titles but make the world run is often more useful.

A friend of mine who worked at O'Hare International Airport told me a story that illustrates this point. He saw a passenger screaming at an airline ticket agent. The ticket agent, however, remained completely calm. After the tirade was over, my friend asked her how she could remain so calm, and she said, "That's easy. He's going to Paris, but his bags are going to Sydney."

1. **Understand the dynamic.** Like it or not, here's how the world works: If you want something, you should be nice to the person (let's call him Biff) who can grant you that something. It doesn't matter whether you are more powerful, more famous, richer, better looking, or better educated. Biff has the power, so deal with it. Returning to the ticket agent episode, it makes no sense to piss off the one person who can help you. In such a situation,

there is no such thing as sucking down. You're always sucking up when you want something.

2. **Understand their needs.** You should try being a ticket agent, flight attendant, secretary, receptionist, waiter, or customer service rep for a day. Then you'd learn that they're not getting paid a lot of money to put up with your crap, and they're dealing with their own sets of issues: a broken-down car, an unhappy spouse, a sick child at home, and maybe even a bozo boss. These people want to do a good job, make a living, and be happy, just as you do. The key word here is *empathy*. If you can empathize with them, you'll be much more successful dealing with them.

3. **Be important.** If you want to be treated as an important customer, then be an important customer. That is, always fly the same airline, eat at the same restaurant, and play hockey at the same rink. If you spread your business around, then don't be surprised if you get jacked around. I only eat at three restaurants in all of Silicon Valley: Gombei, Juban, and Buck's. I can get in anytime I want at these three restaurants—but only these three restaurants. I fly on United seventy-five to a hundred times a year. It takes great care of me. I fly Air Canada once a year. It puts me in a coach class, center seat, between two screaming babies. That's life.

4. **Make them smile.** A window occurs in the first thirty seconds of your interaction with Biff. In that brief time, if you can make him smile, you will differentiate yourself from 95 percent of the orifices that he deals with. Then you're much more likely to get an aisle seat, an appointment with the boss, an outside table, or step-by-step instructions to make Word print.

Simply beginning a conversation with, "How is your day going?" can break the ice. You know, and he knows, that you don't really care how his day is going, but at least you're civil enough to ask. That separates you from the pack of hyenas. Here are some other opening lines that have worked for me:

- Restaurant maître d': "Do you have reservations?" You answer: "I have no reservations whatsoever. I am absolutely certain that I want to eat here."

- Airline ticket agent: "How can I help you?" You answer: "You could give me an upgrade to first class and ensure that my bag is the first one off the conveyor when I get there, but I'd be happy with an aisle seat."
- Secretary: "Will she know what you're calling about?" You answer: "Not unless she's a clairvoyant masochist. But may I try to explain why you should grant me an audience with her?"

5. **Don't try to buy your way in.** Don't try to buy a person with flowers, candy, or an iTunes gift card. Realistically, the downside risk far exceeds the upside, because you're likely to insult Biff by implying that he can be bought. Just be honest, be important, and have a legitimate rationale. That's a good enough case.

   I don't recommend trying to buy your way in, but once you are in, then it's appropriate to express your gratitude with gifts that are kind, but not extravagant. As my mother (and Wilson Mizner) used to say, "Be nice to people on the way up because you'll meet them on the way down." You never know when you'll need help from Biff again.

6. **Never complain.** Let's say that you don't get what you want. Should you go over Biff's head and complain? This is seldom effective. Assuming that Biff is competent, he's not going to get fired because of your whining. Historically, piss is seldom more effective than honey. Persevere, and wear down Biff's defenses with humor, dedication, and empathy, but never go over his head.

7. **Rack up the karmic points.** There's a karmic scoreboard in the sky. It keeps track of how many points you've earned and how many you've used. Therefore, when you have the opportunity to help others, do so—and do so with glee. You'll build up points, and someday your kindness will be returned to you. However, understand that you need to accrue these points before you need them—you cannot go negative.

8. **Accept what cannot be changed.** Sometimes things are just not meant to be: There are no more aisle seats, all the outside tables are taken, and the boss doesn't want to talk to any sales reps. If that's the case, shut up

and move on with life. Don't flatter yourself and believe that the airline is out to get you by assigning all the aisle seats to others. Life is too short to get upset by things like this.

I almost always get an aisle seat, almost always get upgraded, and almost always get my luggage back. I attribute my good fortune to understanding the art of sucking down in a world where most people think it's OK to trash the anyone "beneath" their station in life. Those people are still waiting for their luggage.

CHAPTER 59

The Art of Sucking Up

Flattery is a counterfeit money which,
but for vanity, would have no circulation.

~ FRANÇOIS DE LA ROCHEFOUCAULD

The art complementary to sucking down is sucking up. Sometimes a situation requires it—though I wish this were true less often. Done too blatantly, sucking up will backfire. Done too weakly, you won't get what you want. If you have to do it, you might as well do it right. The perfect suck-up contains the following elements:

- **Credibility.** No matter how good you suck up, if you don't meet the requirements for placement, a job, an interview, or whatever, it won't matter, so you need to deserve what you're asking for.

- **Empathy.** Who can resist a little play on emotion? "Please help us . . . we're just a little company trying to make a go of it." Actually, I'll tell you who can resist this: buttheads who aren't worth sucking up to.

- **Utility.** The best suck-ups are mutually beneficial. You are not only getting something, you are also providing something. Or, if you're in no position to do it right away, show that you will provide something of value in the future. Great suck-ups are always win-win propositions.

- **Gratitude.** If you're trying to get something, express gratitude for what you already have. This works much better than acting pissed off and wronged. You can seldom bludgeon someone into helping you.

- **Obligation.** As we learned from Robert Cialdini, the author of *Influence*, whom I interviewed earlier, if someone does something for you, you're pretty much compelled to do something in return. If you've already done something useful for me, how can I resist doing something for you?

- **Fluidity.** If you're going to ask someone to do something, make it a friction-free effort. You've probably got one shot, so assume the answer will be yes, and provide the action items.

- **Flattery.** You might think that this is the most important element in a suck-up, but it isn't. This is because most of the people you'll be sucking up to are frequently flattered (deservedly or not), so don't make this a central part of your pitch. One sentence at the beginning is enough; then focus on credible reasons why the person should help you.

Suck-up in Action

Remember Alltop from earlier in the book? It's the news Web site that aggregates feeds from Web sites and blogs, organized by topics—travel, wine, economics, politics, sports, and so on. Feeds that are earlier on the page receive more readers because less scrolling is necessary, so people suck up to get higher placement because we explain in our FAQ (frequently asked questions) that we take care of people who take care of us. This is an excellent illustration of a good suck-up:

> Here goes. My name is Brad Ward, a cofounder with Matt
> Herzberger of www.BlogHighEd.org, which is featured in your
> Education section on Alltop.com. Right now, we're all alone,
> hanging out on the bottom row. We are very appreciative and
> excited to be included, but with an FAQ question like that, we
> couldn't resist attempting to move ourselves up the totem pole.

We're pretty cool, though, trust us. Here's what we do at
BlogHighEd.org: We are aggregating twenty of the best higher
education bloggers out there, from Webmasters to marketers to
admission counselors to vendors to consultants and more. Sound
familiar? We're like Alltop's little brother or something. So how
about a little love? We've already given you some on our blogs.

Truth be told, we're not the *Chronicle of Higher Education*. We're
not Inside Higher Ed or the *Washington Post*. And we never will
be. But you know who we are? We are the ones who are taking the
leaps and advances that make things happen. We're the ones
brainstorming and figuring out how we are going to implement
this stuff months before it hits the press. We're presenting a
combined 100+ times a year at conferences. We write for
University Business. We run EduStyle.net. We run TargetX. We
are accomplished campus photographers. We are keynote speakers
(both of them, in this instance). We combine for thousands of RSS
subscribers.

Above all, we are a community, deeply committed to each other
and the greater good of higher education, and even more to the
success of BlogHighEd.org. Have no doubt that we'll stick around
and continue to grow. We don't make money from blogging. No
ads, no fluff. We're doing it after the 8–5, on the weekends, and
over lunch (like right now). And if that isn't awesome enough to
move us to the top of the Education section, I'm not sure what is.

Thanks for your time.

Brad

Did we move his feed up the page? But of course. You can check it out at
Education.alltop.com; look for BlogHighEd.org.

CHAPTER 60

How to Suck Up to a Blogger

Put it before them briefly so they will read it, clearly so they will appreciate it, picturesquely so they will remember it and, above all, accurately so they will be guided by its light.

〜 JOSEPH PULITZER

Blogging has flipped traditional PR on its head. It used to be that press begat buzz. Nowadays buzz begets ink. Life was simple in the old days: You sucked up to the *Wall Street Journal*, one of its reporters wrote about your product, and the buzz began. Journalists no longer create buzz: rather; they react to it: "Everyone is buzzing about Facebook. There must be something to this, so I have to write a story about it." This chapter explains the specific techniques for beguiling bloggers.

1. **Befriend as many bloggers as you can.** As you've already read, focusing on the influentials is a dubious strategy (see "Forget the Influencers After All?"). The support of many bloggers with moderate connections is more powerful than the support of a few big-name bloggers with large connections. And some of these unknown bloggers may become big names in the future. As my mother used to say, "You can never know too many bloggers or have too hard a slap shot."

2. **Create a great product or service.** There is a big catch to this democratization of buzz creation: Bloggers have a very low tolerance for bull shiitake. It's easy to say you're going after bloggers, but this assumes that

they'll like your product or service. The most important thing you can do to attract them is to create a DICEE product or service.

3. **Cite and link.** "Linking is the sincerest form of flattery." Imitation no longer sits atop this throne. It's hard to trash a company, product, service, or person who links to your blog. Personally, I've never met a person who linked to my blog whom I didn't like.

4. **Stroke them.** At the very least, read the blogger's site. Many marketers begin with such a generic pitch that the blogger can tell he hasn't even read the blog. Beyond this, you can send the blogger e-mails with these kinds of messages, but only if they are sincere:

   - "Not a day goes by that I don't read your blog."

   - "Why don't you publish your blog in a book?"

   - "You could easily break up your daily entries into several parts, because they have so much content."

   - "I've forwarded your blog to many of my friends."

   - "I 'digg' your blog almost every day."

5. **Give gifts.** In case you hadn't noticed, most bloggers don't make a lot of money from their blogging efforts. Thus, samples of your product, T-shirts, and pens can go a long way with bloggers, as it does with evangelists. I'm not saying you can buy bloggers, but you can make them happy pretty easily. Dollar for dollar, schwag for bloggers is one of the best marketing investments (though it isn't effective for journalists, as *Fortune*'s Adam Lashinsky explained earlier).

6. **Be responsive.** This is a common-sense duh-ism that is violated almost every day: If you want buzz, you have to return the phone calls and e-mails of bloggers. You are operating on their schedule; they are not operating on yours, so get used to it. Sure, if you're a Steve Jobs, you can make the rules, but until you reach his level, you have to play by the rules.

7. **Use a rifle, not a shotgun.** Any company that carpet bombs bloggers should be shot. The effect is the same as sending two dozen people the same e-mail requesting help. Not only will this approach fail, bloggers will conclude that you're a bozo to boot. Your job is to find out exactly whom you are relevant to. It is not the blogging community's job to sort through your bull shiitake.

8. **Be a foul-weather friend.** Anyone can be friendly, happy, and available when times are good. The big test occurs when the weather turns foul: Your company screws up, or the blogger writes something negative (justified or not). When this happens, some companies erect barriers and hunker down—a big mistake.

9. **Be a source.** Face it: There are times when your company simply isn't worthy of coverage. Don't take your ball and go home. Instead, "pay it forward" and help the blogger with her entry by acting as a source of information, by introducing her to other sources, and by offering insightful analyses. The next time, you may be the subject of the blog, not just a source.

10. **Make connections after you need them, too.** Let's say you're successful, and your great product has garnered the attention of bloggers. This doesn't mean you can rest; instead, keep working the relationships, because you'll need these connections again. Even if you didn't garner any attention, keep at it for the next time you need help. Sucking up is not an event—it's a process.

11. **Pitch reporters through their blogs.** It's difficult to pitch journalists "through the front door" of their big-time publication when the contact is info@newsweek.com. The probability of your e-mail getting to the reporter is zero. However, many journalists have personal blogs, and they are much more accessible through these than through their day-job publications.

The development that buzz generates press has fried many a marketer's mind. You might as well get used to it, though, because blogger buzz is only going to get more powerful and the press less powerful. If you want to maximize your marketing, you will need to master the art of sucking up to bloggers.

CHAPTER 61

The Art of Partnering

Friendship is but another name for an alliance with the follies and the misfortunes of others. Our own share of miseries is sufficient: Why enter then as volunteers into those of another?

~ THOMAS JEFFERSON

During the dotcom days of 1998–2000, *partner* became a verb when many startups didn't have a business model, and they had to blow smoke about having "partnered" with big firms. The logic was that if a company partnered with a Microsoft or an IBM, it would be successful.

To this day, whenever an entrepreneur uses *partner* as a verb, I hear, "Bullshiitake relationship that isn't going to increase revenue." However, I am not an angry little man, so in the spirit of improving what has become a flawed process, this is the art of partnering.

- **Partner for spreadsheet reasons.** Most companies form partnerships for the wrong reason: to make its CEO and the press and analysts happy. This is stupid. The right reason to form a partnership is to increase sales or decrease costs. Here's a quick test: Will you recalculate the spreadsheet model of your financial projections if the partnership happens? If not, then the partnership is doomed. You can wave your hands all you like about "visibility," "credibility," and "acceptability," but if you can't quantify the partnership, then you don't have one.

- **Define deliverables and objectives.** If the primary goal of a partnership is to deliver spreadsheet reasons, then execution is dependent on setting deliverables and objectives, such as additional revenues, lower costs, penetration of new markets, and new products and services. The only way to determine whether a partnership is working is to answer quantifiable questions such as "How many more downloads of software occurred because our two Web sites are now linked?"

- **Ensure that the middles and bottoms like the deal.** Most partnerships form when two CEOs meet at an industry boondoggle. The next thing you know, they've concocted a partnership that "the press and analysts will love," and the next step is to get the PR people to draft an announcement. Is it any wonder partnerships seldom work? The partnerships that work have the support of the middles and bottoms of both organizations. Indeed, the best partnerships occur when the middles and bottoms work together and create a de facto partnership that didn't involve top management until it was done.

- **Designate internal champions.** Long after the press conference and announcement, one person inside each organization must remain the champion of the partnership. "A bunch of people contributing to the partnership when they can" doesn't cut it. For example, during the desktop publishing days of Apple, John Scull (not Sculley) was "Mr. Desktop Publishing" at Apple. His counterpart at Aldus was Paul Brainerd. So the responsibility for the success of desktop publishing came down to John and Paul—not John, Paul, George, and Ringo plus a host of other, part-time contributors.

- **Accentuate strengths, don't hide weaknesses.** Companies form most partnerships to hide their respective weaknesses. For example, Apple and DEC formed such a partnership in the 1980s. Apple's weakness was a lack of data-communications strategy. DEC's weakness was a lack of a personal-computer strategy. So the two companies tried to put two and two together. In the end, two and two didn't even add up to four, because DEC's data-communications strategy couldn't help Apple, and Apple's personal-computer strategy couldn't help DEC. The deal between Apple and Intel is better, because it is based on each company's strengths: Apple's ability to design great consumer devices, and Intel's ability to build fast chips with low power requirements. And this partnership certainly has spreadsheet reasons for both parties.

- **Cut win-win deals.** A partnership seldom takes place between equals. As a result, the more powerful side is tempted to squeeze the other party. The weaker side, for its part, will begrudgingly accept such deals and try to get what it can. Bad idea. Bad karma. Bad practicality. If the partnership is a win-lose deal, it will blow up, because concrete walls and barbed wire cannot hold a partnership together. Only mutually beneficial results can. In the long run, the bitter seed of resentment planted at the start of a partnership will grow into a giant, destructive weed.

- **Include an out clause.** No matter how great the deal looks, put in an out clause so that both parties may terminate the partnership relatively easily. This may seem counterintuitive, but if companies know that they can get out of something, they'll work harder to make it successful. This is because easy out clauses can increase motivation: "We'd better keep up our end of the bargain, because we need these guys, and they can walk." Frankly, if all that's holding the partnership together is a legal document, then it's probably not going to work, anyway. It's hard to imagine indentured servitude as a motivating model of employment.

- **Ask women.** Men have a fundamental genetic flaw. Actually, they have many fundamental genetic flaws, but I am only concerned with one here: the desire to partner (verb!) with anything that moves. They don't care about practicalities and long-term implications. If something is moving, men want to partner with it. Women, by contrast, do not have this genetic flaw. When you come up with an idea for a partnership, don't bother asking men what they think about it, because they will almost always think it's a good idea. Instead, ask women, and gain some real insight as to whether the partnership makes sense.

- **Wait to legislate.** Don't use an e-mail or letter to get negotiation started. After you've reached closure on the deal terms—the result of many meetings, phone calls, and e-mails—then draft an agreement. You should do this at the end of the process because you want the people to have psychologically committed themselves to the partnership. If you start the drafting process too early, you're asking for nitpicking delays and blowups. Incidentally, if you ask for legal advice too early, you'll kill the process. The best way to deal with lawyers is to simply say to them: "This is what I want to do. Now keep us out of jail as we do it."

Unfortunately, partnering with a large company, even under the best conditions, is like being stuck in the belly of a snake. These techniques will help create an effective partnership if one is possible at all. The next step is understanding how big companies lie to you, and that's the subject in the next chapter.

CHAPTER 62

The Top Ten Lies of Partners

**Any alliance whose purpose is not the intention
to wage war is senseless and useless.**

~ ADOLF HITLER

A re you feeling that a snake is about to swallow you? To prevent those
jaws from closing around you, listen for these lies and view them as
warning signals if you hear them.

1. **"We want to do this for strategic reasons."** This is corporatese for, "I
have no idea why we're doing this. My CEO met your CEO at a boondoggle conference and told me to talk to you guys." Ideally, what you'd hear
instead is, "We think we'll make more money by partnering with you."
In other words, the large company wants to do this for solid tactical
reasons.

2. **"Our management really wants to do this."** There are two ways you
can take this. First, you have a great product, the large company gets it,
and life could be great. Second, the large company is clueless and desperate. As a rule of thumb, if you're not 110 percent sure it's the former, then
it's the latter. Then you should question the wisdom of partnering with the
organization at all.

3. **"We can move really fast."** This means that so far, very few people in
the organization have been exposed to the idea. As more people get

involved and the turf wars begin, progress will slow down, if not reverse. It could also be that this isn't a lie because "really fast" means nine to twelve months from the large company's perspective.

4. **"Our legal department won't be a problem."** In other words, the legal department hasn't seen the proposal yet. There are two kinds of legal departments in large companies: the kind that automatically says no when asked, "Can we do this?" and the kind that automatically says no when asked, "Can we do this?"

5. **"The engineering team really likes it"** or **"the marketing team really likes it."** Respectively, these lies mean that the marketing team hasn't seen it yet, and the engineering team hasn't seen it yet. Look at the bright side: Once you get past marketing, engineering, and legal, only accounting is left.

6. **"We want to time the announcement of our partnership with the release of a new version of our product."** This is a lie of good intentions. Unfortunately, it means that the gating item of your partnership is a large company's ability to deliver a new product. May God be with you.

7. **"Our primary concern is whether you guys can scale."** Technically, this isn't a lie. They *are* concerned about this—as they should be, because your team has never shipped a product before, and you only have six months of cash in the bank. It's simply that *their* ability to scale should concern *you*, too, because big companies with infinite resources often can't necessarily scale because of ineptness.

8. **"We'd like your servers to host most of the code and functionality."** This isn't a lie per se. It's more a frightening admission that the large company's product is held together by baling wire, duct tape, and chewing gum, so making any changes could make it blow up. Welcome to corporate partnering: One of the things that you'll learn is that the emperor has no code.

9. **"We're forming a cross-functional team to ensure the success of this project."** This ensures that no one is responsible for the success of

the partnership, nor is there anyone who's going to take the blame. Instead, you want the large company to identify one champion for the partnership. One champion is always better than a cross-functional team.

10. **"I'm leaving soon, but I've found a great person to take over my role in this project."** Now your champion is splitting, and the person who was arguing against the partnership is going to be in charge of implementing it. You've got some major evangelism and bridge repairing to do. May the force be with you.

Despite these warnings, partnerships can work. The main quality to focus on is that both organizations will either increase sales or decrease costs—aka spreadsheet reasons. As long as they exist, a partnership can work.

CHAPTER 63

Ten Questions "with" Jackie Onassis

Even though people may be well known, they hold in their hearts the emotions of a simple person for the moments that are the most important of those we know on earth: birth, marriage, and death.

~ JACKIE ONASSIS

The final chapter of this section is based on a book called *What Would Jackie Do? An Inspired Guide to Distinctive Living* (Gotham, 2006). The coauthors are Shelly Branch of the *Wall Street Journal* and Sue Callaway, the former vice president and general manager of Jaguar Cars U.S. The book explains what Jackie Onassis "would do" in various situations. The book is relevant to the art of beguiling because it deals with noblesse oblige, that is, the concept that the exceptionally fortunate have exceptional social obligations. Here is an excerpt from the book:

> Jackie preferred hailing taxis to get about in New York City. And in those yellow chariots, she would sometimes lean forward and do what so few ever bother to do: ask how the driver's day was going. In one case, she beseeched the cabbie to quit his shift in order to get home safely in soggy weather. What good is it, after all, to be a cut above if you don't let your own splendid qualities trickle down to others?

- **Coddle bit players.** It's terribly wicked not to give props to all of the people who make your path smoother in life. These include the doorman, the mailman—and if you're so lucky—the cook and pilot. In Jackie's case, the list also extended to all sorts of minor politicos. Go beyond tips and nods. As a campaign wife, Jackie was able to recall the names, unprompted, of umpteen mayors and convention delegates. And in the White House, she stunned her new staff by properly addressing members upon their first face-to-face meeting.

- **Don't (publicly) criticize your enemies or opponents.** Leave such base behavior to modern-day politicians and reality-show contestants. Particularly resist the temptation to bad-mouth people by e-mail: There's nothing worse than electronic slurs, which can be endlessly forwarded. Though surrounded by enemies (political) and jealous types (frumpy women), Jackie refused to get nasty. During the 1960 campaign, she declined to take potshots at Hubert Humphrey. And two decades later, when Nancy Reagan got swamped with negative publicity, Jackie waxed empathetic, going so far as to call her to offer advice on handling the press.

- **Tap higher powers to help the helpless.** After you've maxed out your immediate resources, look to your left and right, above and below to harness those six degrees of separation between you and the solution to the problem at hand. Don't be too proud to ask an influential friend to step in on behalf of someone you know—even if the two have never met. That's what connections are really for.

  In 1980 Jackie summoned medical philanthropist Mary Lasker to help an impoverished sick boy, the son of a manicurist, gain access to proper treatment. As a follow-up to the favor, Jackie wrote her friend Mary a heartfelt note: "Now they don't feel that they are just a cipher because they are poor," she scrawled on her Doubleday stationery. "Whatever happens, they know that someone with a noble heart made it possible for them to get the best care they could."

- **Turn the other silken cheek.** Sometimes you must show people what you are made of by staying elevated when you'd least like to—say, when someone zips into your primo parking space, or snatches the last pair of Loro

Piana gloves on sale at Bergdorf's. Like Jackie, you'd do well to let mild acts of ugliness pass without much fuss.

Traveling with Thomas Hoving, then-director of the Metropolitan Museum of Art, Jackie was stunned—and frightened—by the French paparazzi that swarmed her at a low-key Left Bank restaurant. An infuriated Hoving returned to their hotel, the Plaza Athénée, and demanded that the doorman who disclosed their whereabouts be fired. Informing Jackie of the *fait accompli,* Hoving recalls, "She got mad at me." She said: "You suffered a man's livelihood because of that?"

- **Mute the call of mammon.** The classiest cash is also the quietest. So if you're fortunate enough to have an endless supply of crisp bills, just don't crumple them under the noses of those with less. This doesn't mean you should deprive yourself of fine things. Certainly our lady did not. But wealth does require you to be somewhat stealthy about what you've got.

- **Don't gab on about money, either—yours, your parents', your boyfriend's—or your over-the-top plans for it.** When Jackie received a $26 million settlement from Aristotle Onassis's estate, society types needled the widow about how she intended to spend the windfall. "You don't talk about things like that" was her stunned reply.

- **To be a cut above, don't cut.** Even if your social status or connections somehow permit it, resist any temptation to leapfrog over more common folks. This means no line jumping at Disney World, no flashing that Burberry plaid to snare the next cab. In New York, Jackie waited in crowds like everybody else—or avoided them altogether—rather than nudge her way to the front of movie-house and museum queues.

You've got to love Jackie O. What a woman. I wish I had gotten to know her—this book is as close as I've come. I also owe something to my father for teaching me the art of beguiling, because ever since my success at Apple he has pounded into me the concept of noblesse *oblige.*

The Reality of Competing

At some point, you will compete with other organizations. Actually, if you don't compete with anybody for very long, it may mean that you're trying to serve a market that doesn't exist. I've had to compete with IBM and Microsoft, as well as with many startups as a CEO later in my career. This section contains the lessons that I learned while doing things both right and wrong.

CHAPTER 64

The Art of Defensibility

The purpose of competition is not to beat someone down, but to bring out the best in every player.

~ WALTER WHEELER

A reader once asked me, "What should an entrepreneur say when she's asked what makes her company defensible?" You'll usually face this question in the process of fund-raising, but it can also come from potential employees, partners, and customers, too. It goes to the heart of competing in the marketplace.

This seemingly simple question is one of the hardest for an entrepreneur to answer. A good response requires a combination of clairvoyance, luck, street wisdom, humility, honesty, and cockiness. Also, it's often a trick question to see what you're made of. First, these are the worst answers that you can utter:

- **"Patents make our business defensible."** Go ahead and file them, because you may someday achieve huge success and therefore have the time and resources to go to court. However, the most valuable outcomes of a patent are often impressing your parents and filling up space in your MySpace profile. (Exceptions to this rule are biotech, chip design, and medical-device businesses, in which a patent really means something.)

  It's highly unlikely that patents will make your startup company defensible, because you won't have the time or money to do battle with a

Microsoft-size competitor. Sure, every few years you hear that Microsoft has to pay a company tens of millions of dollars, but suing Microsoft isn't a viable (or attractive) business strategy.

- **"We're the only guys who can do this."** This is a signal to investors that you're clueless and don't even know how to use Google. There are very few teams that have a monopoly on knowledge or implementation skills. This is like Terrell Owens claiming that he is the only wide receiver who can help a football team win the Super Bowl, so skip the grand delusions.

- **"[Big-name potential competitor] won't compete with us; they'll simply have to buy us out."** Speaking of grand delusions, this is even worse than TO's. Espousing the theory that what makes your company defensible is that potential competitors will buy you out will put you in the main display of the Bozo Hall of Fame.

Now that you know what not to say, here's a top ten list of what not only to say but also to believe. However, as my boss in the jewelry business used to tell me, "Don't be a *chazzer*" (Hebrew for "pig") by using them all, because your answer won't ring true if you do.

1. **"We know that there are no 'magic bullets' that make us defensible."** This is a great way to start your answer. It shows that you've been around the block and understand how the world works. An experienced investor will breathe a sigh of relief; an inexperienced one will want to call his mother.

2. **"We have filed for patents, but we know that we cannot depend on patents as a major component of defensibility."** This is the perfect treatment of patents: You filed for them just in case you can someday use them as a legal tool; however, you realize that until those halcyon days, you will have to fight with different weapons on the battleground called the market, not the legal system.

3. **"We have an x-month head start, and what we're doing is hard. We know we have, at best, a temporary lead. It's so hard that few**

established companies would defocus themselves by trying to do what we're doing." This shows that you're both ahead of the market but "clueful" (as opposed to clueless) enough to know that leads don't last. Plus, investors want to believe they're ahead of the pack.

4. **"We've built similar businesses before."** This makes the case that you have an advantage on your side: You've done this before, so that even if others are doing it, you can do it better and faster.

5. **"We've amassed a ton of relevant domain expertise because our founders sold to these customers before."** Now you're talking. You've got an inside track with established contacts and established reputations. This is getting interesting.

6. **"We used to work at [big-name company], so we know it won't be a competitor. In fact, we quit the company to start this because our management refused to address this lucrative market."** This is a twofer: believable inside info about a worrisome potential competitor and another way to claim domain expertise.

7. **"We don't know if we're the only people who can or are doing this, but we've already signed up key customers like [insert the biggest names that you truthfully can] to use our product. You'd think they'd know of better solutions if they existed."** The point of this is to use external confirmation of what you're doing.

8. **"We came to you because we believe that the backing of a firm like yours will dissuade other firms from investing in competitive companies. We also know that you have a world-class Rolodex as well as access to the best talent."** You need to say this with a straight face because it is a suck-up, but investors love to be sucked up to. Something like this is a lot easier to say at a Sequoia Capital, Draper Fisher Jurvetson, or Kleiner Perkins than at, say, Chaim, Yankel, and Pippel, LLP.

9. **"We expect that there will be competition because we're not working on a get-rich-quick gimmick. This is a real business that**

we think is going to be big." This is music to an investor's ears: A big market that has competition beats the hell out of dominating a market that doesn't exist.

10. **"It's a race, and we're going to work like hell to reach escape velocity. That's the bottom line."** This is as good as it gets. What makes a company defensible is that it has scaled to the point where it's achieved critical mass and has become synonymous with a market (online video: YouTube), sector (rental DVDs: Netflix), or task (search: Google). And this achievement renders all the other bull shiitake you can fabricate essentially impotent if not downright laughable.

When all the dust settles, the goal is to paint this picture:

- You're streetwise, so you know that you can't depend on patents.
- You understand that very few companies are truly defensible for reasons other than because they either achieved critical mass or had a nine-month head start.
- You have domain expertise, connections, and what you're doing is hard.
- You're not the only team that can do this, but you're in a better position than most.
- You believe that you can build a business better than anyone (a little cockiness is necessary for an entrepreneur to survive).

One last power point: These explanations will only work on people who already believe in what you're doing. If a person doesn't believe, then there's probably nothing that you can say that will convince him of your defensibility. Nor, frankly, is defensibility the sole reason why he's not interested. If this is the case, move on, with the understanding that achieving success is the sweetest revenge.

CHAPTER 65

Counterpoint: Patents and Defensibility

We have to distrust each other.
It is our only defense against betrayal.

~ TENNESSEE WILLIAMS

After reading the previous chapter, three of my buddies who are patent attorneys disagreed with my diatribe against patents as a key component of a startup's defensibility. They are patent attorneys at Rethink(IP): J. Matthew Buchanan, Douglas J. Sorocco, and Stephen M. Nipper. Being the open-minded Guy that I am, I offered to publish their counterpoint so that you can obtain a broader perspective of intellectual property issues for startups.

Patent law is currently a sea of chaos, and the net effect is that patents simply don't pack the oomph that they once did—particularly for startups. For example, the Supreme Court recently issued a decision in *eBay* v. *MercExchange,* which many people expect will change the value of patents for small companies that don't actually make and sell a product.

In the wake of the Court's decision in the *eBay* case, tech startups simply cannot count on their patents as an effective and efficient tool to shut down the Microsofts of the world. And that's after you actually have a patent. Just getting to that point could take years . . . and years. . . and years.

Also, the application backlog at the Patent and Trademark Office is at an all-time high. Current statistics show that the average patent application takes longer than thirty months from the date of filing to the date of issue. Factor in some of the more backlogged tech areas, such as Web business and Internet business methods, and it will realistically be at least five years before the Patent Office even starts to examine your application.

We've even heard of delays up to and beyond ten years in certain technology areas. Your competition could run you over by then, and it's more than likely we'll all be on to Web 5.0 by the time you get the pretty ribbon copy of your patent.

We're not changing our day jobs anytime soon, though, because patents still play an important role in building a defensible business—they're just not the whole enchilada. In most cases, entrepreneurs need to avoid the knee-jerk reaction of "Patent Everything!" and should instead follow a carefully planned, comprehensive intellectual-property strategy to achieve defensibility. Here are a few tips about how to do this:

- **Put patents in the right place.** Don't mistake this point as a statement that patents aren't important. They are. You just need to keep them in proper perspective, which is the underlying theme of Guy's comments. Practically speaking, this means asking, "Should we patent?" at the end of the invention management. Then consider these issues:

  - How are your competitors using patents? In some industries, like biotech, pharma, and medical devices, you can't get past Go without them.

  - Is your invention better protected as a trade secret? Trade secrets are any formula, pattern, machine, or process of manufacturing used in one's business that may give the user an opportunity to obtain an advantage over its competitors who do not know it. The formula for Coca-Cola is an example.

    Not all information can be kept a trade secret. You need to be able to maintain the secrecy in-house—limiting access to the information—and your competitors can't be in a position to reverse engineer your product/service and figure out how you did it. One drawback to trade secrets is that if one of your competitors later invents the same thing and obtains a patent, your "secret" use will not insulate you from patent infringement.

- Could making the invention publicly and freely available create greater value for the company? Making source code and API publicly available might get you that all-important community support that can lead to life-sustaining critical mass and momentum.

- Can placing the invention in the public domain by making a "defensive publication" work for you? A defensive publication is the publication of information and knowledge with the goal of preventing a later competitor from obtaining patent coverage on the exact same invention.

  Many large corporations have used this tactic, i.e., IBM's Technical Disclosure Bulletin. One evil variation of this strategy is to publish the document not in the United States, but instead in Elbonia, Kazakhstan, or some other far corner of the earth in order to keep it generally secret but "published" for the intent of "prior art" status under the Patent Act.

  This won't give you any rock-solid rights, but it might prevent your competitor from obtaining protection on it. Keep in mind that this tactic truly is a donation, though. Once released, this genie can't be put back in the bottle.

- **Look beyond the value in a legal action.** When considering the role of patents in your overall strategy, remember that they can add value beyond just the ability to sue a competitor. This is the fundamental point that Guy missed. Blocking your competitors from getting patents can keep them from suing you. At least you can countersue, and the threat of a countersuit can prevent a suit or force settlement out of court. Also, they should know that paying you a nuisance-value settlement to license the patent is cheaper than battling you in court. Finally, a portfolio of patent assets may have value for future acquirers of your company, and they may be able to afford to sue.

- **Consider the role that inventions will play in your business.** Notice that we say "inventions" and not patents. Never forget that patents come second in this game. Think of the inventions and their role in your business first: Are they an important component of the value and growth of the company?

If inventions are important in any way, develop an efficient system for identifying and managing them. You should have well-designed invention disclosure forms, clearly designed processing systems, regular meetings for reviewing disclosures, and a cataloging meeting with your internal decision makers at least once each year.

- **Get trademarks that are strong and protectable.** If your trademarks aren't protectable, go back to the drawing board. As you consider trademark strength, also look at domain name availability. Time after time, we counsel folks who don't spend enough time to find out if they actually can use a word or symbol. They just assume that it is OK to use.

- **Get the domain name.** You cannot afford to lose this race. Be creative and find something that fits in with your branding strategy. And don't forget typos and other obvious variant domains that people might accidentally enter when seeking you out. (Try going to Utube.com and Youtub.com.) Spending an extra nine bucks here and there on GoDaddy today might help you avoid needing to pay an attorney thousands of dollars later. Consider this domain-name insurance.

- **Develop an overall branding strategy for your trademarks, including your domain name.** Many entrepreneurs simply wait too long to consider this important and incredibly valuable aspect of intellectual property. If you're wondering about the importance and value of a solid brand, ask yourself this question: If I were starting a search company, how great would it be if I could call my company Google? Guess what: You can't. Solid branding with appropriate protections creates significant value. Period.

  Branding is as important as your technology is, and it sucks to have to rebrand everything twenty months into your corporate life just because you didn't spend the time and money to get a legal opinion on the availability of a name.

The bottom line is that if your patent attorney tells you that you must patent everything without regard to the big picture, do yourself a favor and find a new one. A good patent attorney looks at the big picture and proposes a strategy—not a bunch of disparate tactics.

Patents aren't the end-all answer to the defensibility question. And, yes, you might look clueless if you base your defensibility on nothing more than "We've got tons and tons of patents!" A strong intellectual property strategy designed in the context of the relevant industry can, however, give you defensibility.

CHAPTER 66

The Art of Driving Your Competition Crazy

**If any of my competitors were drowning,
I'd stick a hose in their mouth.**

~ RAY KROC

I 'm not sure that "the best defense is a good offense" is true for sports, but it is true for business. If you are constantly innovating and serving your customers, you will keep your competition off balance. However, companies go astray when defeating the competition becomes more important than taking care of customers—with all due respect to Ray Kroc. When companies become obsessed with the pursuit of excellence, by contrast, they often reach new levels of greatness. Here's how to avoid the former and achieve the latter.

- **Know thyself.** Before you can drive your competition crazy, you have to understand what your own company stands for. Otherwise, you'll only succeed in driving yourself crazy. For example, Apple stands for cool technology. It will never represent a CIO's safe bet, an "enterprise software company," or service and support. If it decided it wanted to drive Microsoft crazy by sucking up to CIOs, it would drive itself crazy—that is, if it didn't perish trying.

- **Know thy customer.** The second step is to truly understand what your customer wants from you—and, for that matter, what it doesn't want from you. One thing that your customer seldom wants to do is to help you drive your competition crazy. That's in *your* head, not your customer's. One more thing: A good company listens to what a customer says it wants. A great company anticipates what a customer needs—even before she knows she wants it.

- **Know thy enemy.** The third step is to truly understand your competition. You cannot drive your competition crazy unless you understand their strengths and weaknesses. You should become your competition's customer by buying their products and services. I never truly understood what it was like to be a customer of Microsoft until I bought a Sony Vaio and used Windows. Sure, I had read many comparisons and competitive analyses, but they were nothing compared to hands-on experience.

- **Focus on the customer.** Here's what most people find surprising: The best way to drive your competition crazy is not to do anything to it. Rather, the best way is for you to succeed, because your success, more than any action, will drive your competition crazy. And the way you become successful is not by doing things *to* the competition but *for* the customer. Thus, for most companies, the key to driving the competition crazy is outinnovating, outservicing, and outpricing it.

- **Turn customers into evangelists.** There are few things that drive a competitor crazier than an unpaid, thunder lizard group of customers who become evangelists for a company. I covered this topic in detail in the chapter called "The Art of Evangelism," but the gist is this: Create a great product or service, put it out there, see who falls in love with it, open up your arms to them (they will come running to you), and then take care of them. It's that simple.

- **Make good by doing good.** Doing good has its own, very sufficient rewards, but sometimes you can make good and do good at the same time. For example, if you own a chain of hardware stores, you can help rebuild a community after a natural disaster. You're bound to get a lot of publicity and create bonds with the community. This will drive your competition crazy. And you'll be doing something good!

- **Turn the competition into allies.** One way to get rid of your competition is to drive it out of business. An alternative way is to turn your competition into allies. My favorite author of children's books is Tomie DePaola. My favorite DePaola book is *The Knight and the Dragon* (Putnam Juvenile, 1980). This is the story of a knight and a dragon who train to slay each other. They are smashingly unsuccessful at doing battle and eventually decide to go into business together. Using the dragon's fire-breathing ability and the knight's salesmanship, they create the K & D Bar-B-Q. For example, if a Home Depot opens up next to your hardware store, let it sell the gas barbecues, and you refill people's propane tanks.

- **Play with their minds.** If you're doing all this positive, good stuff, then it's OK to have some fun with your competition—that is, to intentionally play with their minds. Here are examples to inspire you:

  - Hannibal once had his soldiers tie bundles of brush to the horns of cattle. At night, his soldiers lit the brushwood on fire, and Hannibal's Roman enemies thought that thousands of soldiers were marching toward them.

  - A pizza company that was entering the Denver market for the first time ran a promotion offering two pizzas for the price of one if customers brought in the torn-out Yellow Pages ad of its competition.

  - A national hardware store chain opened up right next to a longtime community hardware store. After a period of depression and panic, the store owner came up with a very clever ploy. He put up a sign on the front of his store: MAIN ENTRANCE.

  - When Security Pacific Bank merged with Bank of America, many Security Pacific branches were closed. First Interstate Bank rented trucks and parked them in the lots of the branches that were closing. Then First Interstate employees in those trucks helped people open new accounts as they were leaving the banks.

  - In 1986 British Airways ran a promotion to give away 5,200 seats for travel on June 10. Virgin Atlantic Airways ran ads that said, "It has always been Virgin's policy to encourage you to fly to London for as little as possible. So on June 10 we encourage you to fly British Airways." The British Airways promotion generated a lot of news coverage, but most of the news coverage also included a mention of Virgin's funny ad. It cost British Airways a lot more than Virgin to get this coverage.

- A research company surveyed 750 white-collar workers around the United States. The research showed that 81 percent of the people believed that casual dress improved morale; 47 percent believed that it increased productivity; 46 percent said they considered casual dress an attraction to work for a company; and only 4 percent thought a casual-dress standard would have a negative impact. When Levi Strauss found out about the study, it let thousands of publications know about it. The company also even put in a toll-free hotline to help companies implement a casual dress standard. Guess who was sure to benefit from greater knowledge of this study? Levi Strauss, of course, because of its Dockers line of clothing.

- A Goodyear store in Chattanooga, Tennessee, faced a predicament: It wanted to put up two Goodyear signs. However, the local law stipulated a one-sign limit. Undaunted, the store manager spelled out Goodyear in marigolds in a flower bed. The city inspector considered this a violation, but the public supported the store, so the city government backed off.

- An electrician with only one truck was constantly razzed by his competition because his company was so small. To fake them out, he finally painted three different truck numbers on the right, left, and rear of the truck.

- International Harvester couldn't get steel to its factory in Melrose Park, Illinois, because of a truck drivers' union strike. The company couldn't use nonunion labor because of snipers on the freeway. Finally, the company rented school buses and dressed drivers as nuns, loaded the buses with steel, and made the deliveries. No one would shoot at school buses driven by nuns, right?

I love these stories about how companies drive each other crazy, but I don't want you to think that these kinds of actions are the key to driving your competition crazy. Above all, focus on making your customers happy so that you are successful. Then you can do funny stuff like leaving condoms around where your competitors hang out.

CHAPTER 67

How to Remain Sane

**I hate to advocate drugs, alcohol, violence, or insanity
to anyone, but they've always worked for me.**

~ HUNTER S. THOMPSON

The flip side to driving your competition crazy is to remain sane yourself. The purpose of this chapter is to help you avoid being driven crazy by your competition. This isn't a top ten—it's only a top five, because the key to maintaining your sanity is to keep things simple.

- **Delight your customer.** "The best defense is a good offense." If you continue to delight your customer, it's unlikely that your competition can get to you. There are two reasons this is true. First, you'll be successful at driving your competition crazy, and not vice versa. Second, you'll be so busy that you won't have the time to worry about the mundanity (mundane + insanity) of what your competition is trying to do to you.

- **Don't assume that "perfect information" exists.** It was bad enough before Google alerts and other news-gathering services, but companies have begun to assume a world of perfect information as a result of such technology. They think that the minute the competition announces a new feature, service, or partnership the entire marketplace is aware of it—and likes it. In reality, only you, your competition, and Google's servers know what was announced. By overreacting, you may inadvertently increase awareness and exacerbate the problem.

- **Take a chill pill.** Never let your competition see you sweat. Instead, keep focusing on delighting your customer. Certainly you shouldn't lash out and inflame hostilities, because you'll probably do something stupid. In the story of Sinbad, there is an episode in which his sailors threw stones at monkeys in coconut trees in order to provoke the monkeys into throwing coconuts back at them. That's exactly what the hungry and thirsty sailors wanted the monkeys to do, so they could eat coconuts.

  Of course, this doesn't mean that you should ignore your competition. You should know as much as you can about them. If your competition beats you to the punch, you should take it personally and then furiously outinnovate and outimplement them. Don't let your competition see you sweat, because they will gain strength and confidence from your nervousness. I also believe noticing that you're sweating will make you sweat more.

  There is one more time when you should take a chill pill: when your competition has beaten you to the punch, and there is absolutely nothing you can do about it. In this case, as my mother often told me, "Don't worry about things you can't change. Focus on things that you can."

- **Hang a negative on your competition.** When F. W. Woolworth opened his first store, a competitor who had served the community for years hung out a sign that said: THIS SAME SPOT FOR FIFTY YEARS. Nice shot, huh? Except Woolworth then put up a sign that said A WEEK OLD. NO OLD STOCK. The lesson is to try to find a crucial negative that you can hang on your competition. Maybe they will leave you alone next time.

- **Act like a maniac.** Yes, this is an apparent contradiction to taking a chill pill. What can I say? I'm a complex person. To continue the theme of making your competition leave you alone, one effective strategy is to convince them not to attack you because you might do something really crazy. Virgin Airlines personifies this behavior. Who would want to get in a battle with an airline that offers free motorcycle and limousine rides to the airport, provides in-flight massages and manicures, and accepts the frequent-flyer miles of its competition? Most rational companies would conclude that it's smart not to engage a maniacal competitor.

Ultimately, if you want to remain sane and even thrive, focus on making your company better instead of your competition worse. Ray Kroc, the founder of McDonald's, who would stick a hose in his drowning competitor's mouth, also said:

My way of fighting the competition is the positive approach. Stress your own strengths, emphasize quality, service, cleanliness, and value, and the competition will wear itself out trying to keep up.

The Reality of Hiring and Firing

Hiring and firing are black arts for most people. Few people are trained for hiring—instead we are led to depend on our gut. Few people are trained for firing—instead we are led to believe that companies never make hiring mistakes and always develop their employees properly, so you'll never have to fire anyone. The reality is that hiring and firing are difficult processes, and this section will make you better at both.

CHAPTER 68

The Art of Recruiting

The Church recruited people who had been
starched and ironed before they were washed.

~ JOHN WESLEY

The *Washington Post* convinced a world-class violinist named Joshua Bell to act as a street musician to see how many people would stop to listen to him play and how many would donate money. Bell played Johann Sebastian Bach's "Partita in D minor for solo violin" on a $3.5 million violin made by Antonio Stradivari.

To summarize: This experiment involved a top musician playing Bach on a Stradivarius in a Washington, D.C., Metro station at 7:51 for forty-five minutes one Friday morning while approximately 1,097 commuters walked past. Before I tell you the results, what do you think happened?

    a. He closed down the Metro because people stopped, and they refused to leave the station until he was done; or

    b. Roughly 1,096 people didn't figure out who he was. He collected $32
·   and change.

The answer is that he went unrecognized and unrewarded. The reality is that people make assessments about quality based on context and the opinions of the rest of the herd. Or, maybe it illustrates what happens to people who are around politicians, lobbyists, and lawyers all the time. By the way, the reporter of this story, Gene Weingarten, won a Pulitzer Prize for this article ("Pearls Before Breakfast," *Washington Post,* April 8, 2007, p. W10).

Recruiting is an art, and this chapter explains what it takes to excel at this art.

- **Ignore the irrelevant.** This is the point of the Joshua Bell story. Often a candidate's educational and work experience is relevant on paper but irrelevant in the real world. Would a senior vice president from Microsoft with a PhD in computer science be an ideal employee of a startup? Not necessarily—this guy was working for a company with $60 billion in cash and 95 percent market share, and he woke up every day worried not about the competition or customers but the Antitrust Division of the Department of Justice. The flip side is also true: The candidate without the perfect background could be a diamond in the rough.

- **Hire infected people.** Organizations typically look for candidates with the "right" educational background and work experience. I would add—or even substitute—a third quality: Is the candidate infected with a love of your product? Because all the education and work experience in the world doesn't matter if the candidate doesn't "get it" and love it. On the other hand, an ex–jewelry schlepper like me can make it in technology if he's infected with a love of the product.

- **Hire better than yourself.** In the Macintosh Division, we had a saying, "A players hire A players; B players hire C players"—meaning that great people hire great people. On the other hand, mediocre people hire candidates who are not as good as they are, so they can feel superior to them. (If you start down this slippery slope, you'll soon end up with Z players; this is called the Bozo Explosion. It is followed by the Layoff.) I have come to believe that we were wrong—A players hire A+ players, not merely A players. It takes self-confidence and self-awareness, but it's the only way to build a great team.

- **Double-check your intuition.** The problem with intuition is that people only remember when their intuition was right. In fact, their intuition is probably wrong as often as right. My recommendation is that you ask every candidate the same questions and take extensive notes. You might even conduct the first interview by telephone so you cannot judge the candidates by their appearance. In particular, founders believe they have a good "gut feel" for candidates, so they conduct unstructured interviews that are too subjective, and they end up making lousy hiring decisions.

- **Issue a challenge.** Don't assume that everyone is looking for an easy job to do. The best people are seeking great jobs, and great jobs usually involve great challenges. Thus, don't be afraid to issue a challenge to attract a candidate. When Steve Jobs recruited John Sculley to become the CEO of Apple, this is what he said: "Do you want to spend the rest of your life selling sugared water or do you want a chance to change the world?" OK, so maybe things didn't quite work out the way Steve intended, but my point is still valid.

- **Check independent references.** How many of us have limited reference checking to only those provided by the candidate? I know I have. Can we be more stupid than this? This often happens because we don't double-check our intuition: We like the gal, so we only call the references she's provided, because we don't want to hear that we like a bozo. Do as I say, not as I did: Check independent references—preferably at least one person whom she worked for and one person who worked for her. LinkedIn, the service that enables people to establish networks of professional contacts, is very useful for this.

- **Apply the Shopping Center Test.** As the last step in the recruiting process, apply the Shopping Center Test. It works like this: Suppose you're at a shopping center, and you see the candidate. He is fifty feet away and has not seen you. You have three choices: (1) beeline it over to him and say hello; (2) say to yourself, "This shopping center isn't that big; if I bump into him, then I'll say hello, if not, that's OK too"; (3) get in your car and go to another shopping center. My contention is that unless the candidate elicits the first response, you shouldn't hire him.

- **Use all your weapons.** Once you've found the perfect candidate, use all the weapons at your disposal to land her, not just salary and options. For example, the attractiveness of your vision and the quality of employees (who doesn't like to work with smart people who are kicking butt?) are important weapons, too. To this arsenal, ask your board of directors and advisers to use their sway to sign her up. And finally, throw in the résumé-building potential of working for a great organization like yours (let's not be naïve, here).

- **Sell all the decision makers.** A candidate seldom makes a decision all by herself. There can be several other people contributing to the decision. The obvious ones are spouses and significant others, but kids, colleagues, and friends often play a role. With Asian Americans, parents play a big role because Asian Americans are perpetually trying to make their parents happy. In the interviews, simply ask, "Who is helping you make this decision?" And then see if you can make them happy, too.

- **Wait to compensate.** A common mistake that many organizations make is using an offer letter as the starting point for negotiation. This is very risky because you don't know what reaction this first data point is going to have. If the candidate is Asian American, for example, he might show it to his mother, and your lowball offer may offend her. Then she'll tell the candidate to forget your organization because it's dishonored his family. An offer letter confirms what everyone has agreed upon. It is the last step in negotiations, not the first one.

- **Don't assume you're done.** Garage Technology once recruited an investment banker (mea culpa #1) from a large firm (mea culpa #2). After weeks of wooing and several offers and counteroffers, he accepted a position with us. He even worked for us for a few days, and then he called in sick. Late the next night, he sent me an e-mail saying that he had accepted an offer from a former client of his old investment bank. I learned a valuable lesson: Never assume that your recruiting is done. Frankly, you should recruit every employee every day, because when they go home at night, you might never see them again if you don't keep the lovin' going.

Recruiting is one of the purest forms of evangelism, because you are getting people to believe in your company and bet their lives on working for your company. This is more serious than merely trying your product or service. With what you've learned in this chapter, plus a great product or service, you should be able to recruit anyone you want.

CHAPTER 69

Real-World Recruiting

> RECRUIT, *n.* A person distinguishable from a civilian
> by his uniform and from a soldier by his gait.
>
> ~ AMBROSE BIERCE

Craig James is the chief technology officer of eMolecules. He read the previous chapter and provided me with his recommendations for the art of recruiting. Craig has worked with chemistry, chemists, and chemical databases his entire career, including management of a low-cost mass spectrometer project while at HP Scientific Instruments (now Agilent) and as director of core engineering for Accelrys.

I had the pleasure of being on the Hewlett-Packard recruiting team that had the highest success rate in the company as measured by the retention rate and the eventual performance of the people we hired. Our team leader taught me things that you don't mention at all in your chapter on recruiting, because you discuss what you're trying to learn, but not how to go about learning it. That's the real art of recruiting. We treated the interview like any other project. There was a team leader, and each person specialized in a particular task. Every interview followed the same project plan.

- **Host.** This person's job is to greet the candidate, welcome him, give a tour of the facility (if appropriate), explain the interview process and the other people the candidate will be meeting, and answer initial questions. Twenty to thirty minutes.

- **Technical #1.** This person's job is to grill, hard, on technical topics. This is the toughest interview of the day, and is designed to find out if the candidate is technically competent. Problems, often real-life, that the team is currently facing are presented, and the interviewee must show competence in answering. The candidate must answer basic questions about his field; for example, an electrical engineer must be able to solve circuit problems, find flaws in a circuit diagram, etc. This interview usually leaves the candidate rather rattled. One hour.

- **Project manager.** The hiring manager gives a nontechnical interview, but with focus on the specific job: Does the candidate seem suited? Is the candidate interested? The candidate can ask questions about the project, etc. Forty-five minutes to one hour.

- **Lunch.** Project manager, plus one project team member. Informal, chitchat, ask about candidate's background, school, etc.

- **Human resources.** HR presents company benefits, etc., asks for references, answers candidate's questions about the company, and so on. Thirty minutes.

- **Technical interview #2.** Like Technical #1, but usually less intense. Delve more into candidate's specific accomplishments, ask about candidate's best achievements as well as most dismal failures. Ask the candidate to describe one project in detail, and "deep dive" into the candidate's explanation. This puts the candidate on his own territory, where he should shine. One hour.

- **Host (reprise).** Follow-up questions, explain what's next, thank the candidate. Fifteen to twenty minutes.

We also arranged interviews so that for one job opening, all candidates would be interviewed in as short a time span as possible (usually in a single week). That gave us a good comparison of each candidate to the others, and also allowed us to give the candidates our final decision in a short time.

At the end of the interview day, there was a required team meeting. The leader would ask each team member to give his/her findings and opinion. Then there was a discussion. It was remarkable how a consensus would almost always emerge—I can't remember a time when it wasn't obvious whether to offer the job or not. Almost universally, if one interviewer said no, that was it.

It's critical that you keep the same members on your interview team. They get better and better at it; they get to know each other; and their shared experience gives them perspective and a set of common reference points for discussions. If one of your team isn't good at it, get rid of him and find someone else who has the intuition needed to be on your team. And just because you're the boss doesn't mean you should be on the interview team!

A curious thing about our interviews: We were very hard on the candidates (particularly the tech interviews), but instead of resenting it, the candidates uniformly were impressed and wanted to work for us. They knew that if they joined, they'd be joining a top-notch R & D group.

I have been a candidate on interviews in which it seemed that my interviewers didn't even know each other; their questions overlapped, they missed entire areas of stuff they should have asked me, and so on. I turned down their offers.

There's a lot of wisdom in Craig's recommendations, so add some structure to your interview process. You'll probably discover that the more disciplined and rigorous the process, the better employees you'll attract to your company.

CHAPTER 70

Thirteen Questions with Libby Sartain, Chief People Yahoo!

It is all one to me if a man comes from Sing Sing Prison or Harvard. We hire a man, not his history.

~ MALCOLM S. FORBES

L ibby Sartain was responsible for leading Yahoo!'s global human resources efforts and managing and developing its human resources team. Prior to joining Yahoo! in August 2001, Sartain was "vice president of people" at Southwest Airlines. In this interview, she explains the reality of a big technology company's employer's perspective on the recruiting process, circa 2006.

Q: At any given moment, how many jobs are you trying to fill?

A: Our number of open requisitions fluctuates, but if I had to average, I would say about a thousand at any given moment and a total of twenty-five hundred or so per year.

Q: On average, how many applications do you get per job?

A: For the last few years, we have received more than 120,000 résumés a year. So, we start with about a fifty-to-one ratio, but when we narrow that down to actual qualified candidates, we see about ten for every job.

Q: How can a candidate break through the noise?

A: The biggest mistake candidates make is sending in a résumé but not map-ping it for a specific open position. With so many résumés, and recruiters looking to fill what is open today, they might be missed. So the best thing is to apply for the one or two jobs that are open and for which your skills are a direct match. It is also helpful to be referred by someone inside the company, but be sure it is someone who can vouch for you and your work.

Q: What makes a cover e-mail and résumé "pop" for you?

A: In the cover e-mail, or summary when submitting your applications through an online jobs site like Hot Jobs, we look for your personality to show through. You should be able to come up with a succinct summary of who you are, what you bring to the table, and why we should hire you . . . but your unique personality should "pop."

I suggest that you write an "elevator pitch" for yourself to have at the ready while you're looking for a new job. You can summarize in your cover e-mail or online submission: Who are you? What do you stand for? What is your next big personal objective? How would you like to contribute in your next role? Sitting down and writing a fifty- to seventy-five-word elevator pitch for an imaginary listener is a wonderful experience of self-discovery. To be able to boil down your entire existence into such a short package is one way to discover your essential personal statement to the world. At least, what you'd like your essential personal statement to be. Getting comfortable with the pitch also helps when you are being interviewed.

Q: What do you dread seeing in a résumé?

A: I dread seeing résumés that don't tell me where you have worked and what you have accomplished there. Many people have taken to writing capabilities statements, but most don't have any meat to show how and where they developed the capabilities they claim they have. Overinflating your jobs and experience also works against you. And when you have seen as many résumés as our recruiters have seen, this overinflation is completely obvious.

This sounds strange in the Silicon Valley, but I also like to see some stability. If someone held every job for two years or less, alarm bells go off in my head. I wonder if the candidate has worn out his or her welcome.

Q: Does a résumé that's over one page long hurt a candidate's chances?

A: We are looking at résumés electronically, so the pages aren't really the issue. They should be succinct, but if they are two pages, or three pages . . . and great, that works. Anything over three pages is too much.

Q: How would you rank education, experience, and enthusiasm as desirable qualities of a candidate?

A: You have to have the whole package, but enthusiasm goes a long way with me. I look for people who will fit in our culture and who are smart, fun, friendly, and passionate about what we are doing.

Q: How do your criteria differ from other Silicon Valley companies, like Apple or Google?

A: We offer a distinct opportunity. We can usually offer a candidate a variety of different experiences, because we have so many different products and services and the largest audience in the world. People select us over the competition because we offer them a role that fits their interests and objectives. They also like the fact that they can move to another area in the future, so they like the prospects for their career development.

Q: What's the effect of a candidate saying that she wants to help Yahoo! kick Google's butt?

A: We love people who want us to win against our competition, and we have competitors in every product and service we offer. [This is HR-speak for "It's a good thing."]

Q: How can candidates increase the probability of a great interview?

A: Be prepared! You should have at least researched the company and the business/products that you would be working with on the Internet. You should know what you bring to us and convince us that you can do the job. Once again, we want to see your personality, too.

Q: Can an art history major with no technology education or technology work experience get a job at Yahoo!?

A: Sure, but not a technology job. We have folks with art history backgrounds working in a number of areas, like surfing the Internet, user experience and design, marketing, or maybe even human resources. With such a degree, it helps if you have experience in a prior company.

Q: If a candidate doesn't hear back, at what point should she try to initiate contact—or do people basically "send and pray"?

A: Praying might help, but I suggest that candidates always check back if they don't hear. But if they get a response that says we have found another candidate, they need to move on.

Q: By approximate percentages, how do successful candidates for non-officer-level positions come to you?

A: Candidate found listing on Yahoo! Jobs page—30 percent.

Yahoo! employee referred the candidate—30 percent.

Yahoo! internal recruiter contacted a prospect (that is, the person wasn't looking)—20 percent.

Yahoo!-retained headhunter contacted a prospect (that is, the person wasn't looking)—2 percent.

Conversion from contractor or temporary—10 percent.

Hot Jobs and other jobs sites—7 percent.

At the time of this interview, 2006, Yahoo! was already not as hot as Google, so you can assume that it's even harder to get an interview or job at a place like Google or whatever company is hot when you read this book. Now you know what you're up against and how to package yourself.

CHAPTER 71

Career Guidance for This Century

It is never too late to be what you might have been.

~ GEORGE ELIOT

P enelope Trunk is the author of *Brazen Careerist: The New Rules for Success* (Business Plus, 2007). She is also a columnist at the *Boston Globe*. Previously, she was a software executive, and then she founded two companies. She has been through an IPO, an acquisition, and a bankruptcy. Before that, she played professional beach volleyball. I've included her interview because she provides radically different advice from most career advisers.

Q: How much money does it take to be happy?

A: It takes about $40,000. It does not matter how many kids you have or what city you live in—that's splitting hairs, because people's happiness levels are largely based on their level of optimism and the quality of their relationships. So as long as you have enough money for food and shelter, your optimism level kicks in to dictate how happy you are.

Q: Is it more important to be competent or likable?

A: People would actually rather work with someone who is incompetent and likeable than competent and unlikable. Most people nod in agreement when they read this. It's the unlikable people who form arguments in their head.

But there's more. At work, if you are unlikable, people start thinking you are less competent. So stop thinking you can skate by on your genius IQ, because you can't. You need emotional intelligence as well. This situation is so pronounced that there are special-education classrooms rife with kids who could read when they were three. Social skills matter as much as intelligence when it comes to long-term success, even for the geniuses.

Q: Should I sue a boss who is sexually harassing me?

A: In most cases, you will destroy your career if you report sexual harassment. So unless you are in physical danger, you should not. The laws governing sexual harassment don't protect women who report. The law protects companies from being sued by the women who report. Human-resource professionals are trained to protect the company, not the woman who reports.

When you report harassment, it is usually the case that you lose your job through retaliation. Retaliation is illegal but nearly impossible to prove in court. And, even if you could prove it in court, you would go through emotional hell, with no salary, and high-profile drama that makes you unable to get another job. All this for a settlement that will almost certainly not enable you to retire.

This is simply how the legal system works. I am not saying this is OK. But I'm saying that if you care about your career, you'll do everything possible to not report. Most women are not in the position to sacrifice their career—and their earning power—in the name of trying to bring down one harasser. The legal system needs to step in and take care of this.

Q: When should I ask for a promotion?

A: Maybe never. The average salary increase is 4 percent. Is that going to change your life in any meaningful way? On top of that, someone is promoting you up their ladder, but their ladder is not necessarily your best path. So stay focused on where you want to go instead of the paths other people have created for you.

Getting a promotion is so last century. Instead of letting last century's carrots dictate your workplace rewards, figure out what will be really meaningful to you: training, mentoring, flex time, whatever it is that means more than 4 percent more money. These are all things that can really improve your life and your career.

Q: Is being a generalist or a specialist the path to the executive suite?

A: In Hollywood, the best way to get your pick of any role in the industry is to become a specialist—funny guy, tough girl, action hero—get known for being the best at something, and then use that star power to branch out. The same is true in business.

Jobs that don't require a specialty are low level. To move up, you need to be great at something, and you have to let people know what you don't do. No one is great at everything. Even if your goal is not to get to the executive suite, you should specialize. When you want to take five months off to hike in Tibet, if you are easily replaced, you will be. If you have a skill that is hard to duplicate, your job will be there for you when you get back.

Q: What do I do about the gaps in my résumé when I traveled or couldn't find a job?

A: Talk about them well. A gap is really bad if you spent your days on your sofa watching cartoons. But if you watched cartoons to prepare for your next career move into children's programming, then you sound focused and driven. Same TV, same sofa, two different stories. People don't want to hear your life story. This is good news for people with sofa stints. In almost all cases, you learn something during a gap. Tell a great story about what you've learned and where you're going, and your gap won't get center stage. Leaving out details is not about lying; it's about telling good stories.

Q: Will getting an MBA or any other type of advanced degree be a good use of time and money if I can't find a job?

A: No. If you can't find a job, then you should invest in something like better grooming, or a better résumé, or a coach for poor social skills. These are the things that keep people from getting jobs. Instead of running back to school, figure out why you can't get a job, because maybe it's something that a degree can't overcome.

Grad school generally makes you less employable, not more employable. For example, people who get a graduate degree in the humanities would have had a better chance of surviving the *Titanic* than getting a tenured teaching job.

Unless you are going to a top business school at the beginning of your career, you should not stop working in order to get the degree. Go to night school, because you will not make up for the loss of income with the extra credential.

Law school is one of the only graduate degrees that makes you more employable. Unfortunately it makes you more employable in a profession that makes people very unhappy. Law school rewards perfectionism, and perfectionism is a risk factor for depression. Lawyers have little control over their work and hours, because they are at the beck and call of their clients, and many are constantly working with clients who have problems lawyers cannot solve. These two traits in a job—lack of control over workload and compromised ability to reach stated goals—are the two biggest causes for burnout.

Q: What's the ideal length of a résumé in a world where every résumé is electronic and not viewed printed out on paper?

A: One, still. Your résumé is a marketing document, not a summary of your life, so every line should be about an accomplishment. The more amazing your accomplishments, the fewer you need to list. For example, if you can write "Evangelized Macintosh and made it one of the most beloved brands in the world," then you don't need any other sales and marketing bullets on your résumé.

If you have totally lost perspective, and you think you have two pages' worth of incredible and relevant achievements, consider that hiring managers spend ten seconds evaluating a résumé, and a scanner looks for ten key words, which certainly fit on one page.

So unless you have a great connection with the hiring manager, and you know he'll look at both pages, don't bother sending them. And if you do have that great connection, then you are probably going to get an interview even if your résumé sucks.

Q: How should I prepare for an interview?

A: An interview is a test you can study for. So memorize answers to the fifty most common questions. Most interviewers ask standard variations on standard questions, and there are right answers to these questions.

Whether you are a stripper or a CIA agent, the answer to the question, "What is your weakness?" is a story about how your weakness interfered at work—in a specific situation—and you overcame it. Most of your other answers should be stories, too. This means you need to make them up before you get to the interview. Stories of your life are memorable. Lists of your life are not. Be memorable if you want to be hired.

Another way to prepare is to go to the gym right before the interview. It doesn't matter if you never go to the gym—although you should, because people who work out regularly are more successful in their careers. You should go right before an interview because people judge you first on your appearance, and if you do heavy lifting with your back and stomach muscles, you will stand up much straighter in the interview. This will make you look more confident, which is half the battle in being judged by appearance.

Q: What's the right strategy for the search for a first job out of college?

A: Don't place too much importance on your first job. You'll have a lot more. Most people have eight jobs before they turn thirty, and that's fine. It is nearly impossible to know what career will be a good fit for you until you start trying things. So give yourself the latitude to try a lot. And don't get hung up on a big soul search. To land a great job, you don't need to know the meaning of life, just the meaning of hard work.

Q: Do only losers live at home after college?

A: On some level, it would be insane not to move back home, which is why more than 50 percent of graduating seniors do it. Thus, moving back into your parents' house is a smart step toward finding a career that's right for you, because entry-level jobs typically cannot cover the cost of rent, college loan payments, and insurance premiums—all of which are rising faster than wages. If you don't have to worry about paying rent, you have more flexibility to wait for the right job and to take a job that feels very right but pays very poorly. The rise of the prestigious but unpaid internship intersects perfectly with the trend to move back home.

Q: What should I do if I work for a jerk?

A: Leave. I know there are classic Bob Sutton (Stanford University professor who has written about assholes, his material is coming up later in the book) examples of revered jerks like Steve Jobs, but I wonder about the people who put up with him. Can they not find another visionary to work for who is not such a jerk?

Staying in a job like this makes you look bad. People wonder why you put up with it. And, frankly, you should, too. It's like being an abused wife. The wife who stays always defends the relationship by how much she gets out of it, but to everyone else it is obvious that she should leave. The problem is a loss of personal perspective.

The Nine Biggest Myths of the Workplace

I liked Penelope's interview so much that I asked her for more material. Here's her list of the nine biggest workplace myths:

1. **"You'll be happier if you have a job you like."** The correlation between your happiness and your job is overrated. The most important factors, by far, are your optimism levels and your personal relationships. If you are a pessimist, a great job can't overcome that. Think of the jerks at the top. And if you have great friends and family, you can probably be happy even if you hate your job—imagine a garbage collector who's in love.

2. **"Job hopping will hurt you."** Job hopping is one of the best ways to maintain passion and personal growth in your career. And here's some good news for hoppers—as I said earlier, most people will have eight jobs between the time they are eighteen and thirty. This means most young workers are job hopping. So hiring managers have no choice but to hire job hoppers. Ride this wave and try out a lot of jobs yourself.

3. **"The glass ceiling still exists."** The glass ceiling is over, not because people crashed through, but because people are not looking up. Life above the glass ceiling is hundred-hour weeks, working for someone else, and no time for friends and family. And it's not only women who are saying no to the ladder up: Men are as well. People want to customize success for themselves, not climb someone else's rungs. So if no one is climbing to the top, the glass ceiling isn't keeping anyone down.

4. **"Office politics is about backstabbing."** The people who are most effective at office politics are people who are genuinely nice. Office politics is about helping people to get what they want. This means you have to take the time to figure out what someone cares about, and then think about how you can help him or her to get it. You need to always have your ears open for when you can help. If you do this, you don't have to strong-arm people or manipulate them. Your authentic caring will inspire people to help you when you need it.

5. **"Do good work, and you'll do fine."** For one thing, no one knows what the heck you're doing in your cube if you're not telling them. So when you do good work, let people know. It is not crazy to toot your own horn—it's crazy to think someone will do it for you. Also, if you do good work but you're a jerk, people will judge your work to be subpar. So you could say that good work really only matters if your coworkers enjoy hearing about it from you.

6. **"You need a good résumé."** Only 10 percent of jobs come from sending a blind résumé. Most people get jobs by leveraging their network. Once you have a connection, the person looks at your résumé to make sure there are no red flags. So you need a competent résumé and an excel-

lent network. This means you should stop stressing about which verb to use on the second line of your third job. Go talk to someone instead.

7. **"People with good networks are good at networking."** Just be nice, take genuine interest in the people you meet, and keep in touch with people you like. This will create a group of people who are invested in helping you because they know you and appreciate you. Use LinkedIn to leverage those people's networks, and you just got yourself a very strong network by simply hanging out with the people you like.

8. **"Work hard and good things will come."** Everyone can put in a seventy-hour week. It doesn't mean you're doing good work. So here's an idea: Make sure you're not the hardest worker. Take a long lunch. Get all your work done early. Grand thinking requires space, flexibility, and time. So let people see you staring at the wall. They'll know you're a person with big ideas. Taking time to think makes you more valuable.

9. **"Create the shiny brand of you!"** There is no magic formula for having a great career except to be you. Really you. Know who you are and have the humility to understand that self-knowledge is a never-ending journey. Figure out how to do what you love, and you'll be great at it. Offer your true, good-natured self to other people, and you'll have a great network. Those who stand out as leaders have a notable authenticity that enables them to make genuinely meaningful connections with a wide range of people. Authenticity is a tool for changing the world by doing good.

The core of Penelope's message is that you're responsible for your career and happiness. No one (and no company) is going to hand a good career and life to you. But using her radical thoughts can help you achieve both.

CHAPTER 72

Everything You Wanted to Know About Getting a Job in Silicon Valley But Didn't Know Whom to Ask

Failure is not falling down but refusing to get up.

~ CHINESE PROVERB

Many people ask me for advice about getting a job in Silicon Valley, so here's the real scoop. Not everyone will agree with this advice, and I'm no Penelope Trunk or Libby Sartain. Some people will deny outright what I'm saying, but if you use these tips, you will stand head and shoulders above most candidates for jobs in Silicon Valley.

- **Love what the company does.** Passion for what a company makes or does is the most important factor in getting a job in Silicon Valley. Companies here are built on passion—indeed, perhaps more passion than reality. Hence, they hire passionate people who are already in the reality distortion field.

  The best way to show your passion is to make comments that show that you use the company's product or service. You can fake this with a little bit of research, but most candidates don't even do this. Do whatever it takes to prove that you are beyond the run-of-the-mill candidate who has merely "read about" or "looked at" the Web site. If the company is at all enlightened, passion can overcome the lack of a perfect educational background and work experience.

- **Create a solid pitch and bring it with you.** In Silicon Valley, you can tell that a person is pitching because her lips are moving. Think of your résumé as a pitch for you, the product. I hope you've remembered the 10/20/30 Rule of Pitching. Here's the 1/2/3 Rule of Résumés:

- **1 page long.** When some job candidates read this, they will think, "Guy is referring to the hoi polloi and unwashed masses, not me. I have ten years of experience at four different companies covering five different positions. My résumé needs to be two—maybe even three—pages to adequately explain the totality of my wonderfulness. And the more I mention, the more the company might see things they like." As a rule of thumb, if you can't pitch your company in ten slides or pitch yourself in one page, your idea is stupid and you suck, respectively.

- **2 key points.** Your résumé (and interview) should communicate only two, perhaps three, key points. Key points include pertinent work experience, applicable education, or a love for what the company does. One key point is too few, and three is at the edge of too many.

- **3 sections.** "Two key points" means that your résumé should have only three sections: contact information, work experience, and educational background. This specifically excludes "objectives" (do you really think that a company cares what you want to be when you grow up?), "references available upon request" (duh, of course you'll have to give references if you're asked), and "outside interests" (that Lamaze class training will come in really handy when the company stops delivering software by C-section, but not right now).

While I'm at it, here are some additional résumé tiplets:

- **Have some fresh eyes take a look at it.** Fresh eyes will always find mistakes that you missed.

- **Use active verbs.** Words such as "created," "designed," "wrote," and "sold" are good.

- **Explain what you accomplished—not your title or responsibilities.** The best whats are quantifiable results, such as sales, cost reductions, or shipped products. The worst whats are the number of people you managed

and the amount of budget you blew through. The key is not the size of the
staff or the size of the budget—it's what you accomplished with them.

- **Bring copies of your résumé to the interview.** Suppose that one of the
  interviewers asks for a copy of your résumé. It would be nice to have it with
  you, because much of Silicon Valley suffers from attention deficit disorder,
  so once you're out of sight, you're out of mind.

- **Know—or better yet—dislike the competition.** Another form of passion is a dislike of a company's competition. Don't take this too far, because
  no company you'd want to work for will hire a psychopath, but expressing
  the desire to defeat Microsoft at Apple, Google at Microsoft, or Nintendo at
  Sony is a positive thing. If nothing else, it shows that you understand the
  competitive marketplace.

- **Expect the funny farm.** Most likely you'll go through a group grope of
  interviews by four or five people. Most likely only one of them has hired
  and managed people before. Most likely this is the cast of characters that
  you'll meet. Use these stereotypes to prepare answers to their questions and
  concerns.

Stereotype	Description	Key Question	Key Answer
Wunderkind	Dropped out of Stanford B-School while getting an advanced degree. Scored 1600 on the SAT. Still a virgin. Needs a regression equation to buy a pack of gum. On his way to being farmed out (that is, made CTO), but he doesn't know it yet.	How did your PhD orals go?	Fine, how did yours go?

Stereotype	Description	Key Question	Key Answer
Mom	Maybe the only adult on the team. Part office manager, part psychiatrist, part mother, and part school principal. Easy to dismiss as "clerical staff," but she's the go-to lady when the wunderkinds need real-world advice.	Besides work, what are your passions?	I have lovely children. Would you like to see their pictures? Or I'm at that stage in life where I concentrate on my career, but I eventually want a family.
Mr. CPG	Brought in by the wunderkinds to fix marketing, even though they think the company's gizmo is so cool that it doesn't need marketing. Can't do a demo of the product but believes that everything is a consumer packaged good. MBA. Worked for five years for Playtex, marketing tampons. Leases a Cadillac.	What do you think of Kotler's Four Ps of marketing?	They are still important, but the Internet and online communities have made life much more complex for marketers. I'm glad you're running that function here because I can learn a lot from you.
Sunil	Veep of engineering. After six months of searching, the wunderkinds finally settled on someone who they thought could scale the infrastructure and had room temperature IQ. (How hard could it be to support six million simultaneous users?) The venture capitalists were very happy when he was hired. Brother-in-law runs an outsource programming shop in Bangalore that the company uses.	What do you think of Squid Web-proxy caching?	I think that good architecture makes proxy caching unnecessary.

Stereotype	Description	Key Question	Key Answer
Jasmine McGuire	The sales expert. Finally, the wunderkinds found a sales person whom they could stand for more than fifteen minutes. Pissed off that there aren't more women managers in the company. Worked for ten years at an established Silicon Valley firm where she exceeded quota every year. Sporadic guilt pangs about not seeing her kids enough.	What do you think is the key selling proposition of our product?	There are so many possibilities: ease of use, speed, scalability, world-class tech support.... But you're the expert: What's worked for you?
Lifer	Started at the company when it was two guys in a garage. Wants to make sure that it never forgets its roots. Perfectly happy just to be a great engineer. Drives a secondhand Prius.	Did you watch the History Channel special about Arpanet?	Yeah, I sure did; in fact, I recorded it on my Betamax machine. I still think the Beta format is better than VHS.
Grecian Gray	A Mr. CPG who lasted. Knows everyone in the industry but only an inch deep. Too old to go to another startup but too young to retire. Schedules offsites wherever there's a great golf course. Has had several affairs with employees in the company. Leases a Boxster.	What do you think of the 7 Series BMWs?	They're nice, but that's for a family man. Give me a sports car any day.
HR Professional	Loves the company. Loves her job. Been there and seen that. Bullshit proof. You may think she's "just an HR person," but she'll torpedo you if you piss her off. One of the first people you'd recruit if you leave the company to start something.	What would you like to be doing in five years?	I would like to grow into a management position at this company by further developing my skill set.

Stereotype	Description	Key Question	Key Answer
Ms. CEO	Proof that ice water can run in people's veins. Tough, talented. Shattered the glass ceiling into a thousand pieces. Sports a trophy husband. Makes the Merrill Streep character in *The Devil Wears Prada* look like a Girl Scout. Friends with Carly Fiorina.	Did you see that article in *Forbes* about me?	Seen it? Are you kidding? I have a copy right here. Would you autograph it?
Don Corleone	Executive with the company for twenty years. Feared by employees who don't know him. Loved by those who do. Net worth exceeds $50 million. Empty nester but got his kids summer jobs at the company when they were still in the house. Board member. Secretary answers his e-mail.	What makes you think you can contribute to this company?	I've read about how much you contributed to the company over your career, and I can only hope to make a contribution as large as yours.

- **Show up early.** Get to your interview at least thirty minutes early because (a) you might hit traffic; (b) it make take a while to get signed in and badged; (c) you might learn something from the receptionist; and (d) you don't want to be rushed and flustered when you start your interview.

- **Overdress or ask what to wear.** Tech companies are notorious for T-shirts-and-jeans dress codes, but whether this is appropriate dress for an interview depends on the position and on the interviewer. It might just be your luck that the interviewer recently joined from another organization that had a much stricter dress code. A good rule of thumb is to dress one level above the company norm: For example, for a T-shirt-style company, wear a collared polo shirt. If in doubt, ask what's appropriate for the interview.

- **Answer the first question, "How are you?" with a great response.** For example, a great response is, "I feel great. I'm really anxious to learn more about this job and tell you about myself, so that we can determine if we're a good match." In other settings, this question is an unimportant formality. In an interview, it's an opening to blow away the interviewer with your enthusiasm.

Whatever you do, don't answer the question with the truth: "I'm stuck in a dead-end marriage, my kids have chronic diseases, so I need a good medical plan, and the credit card companies are calling." Tech companies do not hire out of sympathy, and this is a job interview, not outpatient psychiatric counseling.

- **Get the scoop from the first interviewer.** A job interview is a sales call: Listen to what the customer says she wants and then explain why you are the solution. Many interviewers will tell you how to sell to their company. The sooner you get this information, the better.

  These are good questions to ask to get the ball rolling:

  - "What are you concerned about in filling this role?"
  - "What are the company's greatest challenges?"
  - "What are the hot buttons of the other people I'll be meeting?"

  Think: Plug and play, plug and play, plug and play. Sorry, but Silicon Valley companies do not develop employees. Metaphorically speaking, we like to open the box, plug in the gizmo, and be up and running, so you should always be answering the question How can I immediately help this company? If you can't help the company immediately, then maybe this isn't the right company for you.

  This isn't to say that you need five years of experience to get a job in Silicon Valley. For example, someone straight out of college (or high school) can help by testing software, answering the phone, answering tech-support questions, whatever. But don't expect the luxury of a long training program before you start contributing to the bottom line.

- **Take notes.** I wouldn't whip out a Windows Tablet PC if I were interviewing at Apple, but taking notes is a good idea for three reasons: First, you can use what you learn in follow-up interviews; second, if an interviewer asks,

"Who have you talked to here so far?" it would be good to be able to answer; and third, it will make you look like a serious, attentive candidate.

- **Confess your sins.** If you did something stupid in your past, the company will find out, so it's better if it finds out from you rather than from a search on the Internet. A tech entrepreneur once told me how he rented out his chest as a billboard and made $2,500 (it's a long story). A woman he met on Match.com found this out, and it was an issue. If a date can find this stuff from your past, you can bet an interviewer will. Let this make you think twice about the stupid things you're tempted to do on MySpace and Facebook.

- **Retract your mistakes.** If you screw up an answer in an interview, it's cool to say, "That was a crappy answer. Let me try again." If nothing else, it shows that you can realize and correct a mistake in real time. It's better to retract a stupid answer than to leave a permanent impression of cluelessness.

- **Prepare five ways that you think the company could improve.** If you are new to Silicon Valley, you'll quickly learn something: We're just as clueless as any other place on the face of this earth. Here the blind lead the blind, and in the valley of the blind, the one-eyed candidate is very attractive. All this means you should prepare five good ideas about what the company can do to improve its product, fix its marketing, and increase sales. When all the dust settles, it would be great if the interviewers remember you as "the guy with the good ideas."

- **Provide references on the spot.** Print your list of references so that you can provide them in the interview, as opposed to providing them later. In general, try to anticipate every possible request that would turn into a follow-up item: providing references, sample work, examples from your portfolio, software that you've written, whatever.

One more thing about references: Provide only people who will swear on a stack of Bibles that you're great. Before you use a person as a reference you should ask the $64,000 question: "I don't want you to provide a reference unless you feel 100 percent comfortable doing it: Are you 100 percent sure?" This accomplishes two things: You eliminate the references who will "damn you with faint praise," and you secure a commitment to a great reference to the extent that such a thing can be secured.

If you really want to play the reference game at the highest level, ask your best reference to proactively call the interviewer. This works especially well if your reference is famous.

- **Tell the interviewer you see a good fit and want the job, if this is the truth.** You'd be amazed at how few candidates go for the close. You should clearly communicate that you want the job, because aggressiveness counts for a lot in job interviews in Silicon Valley. Then ask what else the company needs to learn about you and what the next steps are.

  If you don't think there's a good fit, say that, too. At least you'll be remembered as an honest person. Perhaps the company will have a position in the future that *is* a good fit.

Here's one last tip: With Silicon Valley companies, and I suspect with most growing companies, remain flexible and humble about the job you'll take. Today's intern or receptionist is often next month's assistant product manager, then next year's marketing manager, then eventually the vice president of marketing. Or, for you nerds, tester to engineering grunt to engineering manager to vice president of engineering. Ergo, don't be proud, just get in, and then kick butt.

CHAPTER 73

Nine Questions to Ask a Startup

Every person who has mastered a profession is a skeptic concerning it.

~ GEORGE BERNARD SHAW

Most of the information about getting a job focuses on impressing and pleasing the company. Let's turn the tables and balance the scales by discussing what a hot candidate should ask a private, venture-backed startup before making the leap to "infinity and beyond," as Buzz Lightyear would say. Nota bene: There is a definite order in how to do this. First, get the job offer, then ask these questions!

1. **How many outstanding shares of stock are there?** Most companies offer dazzlingly large stock options. After all, 100,000 shares sure sounds like a big number—especially if the company goes public at, say, $20/share and then Googles on up to $400/share, as you're being led to believe it will. That's $40,000,000. You could buy Larry Ellison's house with that kind of money!

   The number of options that you're offered is a meaningless number unless you know the total number of outstanding shares of stock. Then you can calculate the percentage of the company that your options represent—and that's what counts. For example, 100,000 shares out of 1,000,000 total shares is a lot better than 250,000 shares of 10,000,000 total shares.

   You could simply ask what percentage you're getting, but that's a little crass, and some people may misinterpret crassness for a lack of good judgment. However, just because you know what percentage of the company you're getting, don't make yourself crazy with delusional thoughts of how much you're worth.

Here are some *guydlines* for a startup that has already raised its first round of venture capital of $1–3 million with no more than fifteen employees. Don't just latch on to the top end of the range, because there are many variables to consider, including salary, cash bonuses, geographic location, and most important of all, your perceived value.

Senior engineer: 0.3–0.7 percent

Midlevel engineer: 0.2–0.4 percent

Product manager: 0.2–0.3 percent

Architect, i.e., the "main (wo)man," though an individual contributor: 1.0–1.5 percent

Vice president: 1.5–3.0 percent

CEO, i.e., "adult supervision" brought in to replace the founder: 5.0–10.0 percent

One more thing about these percentages: As the company grows—and perhaps raises more capital—your percentage will go down. It's better to own a small percentage of a large company than a large percentage of a small company. Also, the company can give more options to valuable employees.

2. **What is the monthly burn rate?** *Burn rate*, as commonly understood, is net cash flow. (In most cases, *net* isn't even necessary to mention, because there are no revenues.) You want the answer to this question in terms of cash, not some bullshit, pro forma, paper-profits calculation—unless you can pay your rent with paper profits.

3. **How much cash is in the bank?** This is a straightforward question. Now take this answer and divide it by the monthly burn rate. This will tell you how long before the company runs out of money. If the answer is less than six months, be cautious, unless the company already has signed term

sheets for the next round of financing. If it doesn't, assume it will take at least six months before another round of financing closes.

4. **When will the company achieve positive cash flow?** You should ask this question, because you'll probably be told that there are months and months of cash or that another round of financing is "looking good." If the answer is years away, then you're signing up for more risk, because venture capitalists aren't the most patient, loyal people. More risk is OK—it takes years to build a great company—but you should know what you're getting into.

5. **When will the product ship?** This is just another way of asking about positive cash flow. Obviously, positive cash flow before shipping is improbable, but if the company is saying that positive cash flow will occur shortly after shipping, something is fishy, or the management is clueless. My advice is that you add six months to the "worst case" date, because nobody ever ships on time.

6. **May I talk to any of the outside investors on the board of directors?** If the outside investors are as positive about the company as you're being told they are (and assuming you're truly a superstar applicant for a senior-level position), then the company should agree to this. If it doesn't, then either the investors are getting "tired," or you're not that important. Indeed, if you are a superstar, you won't have to ask, because the management will ask a big-name board member to call you.

7. **May I talk to several beta sites?** This question is another reality check: The company is probably spinning a tale about how all the beta sites love the product. (In my career, every company has always told me that their beta sites "love the product.") If you're told you can't make contact, then either the company doesn't want to bother future customers (which is reasonable) or you're not important (which is possible). Of course, it could even be that the product sucks, so the company is afraid to let you talk to beta sites. It would be nice to know if it's the last reason.

8. **How much of a "liquidation preference" do the investors have before common shareholders get anything?** Suppose the company has raised $25 million and the liquidation preference is only $25 million (it could be multiples of $25 million, depending on how the investors negotiated the terms of investment). This means that the investors get their $25 million back before the employees get anything. If the company is acquired for $25 million or less, then the employees get nothing. If there's a massive liquidation preference, your options may never be worth anything.

9. **Are there any intellectual property issues or lawsuits pending?** This is a housekeeping question. To put it mildly, it'd be nice to know that the company's intellectual property is free and clear, and that there aren't any lawsuits that could tank the company. If you don't ask, don't expect the company to volunteer such information during the recruitment process.

Finally, a word of caution: The management may interpret these questions as evidence of a lack of "believing" or a failure to understand "the big picture." (It merits repeating: Get the job offer first, and then ask these questions.) On the other hand, you might impress the management with your knowledge of how startups and finance really work. Welcome to the complex and contradictory world of startups.

CHAPTER 74

How to Get a Job on craigslist

The nearest to perfection that most people come is when filling out an employment application.

~ UNKNOWN

M any people use craigslist to buy and sell unwanted junk. Companies, especially startups, also use it as a great source for recruiting because of the techy, risk-loving people who read it. When I ran an ad for photo editors for a site of mine, I learned several lessons that you can apply if you ever use craigslist to find a job.

• **Apply fast.** I posted the job at 11:19 P.M. on Thursday, August 2. The first response came in thirty-one minutes later. Fifteen more responses came in the next day. Therefore, 43 percent of the responses came in the first day or so. If you wait a few days, employers who advertise on craigslist may already have filled the job. Indeed, looking for a job is a job, so don't take a few days off (for example, the weekend) from your search.

• **Write a cover e-mail that addresses the position.** Two people simply attached their résumé to their response. I pushed back on one and suggested that he write a cover e-mail. He copied and pasted my job description to let me know, I guess, which job he was applying for. Needless to say, both candidates didn't get serious consideration. I don't know about other employers, but what I can't stand the most is laziness.

- **Rise to the occasion.** The vast majority of the candidates were highly qualified professional designers, photographers, and photo editors. My response to the first thirty-one applicants (who were diligent enough to write a cover e-mail) involved a test to find pictures that illustrated five sample stories. Twenty-six (84 percent) of the recipients immediately completed the test.

- **Apply well.** You should jump right on an opportunity, because if the position is filled there's usually nothing you can do. However, the three people we hired applied on the fifth and seventh days after the listing. They simply picked the pictures that we liked best—which is to say either our tastes were similar or they figured out what we liked, both of which work for me.

- **Apply really well.** The person who was most obviously the right candidate did something that no one else did: He not only chose good pictures, but he also resized them to approximately 140 × 105 pixels. This is the size of the pictures that we use on our site. Thus, he figured out what kind of pictures we liked and what size we used.

  Several other candidates said something to the effect of, "These aren't the right size for your site, but I figured that you just wanted to check my taste, not my ability to resize photos." Actually, we also wanted to see if the candidates were perfectionists. Most companies would love to find the one candidate who stands head and shoulders above the others, so be that person by applying really well. Ask yourself this simple question: "If I were hiring for this position, what would impress me?"

- **Don't be stupid.** I mentioned in the ad that Macintosh expertise was highly desirable—specifically with a handful of apps. One person wrote back, "Quite frankly, I've never even heard of FlySketch, Skitch or MarsEdit, Ecto, or Qumana." Honesty is not the best policy: Either don't mention your lack of qualifications or spend ten minutes to go figure out what these applications do. My conclusion from the candidate's response was that he was lazy, and laziness wasn't in the job description.

By the way, the ad cost $75, and it yielded approximately thirty-seven good candidates—a cost of a mere $2 per candidate. I'd heard from other companies about the extraordinary effectiveness of craigslist, but now I know this is true. And if you're a candidate for a job on craigslist, now you know what you're up against.

CHAPTER 75

How to Not Hire Someone via craigslist

Men wanted for Hazardous Journey. Small wages, bitter cold, long months of complete darkness, constant danger, safe return doubtful. Honor and recognition in case of success.

~ ERNEST HENRY SHACKLETON

After reading my posting about how to get a job on craigslist, my buddy Danny Kay sent me a link to illustrate what employers do wrong on craigslist. I was amazed by this example, which is from the New York edition of craigslist:

We seek a talented, highly motivated & resourceful individual skilled/experienced in web and print design. Minimum 1–2 years professional experience and examples of work done are mandatory for all applicants.

Requirements:

Degree in Graphic/Web Design with minimum 2 years of Web/ Graphic design experience with both print materials and web site design/development.

Exceptional portfolio that showcases solid conceptual, color, layout graphic design skills as well as fully functional web projects.

Proficiency in Adobe Photoshop, Adobe Illustrator, Adobe ImageReady and Macromedia Dreamweaver.

Solid experience with hand-coding HTML, CSS and basic JavaScript knowledge required.

Experience in InDesign and/or QuarkXPress and good understanding of requirements, specifications and concept of the print production design.

Experience with Macromedia Flash and action scripting is a plus.

Must be a highly self-motivated team player, able to work independently and with direction as part of a team.

Work on PC based platform.

Supervisory experience.

Compensation: Commensurate with experience.

I bet it pays $15–20/hour based on "Compensation: Commensurate with experience." This is recruit-speak for "we think we can hire someone great for peanuts, and we'd rather hire cheap, lousy people than expensive, good ones and risk screwing up our out-of-touch pay ranges."

Also, I don't think that Russell Brown, the world's greatest Adobe-products maven, would qualify for this position, because the company is looking for a person who understands print production and Web site production, has created an "exceptional portfolio," and has mastered seven applications and three languages. You could work for twenty years and not achieve this level of profound expertise.

Thus, the job posting is fundamentally flawed. It casts far too big a net, so it will intimidate or exasperate the little fish (that is, people starting their careers), and the big fish (that is, people who are truly qualified) either aren't reading craigslist or will smell a rat: "Compensation: Commensurate with experience."

This is my advice to employers:

- **Sell.** Almost every help-wanted ad focuses on buying, not selling—that is, the qualifications that candidates have to meet and the fences that they have to jump over. However, in the war for talent, this is ass backwards. This ad, for example, should mention things like "award-winning shop," "work alongside famous designers," "interesting projects for Disney, Apple, and Audi."

- **Use the right tool.** craigslist might not be the best place for senior positions and senior candidates at established companies. Better places are Creativeheads.net, Creativecircle, and I.D. However, craigslist is a great place to recruit entry-level employees and independent contractors.

- **Write accurate job descriptions for honest job titles.** Don't try to entice candidates with promises of greater responsibilities or opportunities than are truly being offered. And don't delude yourself: If the cat drags in an overqualified candidate, are you really going to expand the job?

- **Match job and background requirements.** If you have an entry-level job, then write entry-level specs. If you have a mid- or upper-level job, then write more demanding specs, such as five or more years of experience. Unfortunately, most help-wanted ads contain unrealistic demands for the position.

- **Give young people a break.** In the past of great employees are managers who gave them a break. Maybe they didn't have the ideal educational or work experience—for example, an ex–jewelry schlepper. More important than what's on-screen is what's in the mind, soul, and attitude of candidates.

The people who write most job specifications and ads must have never applied for a job. Or, they are still angry about what it took to get their job. How about we change this and you describe what you really want and what you will really pay? You'll probably have a stronger company by doing this.

CHAPTER 76

The Effort Effect of Carol Dweck

He who moves not forward goes backward.

~ JOHANN WOLFGANG VON GOETHE

Moving on from recruiting and being recruited, if you manage any people or if you are a parent (which is a form of managing people), then you'll enjoy the work of Stanford psychology professor Carol Dweck. For thirty years she has studied why some people excel and others don't. (Hint: The answer is not "God-given talent.") She is also the author of *Mindset: The New Psychology of Success* (Random House, 2006).

Her belief is that people have either "growth" or "fixed" mind-sets. People with the growth mind-set view life as a series of challenges and opportunities for improving. People with a fixed mind-set believe that they are "stuck" as either good or bad people. The problem is that the good ones believe they don't have to work hard, and the bad ones believe that working hard won't change anything. These are Dweck's tips:

- Listen to what you say to your kids, with an ear toward the messages you're sending about mind-set.

- Instead of praising children's intelligence or talent, focus on the processes they used. Some examples:

- "That homework was so long and involved. I really admire the way you concentrated and finished it."
- "That picture has so many beautiful colors. Tell me about them."
- "You put so much thought into that essay. It really makes me think about Shakespeare in a new way."

- When your child messes up, give constructive criticism—feedback that helps the child understand how to fix the problem, rather than labeling or excusing the child.

- Pay attention to the goals you set for your children; having innate talent is not a goal, but expanding skills and knowledge is.

- Don't worry about praising your children for their inherent goodness, though. It's important for children to learn they're basically good and that their parents love them unconditionally, Dweck says. "The problem arises when parents praise children in a way that makes them feel that they're good and love-worthy only when they behave in particular ways that please the parents."

Dweck's work explains the inexorable march toward mediocrity of many great companies:

- Stage 1: Your startup is hot. It ships something great and makes money. Thus, it's able to attract the best, brightest, and most talented. Since childhood, these people have been told they're the best. Indeed, being hired by the hot company is more "proof" that they are the A and A+ players.

- Stage 2: Unfortunately, employees develop a fixed mind-set that they're the most talented, and they think that continued success is a right. Problems arise because pure talent only works as long as the going is easy. When the going gets tough, the tough grind it out.

- Stage 3: Now people don't take risks, because failure would harm their image of being the best, brightest, and most talented. When they do fail, they deny it or attribute it to anything but their shortcomings, so they fix very little.

And mark my words, this is the beginning of the end, so heed Dweck's advice and focus on the process worth ethic, not the inherent brilliance, of your employees.

CHAPTER 77

The Art of Laying People Off

You do not get good people if you lay off half your workforce just because one year the economy isn't very good and then you hire them back.

~ KEN IVERSON

I hope that you never have to lay off or fire people, but the reality is that you will as you advance in your career. If you are scoffing ("Guy, you are clueless: We'll never downsize, because we're growing so fast, and I'll never make a bad hire"), then you're my intended reader.

- **Take responsibility.** Ultimately, it is the CEO's decision to make the cuts, so don't blame it on the board of directors, market conditions, competition, or whatever else. In effect, she should simply say, "I made the decision. This is what we're going to do." If you don't have the courage to do this, don't be a CEO. Now, more than ever, the company will need a leader, and leaders accept responsibility. You should also heed Ken Iverson's advice that whipsawing your staff through reactive layoffs isn't effective.

- **Cut deep and cut once.** Management usually believes that things will get better soon, so it cuts the smallest number of people in anticipation of a miracle. Most of the time, the miracle doesn't materialize, and the company ends up making multiple cuts. Given the choice, you should cut too deeply and risk the high-quality problem of having to rehire. Multiple cuts are terrible for the morale of the employees who have not been laid off.

- **Move fast.** One hour after your management team discusses the need to lay off employees, the entire company will know that something is happening. Once people "know" a layoff is coming, productivity drops like a rock. You're either laying people off or you're not—you should avoid the state of "considering" a layoff.

- **Clean house.** A layoff is an opportunity to terminate marginal employees without having to differentiate between poor performers and positions that you're eliminating. It's good for the marginal employee because he's not tainted with getting fired. Finally, it's good for the employees who remain because they will see that you know who's performing and who isn't.

- **Whack Teddy.** Most executives have hired a friend, a friend of a friend, or a relative as a favor. When a layoff happens, employees will be looking to see what happens to Teddy. "Did he survive the cut or did he go? Is it cronyism or competence that counts at the company?" Make sure that Ted is dead.

- **Share the pain.** When people around you are losing their jobs, you can share the pain, too. Cut your pay. In fact, the higher the employee, the bigger the percentage of pay reduction. Take a smaller office. Turn in the company car. Reassign your personal assistant to a revenue-generating position. Fly coach. Stay in motels. Sell the box-seat tickets to the ball game. Give your 30-inch flat-panel display to a programmer who could use it to debug faster. Do something, however symbolic.

- **Show consistency.** I cannot understand how companies can claim that they have to cut costs and then provide severance packages of six months to a year of salary. You would think that if they wanted to conserve cash, they'd give tiny severance packages. Typically, there are three lines of reasoning for generous severance packages:
    - Cutting head count, even with severance packages, is cheaper than keeping the employee around indefinitely, and we don't want any lawsuits.
    - We have lots of cash, so our balance sheet is strong, but we need to cut heads to make our profit-and-loss statement look better.

- Wall Street (or your investors) is expecting dramatic actions, so we need to do this to show the analysts that we've got what it takes to be a leader.

  None of these reasons makes sense. If you need to do a layoff to cut costs (and conserve cash), then provide minimal severance packages, cut costs as much as you can, conserve as much cash as you can, and deal with your guilt in other ways. If nothing else, it's a consistent story.

- **Don't ask for pity.** Sometimes managers go to great lengths to show the person they're laying off (or firing) how hard it is on them. This reminds me of the old definition of chutzpah: A boy murders his parents and then asks the court for leniency because he's an orphan. The person who suffers is the one being terminated, not the manager.

- **Provide support.** Usually, the people getting laid off aren't at fault. More likely, it was the fault of top management—the same top management with golden parachutes. Hence, you have a moral obligation to provide services like job counseling, résumé-writing assistance, and job-search help. There are firms that specialize in helping employees during "transitions," so use them.

- **Don't let people self-select.** We had a joke at Apple during the dark days of the late eighties that went like this: We would announce that employees who want to quit should come to a big meeting. Those who want to stay at the company should not attend. Then we would let the people go who didn't attend the meeting and keep the ones who wanted to quit—because the latter were smart enough to know that we were in bad shape or that they had better opportunities elsewhere.

  The point is that if you let people choose to get laid off or retire, you might lose your best people. Deciding whom to lay off is a proactive decision: Select the go-forward team to ensure that you never have to lay people off again. Do not leave this to chance.

- **Show people the door.** With few exceptions, all you should do is let people finish the day, maybe the week. (My theory is that Friday is the best day to do a layoff because it lets people have a weekend to decompress.) Showing people the door seems inhumane, but it's better for both the people leaving and the people remaining.

- **Move forward.** Let people say good-bye and then get going. This is when leadership counts. In bad times, you separate the men from the boys and the women from the girls. After the layoff, this is what the remaining employees will be wondering about:
    - Guilt: "Why did I survive the cut and my colleagues didn't?"
    - Future of my job: "Will I survive the next round if there are more cuts?"
    - Future of the company: "Will the company survive at all?"

So you set—or reemphasize—goals, explain what everyone needs to do to get there, and get going, because the best way to move beyond a layoff is to get back to work.

Immediately after a layoff, you might want to retreat to your office, turn off the phones, stop answering e-mails, and avoid everyone. These are the worst actions to take. This is the time for you to motivate by walking around. Employees need to see you, talk to you, and get your help and advice. They don't want to think their leader is cowering in some foxhole. The brave face that you put on may be a charade, but it's an important charade.

CHAPTER 78

The Art of Firing

**Nothing bad's going to happen to us.
If we get fired, it's not a failure;
it's midlife vocational reassessment.**

⌐ P. J. O'ROURKE

L aying people off, while distasteful, is easier than firing people, because layoffs usually occur in bad times, and they don't single a person out. A firing, by contrast, can occur in good times as well as bad times, and it's highly personal.

I've fired people a few times in my career, and I hated everything about the process. I'm not sure I did it well when I did it, but I've thought a lot about how it should be done. This is my best shot at the art of firing.

- **Consult impartial people.** As soon as you have misgivings about a person, talk to one or two people who can give you an impartial appraisal of the situation: Is the person truly at fault? Is she a scapegoat? Are the people calling for her firing any better? In my career, I have been blessed with three people who acted as my sounding board in issues like this. All were women, because women are much better at this than men.

- **Get professional advice.** It's a bad sign if you get too good at firing people because this means you're doing it too often. As soon as you think it's necessary to fire a person, consult someone who understands employment law. This is usually a human-resources person, but it could also be outside legal counsel if you don't have a human-resources person.

- **Search your soul.** You should be able to articulate exactly what you think is going wrong. Could it be your fault? Did you make a mistake and hire the wrong person? Is this an impossible job? Have you established clear goals and the tools and training to achieve these goals? If sales were going well, would we be having this discussion? The most telling question you can answer is: *Are you and the rest of the folks who are calling for the employee's termination judging his results against your intentions?*

  For example, are you judging his sales results against your intentions to ship the product on time? In a perfect world, you would do the opposite: Judge the employee's intentions against your results. In a realistic world, you would judge his results against your results. Unfortunately, the only people who usually receive the benefit of the doubt are the people calling for his termination.

- **Give people a second chance.** I don't care if you live in an "at will" state in which you can terminate anyone at any time, it is still immoral to fire people without helping them understand what they need to improve and providing the opportunity to do so.

  There is a line of reasoning that goes like this: "Nobody ever got fired too early. Don't put off a difficult decision, because everyone is wondering why you're keeping the bozo around. You should have fired him long ago."

  I believed in this "rapid fire" theory until I saw a management team act like piranha attacking a drowning calf when it considered firing an employee. No one wanted to give the employee the benefit of the doubt and a chance to turn the situation around. Luckily, the CEO interceded and kept the employee; subsequently, the person turned into a great contributor.

  There are three problems with rapid-fire firing: First, it may not be the employee's fault that things aren't going well. Second, the employee can improve—people do change. Third, although some employees may rejoice, the smart ones will be thinking, "So this is how this company works. There's no warning. If you're not popular, you get taken out."

- **Document everything.** Ideally, you've already got a paper trail describing the employee's job performance, but the moment you think that they might be fired, start keeping detailed records. There are two reasons to do this.

First, frankly, to cover your ass. Second, writing things down forces you to clarify your thoughts. When you read what you've written, it should be obvious that you're doing the right thing.

- **Do it yourself.** You probably hired the person. Even if you inherited the person, you managed him. So you fire him. This isn't something you can delegate or evade. Conduct a brief (fifteen minutes maximum) one-on-one meeting and tell the person your decision. Be as calm and rational as possible. Do not alter your approach even if (or, more accurately, especially if) the person isn't calm and rational.

  If you have great difficulty firing the person, maybe you never adequately communicated with him or her. And if you never communicated with him or her, maybe you're part of the reason for the poor performance, and you should fire yourself.

- **Be firm.** Never go into a "final" conversation thinking that if it goes well, you might not fire the person. Decide and then implement. If you get talked out of it, the odds are that you'll simply fire the person later. However, don't confuse being firm with being mean. You should be firm in your decision but kind in how your decision is communicated and implemented.

- **Don't be guilted into anything.** For example, a common request is to provide job references. Don't promise anything like this because you're feeling guilty. Your personnel department can provide a reference—like the dates of employment—but that's all you should commit to do. You can always decide to do more later, but you can't do less than what you committed to do.

- **Show people the door.** The day you fire someone should be the last day that person is in the office. This is even more true for firings than layoffs. There is very little to gain by having a fired person hang around for a few days or weeks, and there is a lot to lose: ill will, sabotage, and theft. Give the person a chance to collect their personal items and data from their computers and then get keys, delete accounts, and change passwords.

- **Don't disparage the victim.** There are three good reasons for this. First, it's the classy thing to do, and you want to show the remaining employees that you have class. Second, you could be tipping the karmic scales to be on the receiving end of the sword the next time. Third, the person you're firing could end up in charge of purchasing at your biggest customer—as my mother used to say, "Don't shiitake where you eat."

Ideally, the situation should have never come to this. You should have created a reasonable job and hired the right person for it. You should have set and communicated the right goals. You should have provided course corrections, tools, and training. Some of the fault probably belongs to you. It's too late for the case at hand, but it's not too late to prevent this from happening again, so take a good, long look in the mirror.

The Reality of Working

In the beginning, companies are like a clean sheet of paper, post-Zamboni ice, or a groomed ski slope: nothing but opportunity and upside with a chance to make meaning and change the world. Then the reality of work sets in. Building a successful organization is hard—damn hard, actually. This section examines the non-fairy-tale, real-world version of work.

CHAPTER 79

Work as a Prison?

Oh, you hate your job? Why didn't you say so? There's a support
group for that. It's called EVERYBODY, and they meet at the bar.

~ DREW CAREY

This chapter is an interview with Dr. Philip G. Zimbardo, the Stanford University professor who explained the banality of heroism earlier. His work explains the factors that shape human behavior: in particular, how people adopt and adapt to given roles.

Q: What is the sequence of events of the Stanford Prison Experiment?

A: The Stanford Prison Experiment (SPE) was my attempt to determine what happens when you put good people in an evil place: Does humanity triumph, or do situational forces come to dominate even the best of us? My Stanford psychology graduate students, Craig Haney and Curt Banks, and I created a realistic simulation of a prisonlike environment—a "bad barrel" into which we placed twenty-four carefully selected college student volunteers for a two-week experiment.

On the basis of the assessment from a battery of psychological tests and interviews, we had chosen them from among seventy-five who had answered the ad we placed in the city newspaper. By a flip of the coin of chance, half were to role-play guards, the rest took on the role of prisoners. Naturally, the prisoners lived there 24/7 while the guards worked eight-hour shifts. Initially nothing happened the first day as these college students from all over the United States were awkwardly getting into their roles.

But on the second morning, the prisoners rebelled; the guard crushed the rebellion and then instituted stern measures against these now "dangerous" prisoners. From then on, abuse, aggression, and eventually sadistic pleasure in degrading the prisoners became the daily norm. Within thirty-six hours, the first prisoner had an emotional breakdown and had to be released; similar prisoner breakdowns followed on each of the next four days.

Good, normal young men had been corrupted by the power of their role and by the institutional support for such a power differential between them and their humbled prisoners. The bad barrel had proven to have a toxic effect on our good apples. Our projected two-week-long study was terminated prematurely after only six days because it had escalated out of control.

Q: How did the experiment come to an end?

A: The guards were beginning to force sexually degrading "fun and games" on the prisoners. Obviously, I should have ended the study on my own after witnessing the emotional breakdowns and sexual abuses, but I did not because I had taken on the second role of prison superintendent added to that of principal investigator, and prison officials are not bothered by such reactions. Fortunately for me, someone was bothered, bothered enough to force me to shut down this "little shop of horrors."

I had invited a number of outsiders, young faculty and grad students, to interview everyone connected with our experiment, to give me a fresh perspective on what they discovered. One of them was a recent Stanford PhD named Christina Maslach, who was about to become a new assistant professor at Cal Berkeley. I had just begun dating her. She came down to our dungeon on the fifth night of the study, and after observing what had become the "normal" final toilet run of prisoners each night, she got really distressed.

She saw them with bagged heads, ankles in chains, hands on each other's shoulders moving along the corridor like a zombie parade as guards shouted abuses at them. "It is terrible what *you* are doing to those boys," she yelled at me, adding something like, "I'm not sure I want to continue a relationship with you if this is what you are really like!" That double slap in the face was the catalyst for my realizing that the study had worked too well, that those powerful situational forces had also corrupted me. After making all the necessary logistical arrangements, I pulled the plug on the Stanford Prison Experiment the next day.

In my book, *The Lucifer Effect: Understanding How Good People Turn Evil* (Random House, 2008), I detail for the first time the full day-by-day and night-by-night chronology of the events that had such a transformative impact on virtually everyone who got immersed in that setting. It is only by seeing the creatively evil ways the guards invented to break the will of the prisoners to resist that one comes to appreciate how a host of situational forces can combine to make good people do bad things.

I believe that such understanding puts us all in a better position to appreciate what the Lucifer Effect really means. Lucifer, God's favorite angel, was cast out of heaven into hell for his sin of disobedience against God, and became the devil, Satan. My book analyzes lesser human transformations of ordinary, good people as they are seduced by a set of situational forces to take the first steps down evil's slippery slope.

Q: How would you apply what you learned with the Stanford Prison Experiment to what happened at Abu Ghraib?

A: We conducted the Stanford Prison Experiment in August 1971. More than three decades later, the scenario was reenacted with chilling similarity in another prison by other American prison guards. The images flashing across TV screens around the world of the abuse and torture of Iraqi prisoners by U.S. military police were shocking, but not at all surprising to me.

I had seen their counterpart in my basement prison at Stanford, naked prisoners, bagged heads, sexually humiliated. It was inexcusable behavior, but not inexplicable once I discovered that beyond the visual parallels, the same set of psychological principles were operating in the bad barrel of Tier 1A of the Abu Ghraib night shift.

My sense of the sickening similarities between the mock prison of the Stanford Prison Experiment and that all-too-real prison dungeon in the middle of a controversial war was also highlighted in one of the investigations into the causes of this human tragedy.

The investigation by former defense secretary James Schlesinger and his committee concluded that the "landmark Stanford experiment" should have been a cautionary tale for the military. That report cites the untenable situation created in that prison dungeon for creating the volatile environment that became a catalyst for abusive behavior. Good Apples turned sour in a few weeks on duty in that hellhole of a bad prison barrel embedded in the bad barrel of war.

Q: Is there a difference between "good commanders" and "good professors" letting something bad happen?

A: The worst abuses in both prisons occurred on the night shift, when there was least surveillance by me, the good professor, and by them, the good commanders. In both cases, guards were allowed to have too much unrestrained power without top-down oversight.

In Abu Ghraib, I believe the top brass intentionally designed that setting to give permission for these lowly Army Reservists, "weekend soldiers" without mission-specific training, to "prepare detainees for interrogation," to "take the gloves off," to "soften them up" for interrogation.

Tier 1A was the interrogation, "soft torture" center where 1,000 detainees were housed, men and boys whom the commanders believed held the key to the insurgency's success. But most knew nothing, and those who might have had some worthwhile information had only cold, stale information after being confined for months. Pressure from Donald Rumsfeld went down the military chain of command and ended up with military intelligence officers in charge of Tier 1A soliciting the seven MPs on the night shift to step over the line of protecting their prisoners to breaking them down.

Q: How would you allocate blame to the three factors of disposition, situation, and systemic conditions?

A: *The Lucifer Effect* makes evident that blame for such abuse should not be limited to the few grunts at the end of the food chain—the so-called rogue soldiers. If their immoral actions were fueled by the horrible situation they were forced to work in, then we must also put in the docket those who helped to create that situation—the Power Boys running that sorry show. It must include "command complicity" of the architects of the conditions that led to such abuses—those in the Bush administration, and the military commanders who should have known what their subordinates were doing for three long months.

Q: How would you reengineer the system to prevent a reoccurrence?

A: Such abuses do not occur where there is responsible leadership: where commanders and leaders of all institutions make crystal clear that they will not tolerate doing harm, that personal dignity will always be respected, that the rules of engagement will be known by all, that everyone is ultimately personally responsible for their actions, and that any violations of such protocol will be met with public censure and punishment.

In addition, it is imperative for all leaders to appreciate the psychological dynamics operating in situations they create, and to have psychologically trained personnel who are charged with making them work positively, not destructively.

Q: Are people inherently and consistently good or bad?

A: John Milton's classic statement about the power of the human mind is it can "make a heaven of hell, a hell of heaven." I follow with a psychological celebration of the mind's infinite capacity to make any of us villains or heroes by enabling us to be caring or indifferent, selfless or selfish, creative or destructive.

People are not born evil, but rather with survival talents, and remarkable mental templates to be anything imaginable—just as infants readily learn to speak and understand any of a thousand languages in an instant in their development. We get a push from nature in various directions, such as being more inhibited or bold, but who we become is ultimately a complex process of cultural, historical, religious, economic, and political experiences in familial and other institutional settings.

Most of us fail to appreciate the extent to which our behavior is under situational control, because we prefer to believe that it all is internally generated. We wander around cloaked in an illusion of vulnerability, misarmed with an arrogance of free will and rationality.

Instead, few of us really know ourselves or most others in our lives. We can hardly have confidence in assertions of what we would do in a new or alien situation, because we choose to live in familiar, safe, predictable situations. And we play the same roles over and over in each of our various behavioral settings, as do those we think we know.

Those roles come with scripted actions and dialogues that soon are familiar to our audiences, since we are rarely taxed to improvise but say the lines as directed. Another illusion we cherish is that the line between good and evil is impermeable, with those bad people on the other, evil side and we and our kind and kin forever located in the realm of goodness.

A body of psychological science puts the lie to such an illusion by dramatically demonstrating the ease with which ordinary people can be seduced or initiated into the ranks of the other by blind obedience to authority, mindless conformity, diffusing responsibility, dehumanizing, adherence to norms, and rigidly playing our assigned roles. That line between good and evil is not an abstraction but "cuts through the center of every human heart," according to poet and former Stalin-era prisoner Alexander Solzhenitsyn.

Q: What makes people go wrong?

A: There are many reasons why people go wrong; it all depends on the situation—excluding those with mental disorders that can trigger rage and violence. They are hired guns in the mafia or the military or in children's rebel militias. They mindlessly follow seemingly just ideologies that encourage any means necessary to realize their noble ends. They want to be "team players," "to get with the program," "to be in the popular clique," to not be rejected and cast in the out-group.

They go wrong by doing nothing, by being guilty of the evil of inaction, doing what their mothers urged them—not to get involved, to "mind their own business," and let bad shit happen by looking the other way and holding their noses. Good people don't rush in to do evil where angels fear to tread; instead they start by straying only a small way away from their moral center, and each successive step down is hardly different, barely noticeable, until it is too late and their behavior is shocking and may even be awesome or awful.

Q: How does a person resist undesirable influences?

A: Situational forces can make good people do bad things, but that does not translate into either suspending personal accountability or endorsing pessimistic determinism. We are ultimately responsible for the consequences of any of our behavior that is enacted intentionally; however, now we add to the accountability mix those responsible for creating and maintaining evil-generating behaviors.

I am advocating a revolution in legal theory that expands on the narrow individualistic focus by adding situations and systems to calculations of guilt and sentencing. Further, I advocate replacing the traditional medical model of individual disease and cure, which has spilled over into law, psychiatry, religion, and most of our institutions, with a public-health model.

The presence of pathology in a society alerts the search for the "disease vector," which, when found, enables inoculation against its toxicity and environmental modifications to prevent its spread. Finally, I must add the obvious recognition that people create situations and thus with wisdom and goodwill can change them to work for us rather than against us.

My theory is that making some people bosses and some people workers will have results similar to the Stanford Prison Experiment: Both groups will soon accept the typical roles of their positions. This means you should ensure that bosses aren't overstepping boundaries and workers aren't accepting subservient roles. A little bit of anarchy is better than a prison.

CHAPTER 80

How to Not Choke

Be careful what you water your dreams with.
Water them with worry and fear and you will
produce weeds that choke the life from your dream.

∼ LAO-TZU

I used to take an adult hockey class in which each session started with all of us facing the boards and skating backward when the instructor blew his whistle. We were all supposed to stop on a second whistle. Then he grouped us by how far we had skated in the limited time.

The instructor was trying to group people of similar skill levels for a more efficient learning environment. However, I made the case to him that the folks in the slower groups (like me) learned that we sucked, and our heads filled with negative thoughts. As a result, we performed worse than we (theoretically) could have for the rest of the class. Of course, he ignored my brilliant insight—after all, he's from Minnesota and I'm from Hawaii.

According to "The Choke Factor: How Stereotypes Affect Performance" (*Scientific American*, December 5, 2007), I was right. For example, if female students are told immediately before a math test that women are worse in math than men, they score lower in the test than a similar group not given the negative message.

The theory is that by making a group aware of the stereotype, you can introduce "enhanced cognitive load." Intrusive and negative thoughts cause a load that interrupts and harms performance. What do you think will happen when (not if) you are told that you don't know how to run a company?

Entrepreneurs—like wannabe hockey players and female math-test takers—should heed the scientific understanding of choking and the impact of negative stereotypes.

Here are three ways to avoid choking.

- **Avoid negative people.** If you think about what people say about you, it can lead to becoming what people say about you, so simply avoid these folks. If you cannot avoid them, simply ignore them. The best way to avoid and ignore negative people is to create product and serve your customers like hell.

- **Invoke positive stereotypes.** Positivity can enhance performance, according to the article—it's "fighting fire with fire," as the saying goes. For example, entrepreneurs could invoke the positive stereotype that a couple of guys/gals who love technology and aren't "proven" entrepreneurs can start companies like Apple, Yahoo!, Google, YouTube, and Facebook. Perhaps this is one reason that Silicon Valley rocks as a place for young people to start companies: The wunderkind stereotype is a very positive one here.

- **Frame, or reframe, yourself.** You can control which groups you identify with and the strength of that association. We learned this from Dr. George Lakoff earlier. You don't have to identify with "music pirate." You could more strongly define yourself as a "music revolutionary"—or a mom, dad, wife, husband, scholar, programmer, or marketer, for that matter.

Returning to my problem as a lousy hockey player, I don't take that class anymore; I just ignore the instructor when he tells me that I won't get any better, and I frame myself as the best fifty-four-year-old beginning hockey player in Silicon Valley. By the way, there is one more way to not choke: Never take a bite. That is, never try to start a company, create a product, or play hockey. But if this option appeals to you, you probably aren't reading this book.

CHAPTER 81

Mavericks in the Workplace

Managing an advertising agency isn't all beer and skittles. After fourteen years of it, I have come to the conclusion that the top man has one principal responsibility: to provide an atmosphere in which creative mavericks can do useful work.

~ DAVID OGILVY

Polly LaBarre is the coauthor (with Bill Taylor) of *Mavericks at Work: Why the Most Original Minds in Business Win.* The strategies, tactics, and advice in *Mavericks at Work* grew out of in-depth access to a collection of forward-looking companies. These maverick companies are attracting millions of customers, creating thousands of jobs, and generating billions of dollars of wealth.

Taylor is a cofounder and founding editor of *Fast Company.* LaBarre was a senior editor at *Fast Company* for eight years and was one of the best reporters on the topic of entrepreneurship and marketing. In this interview, she provides a reality check for innovation in the workplace.

Q: What's the difference between a maverick and a jerk?

A: Mavericks are so different, so edgy, and so independent of spirit that their personal style or message may not appeal to everyone. But that's precisely the point: Mavericks are defined by the power and originality of their ideas. They stand out from the crowd because they stand for something truly unique. What's more, they take stands—against the status quo, in defiance of the industry elite—and offer compelling alternatives to business as usual.

Mavericks may be fighters, but they're not rebels without a cause, and that is the critical distinction. Their sense of purpose is not only powerfully distinct (think Southwest Airlines' quest to democratize the skies), it's provocative and disruptive (think HBO's declaration of originality: "It's not TV. It's HBO").

Don't confuse mavericks' unswerving commitment to a cause and their lack of patience for the status quo with the egotism, monomania, and powermongering modeled by too many celebrity CEOs and moguls. Mavericks, in fact, have a sense of humility.

Q: "Maverick humility"? That sounds like a contradiction in terms.

A: Just because you have a sharp-eyed point of view doesn't mean you need a sharp-elbowed approach to pursuing it. Sometimes the innovators with the most compelling strategic twists choose to broadcast them with a whisper rather than a shout.

One particularly vivid example of maverick humility is craigslist's adherence to its Nerd Values. craigslist has to be one of the most low-key organizations that ever became a worldwide sensation. Craig Newmark has become kind of a cult figure, but spend some time with CEO Jim Buckmaster (about as soft-spoken, reserved, and minimalist a CEO as we've ever met) and you get a powerful sense of the disruptive idea at the heart of the company: to provide a no-frills public service in an industry filled with overblown claims and in-your-face marketing.

Q: What's your assessment of Steve Jobs?

A: Steve Jobs is without a doubt a maverick who has forever changed the way we relate to computers and animated films. Jobs was smart enough to buy Pixar for $10 million in 1986 and then sell it to Disney for $7.4 billion, but he was even smarter to enlist Ed Catmull and John Lasseter to run the place.

What's most remarkable about Pixar is that it has become the envy of Hollywood because it never went Hollywood. More than a few business pundits have modeled the corporation of the future on the Hollywood model of work: an ad hoc collection of actors, producers, and technicians coming together around a script and financing, and then disbanding when the film is finished. The problem with that model is that it allows for maximum flexibility and minimum loyalty. What's more, it's usually just when the film wraps that the people involved really figure out how to work together.

Turn that model on its head and you get Pixar's version of the right way to make movies: a tight-knit company of long-term collaborators who stick together, learn from one another, and strive to improve with every production. A key component of that model is Pixar's no-contract policy. Famous, talented directors like Brad Bird, Peter Docter, Andrew Stanton, and Lee Unkrich, all of whom could secure lucrative contracts with any studio, are salaried employees of Pixar who contribute to all of the studio's projects rather than just their own pet projects.

This model tackles one of the most enduring people problems in any industry: How do you not only attract wildly talented people to work in your company, but also get those wildly talented people to continuously produce great work together? Or, as Randy Nelson, dean of Pixar University, puts it, How do you do art as a team sport? That question lies at the heart of Pixar's design for work, and the answers include turning the workplace into a canvas for the work and putting everyone in the organization in a position to learn together.

Q: Are mavericks born or made?

A: It's probably a little bit nature, a little bit nurture. We wrote this book to nurture the maverick in all businesspeople. What red-blooded working person wakes up in the morning, looks in the mirror, and says, I think I'll stand for business as usual today?

We all want to make a mark, forge our own path, and express ourselves in the world. It's just that some of us need more of a nudge down that path than others. Hopefully the maverick individuals and ideas we present are inspiring and instructive enough to move people.

The thirty-two companies we feature have vastly different histories, cultures, and business models. We examined glamorous fields like fashion, advertising, and Hollywood, as well as old-line industries like construction, mining, and household products. The maverick leaders of these organizations are young, old, women, men, Americans, Europeans, charismatic and preacherlike, retiring and almost reticent. They just don't fit any one mold.

Q: How does gender play into maverickdom?

A: Some of the most powerfully inspiring and effective mavericks we know are women. What's more, maverickdom in general is mercifully free of the power-suited legions of organization men who have squeezed women out for too long. Mavericks connect and win on the basis of a deeply felt and original sense of purpose; it doesn't matter what package that comes in.

For example, IBM's Jane Harper isn't an unlikely maverick because she's a woman but because she's survived—and thrived—as a relentless challenger of the status quo at IBM for a quarter century. She has worked all over the organization, but her real specialty is creating an entirely new position by pushing the organization in new directions. She took on the role of director of Internet technology and operations after she pushed the company to launch one of the first corporate Web sites in 1994. She got IBM to build a Web site in part by announcing to Lou Gerstner—along with her boss and collaborator, John Patrick—that IBM had bought a huge chunk of floor space at Internet World and needed to create a respectable Internet presence, fast.

In 1999, Harper asked a question nobody else wanted to address: Why would really great people—the best technical and managerial talent in the world—want to come work at IBM? In an era when every young, gifted programmer, engineer, or entrepreneur's first instinct was to write their own business plan or head to eBay or Google, life as a foot soldier in Big Blue's 320,000-member global army was a pretty hard sell. Harper understood that great people want to work on exciting, high-impact projects, with a small team, in a dynamic setting. So she created exactly that in a Cambridge, Massachusetts, lab and launched a wholly original and powerfully effective internship program called Extreme Blue.

Since that initial experiment (for which she had no permission and no budget—hallmarks of a maverick), Extreme Blue has grown to a yearlong set of programs that attract 250 top interns and hundreds of IBMers as sponsors and mentors. In the six years since the program's founding, nearly 80 percent of the participants have accepted full-time positions at IBM (including many with competing offers from Google et al.). What's more, students file a hundred-plus patent disclosures each summer and turn nearly half of the nascent ideas they start with at the beginning of an intense twelve-week summer program into actual products and services for IBM customers.

Q: How does a maverick survive, much less thrive, inside a large, publicly traded company full of MBAs—to state the worst case?

A: A better question might be: How will large, publicly traded companies full of MBAs survive, much less thrive, without a healthy complement of mavericks? But let me answer your question. We encountered a bunch of mavericks inside big traditional companies. They all seemed to have a couple of survival strategies in common:

They unleashed tough questions and critiques of their organization without losing their sense of loyalty to it. They're the kind of questions every CEO should be asking. For example, Jane Harper asked of IBM, Why would great people want to work here? And Larry Huston, now vice president of innovation at Procter & Gamble, argued, "The current business model for R & D is broken. How can P & G possibly build all of the scientific capabilities we need by ourselves?"

Mavericks don't just ask questions, they act. We saw this again and again: They just got started—usually without a budget or formal permission—by designing an experiment around their question. Jane Harper launched Extreme Blue and spent a couple of years begging and borrowing resources until the program's impact became clear.

Mavericks look for peers and fellow travelers outside the boundaries of their company. Not surprisingly, mavericks tend to click when they meet other mavericks. They're great networkers and learners and are always looking for kindred spirits for support and ideas.

Q: Do mavericks drive out bozos or do bozos drive out mavericks?

A: Both. Bozos tend to drive mavericks out of a company, but mavericks often go on to create companies that drive bozo companies out of business.

Q: What's the difference between open-source innovation and listening to the customer?

A: The open-source insight is simply that you don't have to be smart enough to have all the answers; you just have to be smart enough to invite other people to play in your sandbox. Eric von Hippel calls this lead-user innovation, and Tim O'Reilly calls it architecture of participation. What it's really about is tapping into shared passion.

If you want to create an enduring, emotional bond with customers, create a sense of shared ownership and participation among customers themselves. The more you invite people in to shape your company's personality and products, and the more you enable them to share their ideas with one another, the greater their stake in what your company does. Shared ownership is much deeper than simply listening to the customer.

For example, Jones Soda is a Seattle-based company that targets the twelve- to twenty-four-year-old demographic with flavors like Fufu Berry, Blue Bubblegum, and WhoopAss and special holiday drinks like Brussels Sprout with Prosciutto. When Peter van Stolk started the company, he realized the world didn't need another soda but that everybody needs something to connect with. That forced the team to think very differently about the design of the company.

Everything they do is about sharing ownership of the brand with the customer. One key to the brand identity of a packaged good like soda is, well, its packaging. Jones handed that over to its customers by inviting them to submit photos to feature on its labels. Over the years, Jones has received around four million photos from customers; people then vote for which photos go on labels.

Customers also e-mail favorite sayings, aphorisms, and messages, which are then used as under-the-cap fortunes. In 2004, Jones launched a Web site called Jones Independent Music, where bands post songs, images, bios, and contact information. Jones customers can download the tunes for free, rate songs and bands, and create playlists to share with one another. Every month some twenty bands appear on the bottle labels.

Why would a soda company offer a music service? Again, the message is never about selling soda, it's about making the brand connect with its customers. All this is about more than just listening to the customer. It's about sharing ownership of the brand with the customer. Jones doesn't preach to customers about the virtues of its brand; it unleashes the energy and creativity of its customers to give the brand its virtues. Jones is trying to turn soda into a platform for social interaction.

Q: What's the best idea in the book?

A: Companies competing on the basis of purpose is hardly without precedent, but maverick companies exude an *undeniable* sense of purpose. A maverick's strategy tends to be as edgy as it is enduring, as disruptive as it is distinctive, and as timely as it is timeless. In an era of hypercompetition and nonstop innovation, the most powerful ideas in business are the ones that set forth an agenda for reform and renewal—the ones that turn a company into a cause.

We call it strategy as advocacy. Maverick leaders don't start with a business plan; they start with an original blueprint for where their business can and should be going. They offer up a set of ideas that reshape the sense of what's possible for customers, employees, and investors. For example, ING Direct is to banking what Southwest is to airlines: a direct, no-frills savings bank that thrives by challenging the status quo and offering an alternative to the worst practices of its rivals.

The declared purpose of ING Direct is to lead Americans back to savings—to serve as an antidote to a toxic financial culture that encourages individuals to save too little, spend too much, and gamble with their investments. That distinctive and disruptive purpose maps to a simple business model: no branches, no ATMs, and no checking accounts—just a simple menu of savings accounts, CDs, and mutual funds. What the bank doesn't have is minimum deposits, fees, and confusing paperwork. These differences and the bank's edgy critique of the industry really click with people and turn it into a cause.

The Macintosh Division was the largest collection of mavericks in the history of Silicon Valley—at least those of us who worked there think so. We raised a pirate flag over our building. Our cause was the prevention of worldwide domination by IBM and an Orwellian *1984* world. The only quality that doesn't jibe with this interview is that I don't remember much humility in the division. Details, details.

CHAPTER 82

Ten or So Things to Learn This School Year

The difference between school and life? In school, you're taught a lesson and then given a test. In life, you're given a test that teaches you a lesson.

~ TOM BODETT

Every summer, my family spends our family vacation on the campus of the University of California at Santa Barbara. This environment inspired me to write about what students should learn in order to prepare for life after graduation. It seems to me that schools often teach the opposite of what's necessary for the real world.

Perhaps, in school, students have plenty of time and no money, so long papers, e-mails, and presentations are not a problem. However, people in the real world have plenty of money (or at least more money) and no time. This is what I wished I had learned in school before I graduated.

1. **How to talk to your boss.** In college, you're supposed to bring problems to your teachers during office hours, and you share the experience of coming up with a solution. In the real world, you're supposed to bring solutions to your boss in an e-mail, in the hall, or in a five-minute conversation. Typically, your boss either already knows about the problem or doesn't want to know about it. Your role is to provide answers, not questions. Believe it or not, in the real world, those who can do, do. Those who can't do, share with others who can't do.

2. **How to survive a meeting.** Enduring long, boring, and pointless meetings is a key survival skill. There are three key ways to accomplish this: First, assume that most of what you'll hear is pure, petty, ass-covering bull shiitake, and it's part of the game. This will prevent you from going crazy. Second, focus on what you want to accomplish in the meeting and ignore everything else. Once you get what you want, take yourself "out of your body," sit back, and enjoy the show. Third, vow to yourself that someday you'll start a company, and your meetings won't work like this.

3. **How to run a meeting.** Someday you'll be running meetings. When you are, the first thing you need to learn is this: Don't schedule a meeting unless it's necessary. The primary purpose of a meeting is to make a decision. It is not to share experiences or feel warm and fuzzy. With that in mind, here are five key points to learn about running a meeting: (1) Start on time even if everyone isn't there, because then they will be next time. (2) Invite the fewest people possible to the meeting. (3) Set an agenda for exactly what's going to happen at the meeting. (4) End on time so that everyone focuses on the pertinent issues. (5) Send an e-mail to all participants that confirms decisions and reviews action items. There are more power tips for running good meetings, but if you do these five, you're ahead of 90 percent of the world.

4. **How to figure out anything on your own.** Armed with Google, PDFs of manuals, and self-reliance, force yourself to learn how to figure out just about anything on your own. There are no office hours, no teaching assistants, and no study groups in the real world. Actually, the real world is often one long, lonely, independent study, so get with it.

5. **How to negotiate.** Don't believe what you see on reality television shows about negotiation and teamwork. They're all bull shiitake. The only method that works in the real world involves five steps: (1) Prepare for the negotiation by knowing your facts. (2) Figure out what you really want. (3) Figure out what you don't care about. (4) Figure out what the other party really wants. (5) Create a win-win outcome to ensure that everyone is happy. You'll be a negotiating maven if you do this.

6. **How to make small talk.** Generally, "Whassup?" doesn't work in the real world. Generally, "What do you do?" unleashes a response that leads to a good conversation. Generally, if you listen more than you talk, you will (ironically) be considered not only a good conversationalist but also smart. Life is mysterious sometimes.

7. **How to explain something in thirty seconds.** Unfortunately, many schools don't have elevators, or else students would know how to explain things in a thirty-second elevator pitch. Think mantra (three words), not mission statement (sixty words). Think time, not money, as the most important commodity. Think ahead, not on your feet. If you can't explain enough in thirty seconds to incite interest, you're going to have a long, boring career.

8. **How to write a one-page report.** I remember struggling to meet the minimum page requirements of reports in college. Double spacing and 14-point Selectric typewriter balls saved me. Then I went out into the real world and encountered bosses who wanted a one-page report. What the heck??? The best reports in the real world are one page or less. (The same thing is true of résumés, but that's another, more controversial topic for unemployed people who want to list all the .net classes that they took.)

9. **How to write a five-sentence e-mail.** Young people have an advantage over older people in this area, because older people (like me) were taught to write letters that were printed on paper, signed, stuck in an envelope, and mailed. Writing a short e-mail was a new experience for them. Young people, by contrast, are used to IMing and chatting. If anything, they're too skilled in brevity, but it's easier to teach someone how to write a longer message than a shorter one. Whether UR yung or old, d point S dat doptimal Len of an Emsg S 5 sentences.

10. **How to get along with coworkers.** Success in school is mostly determined by individual accomplishments: grades, test scores, projects, whatever. Few activities are group efforts. Then you go into the real world, where the higher you rise in an organization, the less important your individual accomplishments are. What becomes more and more important is

the ability to work with/through/beside and sometimes around others. The most important lesson to learn: Share the credit with others, because a rising tide floats all boats.

What about freeloaders (those scum of the earth who don't do anything for the group)? In school you can let them know how you truly feel. You can't in the real world, because bozos have a way of rising to the top of many organizations, and bozos seek revenge. The best solution is to bite your tongue, tolerate them, and try to never have them on the team again, but there's little upside in criticizing them.

11. **How to use PowerPoint (or Keynote).** I've seen the PowerPoint slides of many professors—what terrible role models these folks are. Maybe they are thinking: "This is a one-hour class, I can cover one slide per minute, so I need sixty slides. Oh, and I've written all this text already in my textbook, so I'll just copy and paste my twelve-point manuscript into the presentation." Perhaps the tenure system causes this kind of problem. In the real world, this is no tenure, so you need to limit yourself to ten slides, twenty minutes, and a thirty-point font—assuming that you want to get what you want.

12. **How to leave a voice mail.** Very few people of any age leave good voice mails. The purpose of a voice mail is to make progress toward getting what you want. A long one isn't going to zip you along to your goal. Think of an oral version of a compelling five-sentence e-mail: The optimal length of a voice mail is fifteen seconds.

Two power tips: First, say your telephone number slowly once at the beginning of your message and then again at the end. You don't want to make people play back your message to hear your phone number. Second (and this applies to e-mail, too), always make progress. Never leave a voice mail that says, "Call me back, and I'll tell you what time we can meet." Just say, "Tuesday, 10:00 A.M., at your office."

One last thing: the purpose of going to school is not to prepare for working but to prepare for living. Working is a part of living, and it requires these kinds of skills no matter what career you pursue. However, there is much more to life than work, so study what you love.

CHAPTER 83

"Why Smart People Do Dumb Things"

A strong mind masks immaturity.

~ DR. MORTIMER FEINBERG AND JOHN J. TARRANT

I ended my summer vacation in 2007 by discovering that my MacBook's hard disk was quasi hosed, though not totally hosed, as in "Accept fate— there's nothing you can do; it's dead." I could somewhat access files and even come close to booting the machine. But I finished my summer cajoling, coercing, and cursing my MacBook's hard disk.

The $64,000 question is, "Why didn't I have my MacBook completely and currently backed up?" During this weekend of aggravation, I read a book (at the suggestion of my buddy Bill Meade) called *Why Smart People Do Dumb Things*, by Dr. Mortimer Feinberg and John J. Tarrant, and it answered my question.

- **Hubris.** Pride to the point that you no longer feel shame, no longer believe that you are subject to public opinion, and no longer need to fear "the gods." Examples: Gary Hart's involvement with Donna Rice, which ended his run for the presidency, and the $2 million toga party thrown by Dennis Kozlowski of Tyco.

- **Arrogance.** From the Latin word *arrogare:* "to claim for oneself." Arrogant people believe they have claim to anything and everything they want—they are "entitled" to it. King David, for example, felt entitled to Bathsheba. the wife of one of his soldiers. Modern-day King Davids feel entitled to corporate jets and an entourage to tell them that their keynote speech rocked.

- **Narcissism.** Self-absorption to the point that you are blind to reality. The world only exists to provide you gratification. Examples: Richard Nixon and Watergate; the Clintons and Whitewater—really just about every politician and CEO who falls from grace.

- **Unconscious need to fail.** If you think failing is hard, try winning. The questions that go through people's minds when they are on the doorstep of success are: Do I really deserve to win? Do I want the pressure of constantly having to win in the future? Can I really handle success? Perhaps this explains why professional athletes still take performance drugs even after watching their colleagues get busted.

The authors go on to discuss maturity (the "capacity to make constructive use of our inmost feelings") and what they call the Six Basic Principles of Maturity.

1. **Accept yourself.** "You're on the road to maturity if you can begin to appreciate yourself without trying to be what you cannot possibly be." The CEOs who failed at Apple did so because they wanted to be another Steve Jobs. They couldn't accept themselves and their own, different capabilities and shortcomings.

2. **Accept others.** "Your relations with other people are a basic test of your maturity. If you don't get along well with others, it's not because you're not smart enough, or because you're smart and they're dumb. It's because you still need to grow up in some vital centers of your being." For example, there are companies in Silicon Valley that maintain a "tyranny of PhDs," under which only PhDs are held in high esteem and sales, marketing, operations, and other functions are fodder.

3. **Keep your sense of humor.** "Your humor reflects your attitudes toward people. The mature person uses humor not as a bludgeoning hammer but rather as a plane to shave off rough edges."

4. **Accept simple pleasures.** "The capacity to get excited over things even when they seem ordinary to others—this is a sign of a healthy personality." For example, some tech entrepreneurs have yachts that can barely pass under the Golden Gate Bridge. I'd be happy if I could skate backward.

5. **Enjoy the present.** "Emotional grown-ups don't live on an expectancy basis. They plan for the future, but they know they must also live in the present. The mature person realizes that the best insurance for tomorrow is the effective use of today."

6. **Welcome work.** "Appreciation of work is a hallmark of mature people. . . . Immature people are constantly fighting certain aspects of their work. They resent routine reports, or meetings, or correspondence. They allow these annoyances to grate on their nerves continually. Satisfaction in doing a good job is blocked out by the dust speck in the eye of resentment over trivia."

This is good stuff. You could photocopy this posting and slip it under the corner-office door of you-know-who. Back to my hard disk. Why didn't I, supposedly a smart person with a computer background with difficult-to-replace files, back up my hard disk?

- **Hubris:** I no longer feared the hard-disk gods.

- **Arrogance:** I was "entitled" to a trouble-free hard disk. Even if it did fail, I have enough connections for some company to jump through hoops to recover it for me.

- **Narcissism:** Hard disk failure cannot happen to me, Guy Kawasaki. Now let me get back to admiring myself.

- **Unconscious need to fail:** Perhaps I had an unconscious need for my hard disk to fail so that I wouldn't have to answer my backlog of 700 e-mails.

As I learned from reading this book, whether you're talking about business, politics, or your hard disk, it pays to be mature. It also helps when Apple introduces a cool backup product like Time Machine.

CHAPTER 84

Why Smart Companies
Do Dumb Things

It's too bad that stupidity isn't painful.

~ ANTON LAVEY

O K, so smart people do dumb things, but you'd think that smart people working together wouldn't mean a company wouldn't do dumb things. After all, they could check and balance each other. You'd be wrong: Companies often do dumb things that range from selling crappy products to breaking laws. The examples go from A (Adelphia) to X (Xerox) with stops at E (Enron) and G (Global Crossing) in the middle. Luckily, *Why Smart People Do Dumb Things* explains why smart companies do dumb things, too.

• **Consensus.** When it comes to doing dumb things, the sum of the parts is less than the whole. Throwing more minds at the problem means more data, more perspectives, more possible solutions, more critiques of these solutions, and more minds (and hands) implementing the solution, right?

Possibly, but there's also the downside of more people: Once consensus starts to build, it's harder to alter a decision. It's one thing to argue against a few people; it's much more difficult to argue against the wisdom of a crowd. Individuals who hold out, question, or disagree are labeled as clueless, uncooperative, and not team players.

- **Conviction.** Consensus rears its ugly head during the decision-making process. The situation can get worse once implementation occurs, because the organization marches along with a firm belief in what it's doing. At that point, a decision takes on a sacred life of its own, and a company cannot see flaws.

  Conviction is not inherently bad, and truthfully, it's an important component of success. The trick is to combine conviction with open eyes and open minds to reduce the likelihood of having a conviction about the wrong thing.

- **CEOs.** There is one kind of consensus that is particularly powerful and dangerous: a CEO (or any top executive) who provides cues about what she likes. (CEO = Consensus Executive Officer?) Then, disagreeing takes on the gravity of career risk. However, smart people don't necessarily turn into thumb-sucking dweebs just because the CEO likes something, so what gives?

  It could be that people, no matter how smart, rearrange reality. They do not simply follow the dumb cues of the CEO. Instead, there's an intermediate step: They see the cues, rearrange the facts in their mind, and then conclude that the CEO is right. The result is the same, though.

- **Experts.** If there's anything that smart people worship, it's other smart people. For example, you don't know much about geography, so you hire a consultant who's an expert in geography, and he tells you that the earth is flat. It's tough to be strong enough to not defer to an expert.

  Most experts have a tough time accepting surprises that are outside their comfort zone. For example, if you come to me with a marketing problem, I will usually tell you that evangelism is the answer.

- **Good news.** The competition, customers, governments, and schmexperts (schmucks + experts) constantly assault a company. Because of this barrage, good news is attractive—like an addictive, illegal, and dangerous drug. It makes you crave more good news, and you refuse to communicate bad news up the chain of command. Ultimately, it may even make you refuse to hear bad news at all. How many commanders-in-chief of armies has this phenomenon brought down over the course of history?

- **Lofty ends.** Lofty ends can justify all sorts of weird and inappropriate means. Look no further than the quests for peace that produce mayhem and violence. Or, the desire to make a profit (something that is good for shareholders and customers) that warps a company's code of ethics even though the company is made up of smart, honest people. Companies trying to achieve a lofty goal can start believing that any means to achieve it is okay.

In addition to what Feinberg and Tarrant discuss, during my career I've noticed three other factors that make smart companies do dumb things.

- **Budgets.** Ideas take on a life of their own in the form of convictions. That's bad enough, but then the implementation of ideas can also take on a life of its own. This is called a budget. It is a holy document that takes the place of management, observation, decision making, and analysis for an entire year. Then the flawed thinking of the budget serves as the basis for the next year's implementations.

- **Greed.** You've heard of the concept of "good to great" by Jim Collins. There's also "good to greedy." When a company wants it all, it often doesn't let rules, regulations, and common sense get in the way. Greed trumps intelligence.

- **Arrogance.** This is greed's twin brother. Arrogance sets in when a company believes success is a God-given right. Arrogance makes a company believe it's above the law, so that no one and nothing has claims against it. Greed can trump intelligence all by itself; if you throw in arrogance, too, intelligence doesn't have a chance.

I would be remiss if I didn't provide ways to prevent or reduce the likelihood that your smart company will do dumb things. These are the best ways to prevent this from happening.

- **Squash arrogance and greed.** This recommendation sits squarely on the shoulders of the CEO. Arrogant and greedy people attract and hire arrogant and greedy people. Let's say you're not arrogant and greedy, but you're not the CEO. Then at least don't hire arrogant and greedy people in your area. Let's say you're not a manager, then at least don't be arrogant and greedy.

- **Delay consensus.** Sometimes the faster you go, the less you see. In particular, the CEO should not rush into a decision, because most employees will not question the CEO. This is hard to resist for management, because the image of decisiveness is so seductive. You should wait until you have enough information and analysis to make a truly informed decision.

- **Cherish diversity.** Say, believe, and act in a way that convinces employees that differences of opinion and diversity of thought are good things. Frankly, a couple of curmudgeons are good for a company. And don't shoot the bearer of bad news, because she is actually doing her duty—and doing you a favor.

- **Spell things out.** If you're in management, it's not wise to say, "Plug this leak in our company" and assume that it will be done legally. You should say, "Plug this leak in our company by using only legal, ethical, and reasonable methods."

- **Move the crown.** When employees go around saying, "We need to do it this way because Bill/Steve/Carly wants it this way," you're in trouble. It means that employees are making decisions based on what they think will make the kings happy—as opposed to what's right for the customer, employees, or shareholders. Good CEOs put the crown on the customer's head, not theirs.

- **Restrict experts to narrow areas.** Don't use experts to create your strategic road map or annual plans unless you want MBAs who have never run anything larger than a school snack bar to decide your fate.

- **Ask for bad news.** Don't assume bad news will find you—you have to find it. You should allocate a time that's specifically for listening to bad news. Better to hear it when it's only bad than when it's horrible news.

- **Approach budgets as working guidelines.** Don't make policies that are set in stone. If your budget doesn't change for the whole year, you're either clairvoyant (there are probably easier ways to make money if you are) or clueless.

This is a depressing topic, so here's an explanation of "Enronomics" to amuse you before we take on bozos in the next chapter.

You have two cows. You sell three of them to your publicly listed company, using letters of credit opened by your brother-in-law at the bank, then execute a debt-equity swap with an associated general offer so that you get all four cows back, with a tax exemption for five cows. The milk rights to the six cows are transferred through an intermediary to a Cayman Island company secretly owned by the majority shareholder who sells the rights to all seven cows back to your listed company. The Enron annual report says the company owns eight cows, with an option on one more.

CHAPTER 85

How to Prevent a Bozo Explosion

But the fact that some geniuses were laughed at does not imply
that all who are laughed at are geniuses. They laughed at Columbus,
they laughed at Fulton, they laughed at the Wright brothers.
But they also laughed at Bozo the Clown.

~ DR. CARL SAGAN

The previous chapter examined what happens when smart people do
dumb things. Sometimes companies suffer from dumb people doing
dumb things—this is even worse. It's depressing to watch a lean, mean
fighting machine deteriorate into a mediocracy (mediocre + bureaucracy). In
Silicon Valley, we call this process a bozo explosion. This downward slide
seems inevitable after a company achieves success, often during the years
immediately following an IPO. I created Guy's Bozo Aptitude Test or GBAT
to help people diagnose whether their company is slipping toward bozosity.

Take the GBAT

Give yourself one point each time you answer "yes" to the following questions.

1. Are the two most popular words in your company *partner* and *strategic*?

2. Does your management have two-day offsites at places like the Ritz Carl-
ton to foster communication and to craft a company mission statement?

3. Does the company mission statement contain more than twenty words?

4. Does your CEO's admin have an admin?

5. Does your parking lot's "biorhythm" look like this?
   a. 8:00 A.M.–10:00 A.M.—Japanese cars exceed German cars
   b. 10:00 A.M.–5:00 P.M.—German cars exceed Japanese cars
   c. 5:00 P.M.–10:00 P.M.—Japanese cars exceed German cars

6. Does your HR department require an MBA degree for any position?

7. Does your company consider time to be more important than money, so you have a company cafeteria, health club, and pet-grooming service? Moreover, are the company cafeteria, health club, and pet-grooming service the first things that employees show visitors?

8. Does someone whose music sells in the iTunes store perform at the company Christmas party?

9. Is the company paying any employee to do nothing but write a blog?

10. Do employees read this blog to find out what's happening in the company?

11. Does the success of a competitor upset you more than the loss of a customer?

12. Do most of your middle managers have big-name consumer-goods backgrounds?

13. Do you hire a big-name consulting firm that brings in twenty-three-year-old MBAs with one year of experience to rethink your corporate strategies?

14. Did your company like some of these MBAs and hire them away from the big-name consulting firm?

15. Is the front-desk staff getting better looking and less competent?

16. Is the only time that you see your CEO when she's on CNBC?

17. Do you watch CNBC during the day without feeling guilty?

18. Is the ratio of engineers to attorneys below 25 to 1?

19. Has your company created a "company values" poster?

20. Do the phrases "leveraging core competencies" and "maximizing share-holder value" show up in official documents in the same paragraph?

21. Do new executives campaign to improve products before they understand how to use them?

22. Does your company outsource the customer-service function?

23. Is your CEO's chair more expensive than your first car?

24. Do you have more than two execs with the word *chief* in their title?

25. Has the company become a schwag fountain: pens, bags, notepads, messenger bags.

Give yourself two points for answering "yes" to each of these questions:

26. Has your CEO written a book?

27. Has your CEO gone to the World Economic Forum in Davos, where he gave advice to the presidents of Eastern European countries about entrepreneurship?

28. Does your company have a private jet?

29. Is the private jet leased from the CEO?

30. Has your company hired a retired professional athlete as a motivational speaker?

31. Has your company hired a retired politician as a motivational speaker?

Score Sheet

Here's how to score your company:

- **0–5**—You're probably bootstrapping the company and not spending Other People's Money. You're a long way from bozosity.

- **6–10**—The company is still in the young, hungry, and innovative stage. Nothing to worry about yet.

- **11–30**—The inexorable slide to bozosity is starting.

- **31 or more**—Update your résumé because your company will hit the wall soon.

What to Do

Did you gulp? Don't sweat it: You're not alone. In fact, you'd be more alone if you weren't going through the slide. Here are actions you can take to slow down and maybe reverse it.

1. **Look beyond the résumé.** The goal of hiring is to build a great team. One convenient proxy for great employees is a relevant educational or work background. However, the perceived right educational background and work experience are not sufficient conditions for excellence. Hiring a bozo with the right résumé can drag down other employees and increase the probability of hiring more bozos. Not hiring a great person because she lacks the right résumé is a tragic oversight.

2. **Diversify.** Some companies look like the corporate version of the Stepford Wives: Everyone grew up in a white, upper-class family, everyone went to an Ivy League school, and everyone got an MBA. It's a bunch of Me and Mini-Me's. When this happens, it means that form is overruling function, and the way people succeed is by representing the right form, not excelling at the right function. That's back asswards.

3. **Insist that managers hire better than themselves.** For example, an engineering manager should hire a programmer who is a better programmer than she is, not worse. By the way, this principle starts at the level of the board of directors when hiring the CEO.

4. **Eradicate arrogance.** Arrogance manifests itself in two principal areas: first, when your employees describe the competition using terms like

"clueless," "bozo" (ironically), or just plain "stupid." Second, when your employees start believing that the company's "manifest destiny" is to dominate the market. When you find this sort of attitude, pull the employee aside and tell him to wake up and smell the ragweed. Refer back to the chapter called "Why Smart Companies Do Dumb Things" for more about this subject.

5. **Understaff.** Hire fewer people than you're "sure" you need to accommodate that hockey-stick growth you're "sure" you're going to achieve. When you're in a rush to fill openings to respond to growth, you make mistakes. Unfortunately, many companies adopt the attitude of "Hire any intelligent body, and we'll sort everything out later."

6. **Undergrow.** This is the flip side of understaffing. I am suggesting intentionally forgoing sales. Staying small and fine is a perfectly acceptable management policy. At the very least, calculate the entire impact on head count of getting that additional sale, new line of business, or acquisition.

7. **Merge and purge.** You owe it to your employees to provide feedback and direction and give them every opportunity to succeed. However, you also owe it to both the person and the company to fire someone who isn't doing the job. If there's a problem, fix it. If you can't fix it, then make the employee an "exployee."

Honestly, almost every company goes through a bozo explosion. Thus, the salient question isn't, "Will we have a bozo explosion?" as much as "When we have a bozo explosion, will we change our ways?" What makes change in this situation hard is that a bozo explosion usually occurs when (and perhaps because) a company is doing well. Hence the recommendation to understaff and undergrow, painful and illogical as this may seem.

CHAPTER 86

Are You an Egomaniac?

For over a thousand years Roman conquerors returning from the wars enjoyed the honor of triumph, a tumultuous parade. In the procession came trumpeters, musicians and strange animals from conquered territories, together with carts laden with treasure and captured armaments. The conqueror rode in a triumphal chariot, the dazed prisoners walking in chains before him. Sometimes his children robed in white stood with him in the chariot or rode the trace horses. A slave stood behind the conqueror holding a golden crown and whispering in his ear a warning: that all glory is fleeting.

~ GENERAL GEORGE C. PATTON

Steven Smith has spent the past ten years exploring how great leaders use their egos differently than the rest of us. The result of his work is a book he coauthored with David Marcum called *egonomics: What Makes Ego Our Greatest Asset (or Most Expensive Liability)* (Fireside, 2007). The topic of this interview is one of paramount importance to anyone who wants to change the world: Ego. Too much? Too little? How much is just enough?

Q: Does it take a big ego to be successful, or do you start with a normal ego, somehow achieve success, and then get a big ego?

A: First, there's a vital difference between a big ego and big ambition. Successful people usually start with big ambition or big ideas, and a normal, healthy ego. That combination of ambition, ideas, and healthy ego drives their success. If they're not careful, though, their success creates the illusion that it was they alone who achieved that success. And the more publicly visible they are, the more they believe the headlines that attribute their success to just them.

Once they assign all of that success to themselves, their ego whispers how great they are, and that anything else they think or do will be equally great. That's when healthy ego becomes "big" ego, and it's hard to convince ourselves it's not just us, because our self-written history reinforces that we're the one that did it.

Q: The opening line of your book is, "Ego is the invisible line item on every company's profit and loss statement." Why is it invisible?

A: Because it hasn't been measured, and yet people know the costs are there. Over half of all businesspeople estimate that ego costs their company 6 to 15 percent of annual revenue; many believe that estimate is too conservative. But even if ego were only costing 6 percent of revenue, the annual cost of ego would be nearly $1.1 billion to the average *Fortune* 500 company.

The reason ego stays invisible is because we don't talk about it—we talk about everything else, like numbers. It's also easier to talk about lighter topics like communication, decision making, leadership, or teamwork. But the most sensitive, yet most powerful, topic is ego.

We think people should look at management capabilities in the same way Dmitry Mendeleyev looked at the periodic table of elements. He was the first person to organize the elements by weight—lightest to heaviest. The same thing is true in business—each capability has different weights, some lighter, some heavier. The "atomic weight" of the ability to manage the human element of ego is greater than all of them.

There are other important elements on the leadership "table," but ego has the most weight—in large part because of the effect it has on everything else. And yet it's the most avoided. People have been afraid to talk about ego because they don't understand how it functions, especially at work. And the conversations they do have about it are usually at the water cooler and in private. More importantly, it's almost always seen as someone else's problem, and that needs to change.

Q: What are the telltale signs of an overinflated ego?

A: First, let's be clear that most people—99 percent of us—don't have over-inflated egos all the time; just some of the time. When ego overinflates, there are four early warning signs:

    a. Being comparative: Being too competitive makes you less competitive.

    b. Being defensive: Defending ideas turns into being defensive.

    c. Seeking acceptance: Desiring respect and recognition interferes with success.

    d. Showcasing brilliance: Ideas can be overshadowed by your own intelligence and talent.

Let's take just one that gets a lot of people in business, and usually triggers the other three warning signs, being comparative or too competitive. Here are some things you can watch for.

- Seeing someone you work with as a rival and thinking about how to beat them.
- Taking disagreement with your ideas personally.
- Compulsively following a competitor's lead so they're not doing anything you're not.
- Criticizing a competitor's strategies and prematurely discarding them as irrelevant.
- Believing you don't ever deserve to lose—a game, a conversation, a debate, a promotion, a raise, etc.—and not being gracious in defeat.
- Disagreeing with someone's point just because she's the one who made it.
- Feeling worse about where you are when you see what others achieve.

Q: Then what is a healthy ego?

A: Genuine confidence; confidence that doesn't have to exert itself to prove its confidence. Healthy ego keeps us from thinking too highly or too little of ourselves and reminds us how far we have come, while at the same time helping us see how far short we are of what we can be. But to understand what healthy ego is, you have to understand the relationship between ego and humility. For most people, tradition holds that the opposite of excessive ego is humility, when in fact having too little ego is just as dangerous and unproductive as having too much.

When we strike the right balance between ego and humility, we're genuinely confident. In the book, we call that the ego equilibrium. But since there's a natural tendency to deviate from the equilibrium, when we move just right or left of center, we get false confidence, and ego manages us rather than the other way around. As a result, our strengths morph into counterfeits, weaknesses; someone who's passionate now becomes overzealous, or a strong-willed person becomes inflexible. We think it's the same thing, but it's not, and everyone around us notices the difference.

Imagine that the spectrum of ego is magnetic, with the strongest pull coming from the two ends. At the center, the magnetic pull on either side has little effect on us. But the closer we move to the extremes, the more the magnetic pull affects us and the harder it is to make our way back. The longer we stay off-center, the more comfortable we become being off-center. If we don't quickly recover, we're likely to develop bad ego habits.

Q: How can humility survive in a capitalistic, dog-eat-dog market?

A: That's the cool thing we discovered in our work, even though the perceived weakness of humility is the assumption, even in a question like this one. Humility is the only real way to become great, everything else being equal. As a trait, humility is the point of equilibrium between too much ego and not enough. Humility has a reputation of being the polar opposite of excessive ego. In fact, the exact opposite of excessive ego is no confidence at all. Humility provides the crucial balance between the two extremes. When Jim Collins did his work in *Good to Great*, humility was one of only two characteristics he discovered that separated leaders capable of leading good—even very good—companies from leaders who made their companies great performers. And all of those leaders who lifted their companies to greatness and sustained them for over fifteen years did it in the same dog-eat-dog world everyone else was in. Humility was custom-made for the business world.

Q: Is there such a thing as not enough ego?

A: Definitely. In fact, more people and company cultures suffer from this than you might think. It's the junior-high side of ego: We need the approval and acceptance of others so much that we make decisions we wouldn't make if we felt more genuinely confident about who we are.

That lack of enough ego puts others in the driver's seat of our self-confidence, and people start to shape their thoughts and actions to what they believe will be endorsed by others; they become "pleasers" and don't offer what's on their minds. Companies then get "good" ideas from people—but sadly, not their best. Ironically, when they don't get our best, they're less likely to give us the acceptance we deserve.

When our desire for acceptance is healthy, acceptance and respect are still important to us, but they aren't our only goal. We can want acceptance without letting it affect our self-worth or authenticity. When our desire for recognition and respect is balanced, we draw a clear distinction between who we are and what we do.

Q: What is your analysis of Steve Jobs?

A: Steve's gone through a metamorphosis in how he works. He's always been exceptionally gifted as a creator and designer, but he used those gifts in a way that drove people away from his company and minimized the talent and creative IQ of the people around him. Once he was kicked out of Apple, life began to humble him through his own health challenges, his reputation, losing what he created, etc. Interestingly, Steve came out of that time of his life with a healthier ego, because life had humbled him and he accepted the lessons.

At his commencement speech at Stanford a couple of years ago, he said, "I'm pretty sure none of this [NeXT, Pixar, his return to Apple, the iPod and iTunes] would have happened if I hadn't been fired from Apple. It was awful-tasting medicine, but I guess the patient needed it."

Humility is a powerful antidote to unhealthy ego, and we can either humble ourselves or wait for life to humble us. About one year ago, *Fortune* had Steve on the cover, but the two-page spread inside had six or seven people sitting next to him. We thought that picture said it all; he's no longer in this by himself, and it appears that he recognizes that. As a result, he's a much better leader.

Q: How does an egotist reform himself or herself?

A: Therapy! The truth is, true egotists rarely reform. *egonomics* isn't for the small percentage of egotists in the population who need therapy. In terms of reformation, we all need some. Maybe it's the way we present our ideas, defend our positions, think about ourselves, share our talent and expertise, motivate people, etc. But the first step in any kind of reformation is awareness, because where there is no awareness, there is no choice.

And that awareness can't only come from ourselves. Get feedback, ask people how you're doing, and watch for any of the four early warning signs. We give companies who read *egonomics* free access to an assessment that measures how healthy the culture's collective ego is.

Q: What should you do if you work for an egotist?

A: Run to the nearest exit and find somewhere else to work, but if that's not an option, then fighting his ego with your own isn't the answer. An egotist rarely wins unless he's in positional power; then you can't do much. But if he's not your boss, then sit down and talk to him about what you're noticing, and make sure it's not your own ego.

Sometimes we assign other people the worst of what we're seeing in ourselves. We also talk a lot in the book about how to communicate to get someone else to open her mind, back off a locked position, or change the way she's working with you. Bob Sutton at Stanford wrote a very good book called *The No Asshole Rule: Building a Civilized Workplace and Surviving One That Isn't* (Business Plus, 2007), which deals more with the pure egotists. Our work is focused on the rest of us, who aren't assholes but lack just enough humility to reach our real potential.

Q: Which of the presidential candidates do you think does the best job of managing his or her ego?

A: Rather than answer what we think, we'll let a survey answer that question. We Web-surveyed about 1,200 people and asked questions about how voters would rank the humility, curiosity, and veracity of the candidate—things like how they would handle making mistakes, what kinds of people they would put in the Cabinet, how open-minded and forthcoming they are, how curious they are about policies they don't understand, how diplomatic they would be internationally, etc.

About two thirds of the people who responded were Republican. We're not sure how to explain that. But what's interesting is that a Republican didn't win what we called the "presidential egonomics" survey. A democrat, Barack Obama, was the clear winner, with a score of 80.3 out of 100. This means that the respondents saw Obama as the most open-minded, curious, intellectually honest, collaborative, and genuinely confident candidate.

The worst? Edwards, Giuliani, Romney, and McCain all came in at about the same score—all about six points behind Obama. Hillary Clinton was clearly last at 68.4.

Q: How would we change if we did a better job of managing ego?

A: We would be more open-minded about views that differ from ours and less rigid in making changes when we're challenged with them. Closed minds and fixed positions may be the most prevalent outcomes of mismanaged ego. Good leaders keep their minds open. But great leaders open the minds of others in the most intense circumstances, even against the odds of prejudice, politics, and habit.

But in those circumstances, ego can trip all of us, at any time, momentarily, if we confuse our identity, who we are, with our ideas, what we think and believe. When we slip, we stop defending our ideas and *we* get defensive. We stop *sharing* our brilliance and try to dominate the conversation with it. Rather than letting *ideas* compete with each other to let the best one win, we start to compete with each other. All of which has the net result of closing minds and stopping the opportunity for innovation or change in a company. After all, if people's minds are closed—even partially—there isn't much innovation or change happening.

The Japanese have a saying: "There are two kinds of stupid people. One never climbs to the top of Mt. Fuji to see the incredible view of the countryside. The other climbs twice." I worked for Steve Jobs twice, so I guess that makes me stupid. I wouldn't do things the way he does them, but that's my problem, not his. This interview with Smith helped me understand and appreciate people with large egos. I say as long as they can deliver, more power to them.

CHAPTER 87

The No-Asshole Rule

If you act like an asshole one night, [you]
might not remember it. But we will.

~ ROBERT LORENC

This chapter features more wisdom from Bob Sutton. You have to like an author who has the testicles (or ovaries) to walk away from Harvard Business School Press because it wouldn't let him use the word *asshole* in his title. (HBS Press also turned me down once.) While I am not a big fan of profanity, *asshole* is the only word that delivers the proper connotative meaning in some situations, so forgive me for using it here.

Sutton's book, *The No Asshole Rule: Building a Civilized Workplace and Surviving One That Isn't* (Business Plus, 2007), is the definitive guide to understanding, counteracting, and not becoming an asshole. I am qualified to make this judgment because (a) I've been an asshole and (b) I've been a victim of assholes.

The first step is to recognize who is an asshole. Sutton's blog cites one method. It's called the Starbucks Test. It goes like this: If you hear someone at Starbucks order a "decaf grande half-soy, half-low-fat, iced vanilla, double-shot, gingerbread cappuccino, extra dry, light ice, with one Sweet'n Low and one NutraSweet," you're in the presence of an asshole. It's unlikely that this petty combination is necessary—the person ordering is trying to flex her power because she's an asshole.

A second method is to use Suttons's dirty-dozen list of everyday asshole actions:

1. Personal insults

2. Invading one's personal territory

3. Uninvited personal contact

4. Threats and intimidation, both verbal and nonverbal

5. Sarcastic jokes and teasing used as insult delivery systems

6. Withering e-mail flames

7. Status slaps intended to humiliate their victims

8. Public shaming or status degradation rituals

9. Rude interruptions

10. Two-faced attacks

11. Dirty looks

12. Treating people as if they are invisible

A third method—albeit the least reliable, scientific, and fair but the most fun—is to search Google with a person's name (or a profession) plus "asshole." This yields some interesting results:

Steve Ballmer: 8,860

Terrell Owens: 21,200

Guy Kawasaki: 6,850

Lawyers: 280,000

Donald Trump: 61,800

How to Avoid Being an Asshole

The first $64,000 question is, "How does one avoid being an asshole?" I've compiled a top-eleven list to summarize the ways.

1. **Do not make people feel oppressed, humiliated, de-energized, or belittled.** If you find yourself having these effects, it's time to change your behavior, no matter what you think of yourself.

2. **Apologize if you act like an asshole.** I've figured out that the distastefulness of apologizing far outweighs that temporary pleasure of acting like an asshole. Thus, acting like an asshole has little upside for me, because I'll hate apologizing later.

3. **Face your past.** The past is a very good predictor of future behavior. For example, were you a bully in school? If your parents and siblings were assholes, you may have caught the disease. Knowing that you're an asshole is the first step toward change.

4. **Do not mistreat people who are less powerful than you.** One of the sure signs of an asshole is treating service people, like clerks, flight attendants, and waiters, in a degrading manner.

5. **Resist becoming an assholeholic from the start.** The easiest time to avoid becoming an asshole is at the very beginning. Don't think that you can do "what you have to" to fit in and then change later. It won't happen.

6. **Walk away and stay away from assholes.** Don't be afraid to leave a bad situation. It's unlikely you'll change the assholes into good people; it's much more likely that you'll descend to their level.

7. **View acting like an asshole as a communicable disease.** If you have any sense of decency, when you're sick, you avoid contact to prevent spreading the disease. So if you act like an asshole, you're not affecting only yourself; you're also teaching other people that it's OK to be an asshole.

8. **Focus on win-win.** Children (young and old) think that the world is a zero-sum game. If another kid is playing with the Dora doll, you can't. As people get older, they should realize that life doesn't have to be a win-lose proposition—unless, that is, you're an asshole.

9. **Focus on ways in which you are no better, or even worse, than others.** Thinking that you're smarter, faster, better looking, or funnier than others turns you into an asshole. Thinking that you're no better, or even worse, keeps you humble.

10. **Focus on ways in which you are similar to people, not different.** If you concentrate on how you and others have similar goals, desires, and passions, you're bound to be less of an asshole. How can you treat people who are similar to you with disdain?

11. **Tell yourself, "I have enough stuff (money, toys, friends, cars, whatever)."** Discontentment and envy are major factors in becoming an asshole. If you're happy, there's no reason to stomp on others.

How to Deal with Assholes

Let's say that you're not an asshole, but you have to cope with assholes. What can you do? That's the second $64,000 question that Sutton answers.

- **Hope for the best, but expect the worst.** One of the most frustrating aspects of dealing with assholes is that they disappoint you, making you wonder about the very value of humans. Lowering your expectations can help reduce disappointment. Don't solely lower your expectations, though, or you will slip into cynicism (and possibly turn into an asshole, too). Continue to hope for the best.

- **Develop indifference and emotional detachment.** Sutton may be the only author who has the insight and courage to recommend that being indifferent and detached may be a good thing in work environments. I would put this differently: Get tough and deal with it. Life isn't fair.

- **Look for small wins.** Small victories can keep you going. Most assholes pride themselves on total control and absolute domination. Any victory, no matter how small, can keep you going. Rest assured that small victories can lead to winning the war.

- **Limit your exposure.** You can do what you can to avoid meetings and interactions with assholes. This involves finding or building pockets of "safety, support, and sanity," to use Sutton's words. He cites an example of a nurse's lounge as a refuge from an asshole doctor.

- **Expose them.** In his blog, Sutton mentions Marge's Asshole Management Metric. This refers to a four-point system from 0 to 3. Marge, the boss, would point to people who were behaving like assholes and hold up one, two, or three fingers according to this code:

    1 = You are a normal person who can occasionally assert yourself on an issue you are passionate about, but you handle yourself in a nonconfrontational way on nearly all occasions.

    2 = You can consistently assert yourself in a nonconfrontational way and are occasionally an asshole, but you feel horrible about it afterward, and you may or may not apologize (but you probably will have to confess your remorse to someone).

    3 = You can consistently be an asshole, and you either do not recognize this or you simply enjoy it.

    By the way, 0 in her system means you are a very nice person, but very passive. No one can say a word against you, and no one would ever think to call you an asshole.

    If you are safe in your position, then calling assholes out is a good way to deal with them.

- **Band together and expose them.** Maybe you aren't safe in your position, so you cannot individually expose an asshole. In this case, band together with your fellow employees and then expose the asshole. It's one thing if only one person complains, but when several do, the trend is your friend. As my mother used to say, "When three people tell you that you're drunk, you catch a cab home," so get a few people to expose the asshole.

- **De-escalate and reeducate.** This strategy requires that the asshole you're dealing with isn't a "chronic," "certified," and "flagrant" asshole. It means meeting asshole behavior with calmness (instead of either similar behavior or fear) and trying to reeducate the person about how he's behaving.

One more thing about assholes: Standing up to them shouldn't scare you. While I was an Apple employee, I was in a meeting with a highly placed Apple exec and Apple's ad agency. The ad-agency person showed the new television spots and said he'd give a copy to the Apple exec and me. The Apple exec told the agency person not to give one to me. I spoke up: "Are you saying you don't trust me?" The Apple exec answered: "Yes." To which I replied, "That's OK because I don't trust you, either." You know what? The sun rose the next day, and my family still loved me.

CHAPTER 88

Is Your Boss an Asshole?

Love is bullshit. Emotion is bullshit. I am a rock.
A jerk. I'm an uncaring asshole and proud of it.

~ CHUCK PALAHNIUK

Q: How many bosses does it take to screw in a lightbulb?
A: One. He holds up the lightbulb and expects the universe to revolve around him.

At a basic level, determining if your boss is an asshole is easy: Is your boss rude? Asshole bosses keep people waiting, they yell and scream at people, and they are demeaning. They think they can get away with this because they *have* gotten away with this, because society tolerates bullshit from the rich and famous.

I digress, but I've often wondered which came first: Was the person always an asshole or did accomplishing something great (probably by luck) mean that people would tolerate bull-shiitake behavior? One thing is for sure: Not all assholes do great things, so there's no causal relationship.

Your boss is an asshole if he:

• **Thinks that the rules are different for him.** For example, a parking space for handicapped people is really for handicapped people *plus him,* because his time is so valuable that he can't walk fifty additional feet. Or, the carpool lane is for cars with multiple people, hybrids, and her, because she's late for a meeting.

- **Doesn't understand the difference between a position making a person and a person making a position.** The vice president of acquisitions for a big media company is a big deal, but all her power, and therefore the ability to act like an asshole, evaporates without this title. Assholes usually don't understand that their current position affords them temporary privileges.

- **Requires handlers.** This refers to a personal assistant, appointments secretary, public-relations flunky, and chauffeur. Of course, if an asshole didn't have the position/money/status, he could answer the phone, make appointments, talk to the press, and drive himself.

- **Requires the fulfillment of special requests in order to be happy/ productive/efficient.** For example, in order to make a speech, she needs a special brand of spring water from the south of France. Such action is flexing for the sake of flexing; none of this crap is necessary.

- **Relates to people primarily in terms of what they can do for him.** In other words, "good" people can do a lot for him. "Lousy" people aren't useful. The way a lousy person becomes a good person is by showing that he can help your boss in some way.

- **Judges people by his own values, not the employees' or society's values.** Assholes think that what they consider important is what everyone should consider important. For example, a boss may value only professional accomplishments and financial achievements, so that someone who is "merely" a mom or dad with a focus on a family is inferior.

- **Judges employees' results but his own intentions.** Assholes seldom come up short, because they judge their intentions ("I intended to do your quarterly review"), but they judge an employee only by results ("You didn't finish the software on time"). Instead, a boss should judge his results against his employees' results and never mix results and intentions.

- **Asks you to do something that he wouldn't do.** This is a good, all-purpose test. Does your boss ask you to fly coach while she flies first class? Does he ask you to work weekends while he's off at a hockey tournament?

I'm all for using boss time effectively (for example, not making her drop off a package at Federal Express), but were it not that your boss could be doing something more valuable for the company, would she do what she's asking you to do?

- **Calls employees any time of the day.** Rarely, as in once per year for an emergency, this is OK, but any more often and your boss is an asshole. His happiness is not your problem 24/7. You are entitled to your personal time and space and life.

- **Believes that the world is out to get her when faced with criticism or even omission.** For example, bloggers don't write about her because they are all jealous of her. Frankly, it's more likely that she's not worth writing about than the blogosphere is colluding against her. This boss needs to learn that "it's not always about her."

- **Slows down or halts your career progress.** One can forgive or ignore the previous ten issues, but this one is by far the worst thing an asshole boss can do. Usually it's a matter of convenience: "How can you leave me? I need you." For doing this, a boss should go into the *anals* of assholedom. God didn't put you on this earth to make your boss's life better, so don't hesitate to abandon a boss who holds you back.

Mean-spirited morons are still running much of the workplace, and it's time to take a stand. Most nastiness is directed by superiors to subordinates, so before taking a job, do your homework and screen them in advance. After all, avoidance is easier than curing.

To do this, I propose that you check your prospective boss's references just as she's checking out yours. I'm not suggesting that you ask your prospective boss for a list of references (you can try, but it may mean you don't get the job).

Instead, do a LinkedIn reference check. First, look her up to determine if you have any common connections. If so, find out more from people you trust. Second, use the LinkedIn reference-check tool to find people who overlapped with her in the past.

The beauty of this tool is that she doesn't even have to be a member of

LinkedIn. You simply specify the company and years of employment for her, and LinkedIn will show you people in your network who worked at that company during the same time.

Once you've located folks to serve as a reference check, you need to know what to ask. This is where Badass Bob Sutton comes in. He prepared this list of questions for you.

- **Kisses up and kicks down:** "How does the prospective boss respond to feedback from people higher in rank and lower in rank? Can you provide examples from experience?" One characteristic of certified assholes is that they tend to demean those who are less powerful while brownnosing their superiors.

- **Can't take it:** "Does the prospective boss accept criticism or blame when the going gets tough?" Be wary of people who constantly dish out criticism but can't take a healthy dose themselves.

- **Short fuse:** "In what situations have you seen the prospective boss lose his temper?" Sometimes anger is justified, even effective when used sparingly, but someone who shoots the messenger too often can breed a climate of fear in the workplace. Are coworkers scared of getting in an elevator with this person?

- **Bad credit:** "Which style best describes the prospective boss: gives out gratuitous credit, assigns credit where credit is due, or believes everyone should be their own champion?" This question opens the door to discuss whether or not someone tends to take a lot of credit while not recognizing the work of his or her team.

- **Canker sore:** "What do past collaborators say about working with the prospective boss?" Assholes usually have a history of infecting teams with nasty and dysfunctional conflict. The world seems willing to tolerate talented assholes, but that doesn't mean *you* have to.

- **Flamer:** What kind of e-mail sender is the prospective boss? Most assholes cannot contain themselves when it comes to e-mail: flaming people, carbon copying the world, blind carbon copying to cover his own buttocks. E-mail etiquette is a window into one's soul.

- **Downer:** "What types of people find it difficult to work with the prospective boss? What types of people seem to work very well with the prospective boss?" Pay attention to responses that suggest "strong-willed" or "self-motivated" people tend to work best with the person, because assholes tend to leave people around them feeling de-energized and deflated.

- **Card shark:** "Does the prospective boss share information for everyone's benefit?" A tendency to hold cards close to the chest—i.e., a reluctance to share information—is a sign that this person treats coworkers as competitors who must be defeated so he or she can get ahead.

- **Army of one:** "Would people pick the prospective boss for their team?" Sometimes there is an upside to having an asshole on your team, but that won't matter if the coworkers refuse to work with him. Use this question to help determine if the benefit of having the prospective boss on your team outweighs any asshole behaviors.

- **Open architecture:** "How would the prospective boss respond if a copy of *The No Asshole Rule* appeared on her desk?" Be careful if the answer is, "Duck!"

You may believe that only you think your boss is an asshole. If so, I offer the "Kawasaki theory of perfect information about assholes." It goes like this: If you think your boss is an asshole, most likely everyone else does, too. It's seldom true that you think someone is an asshole and everyone else thinks he's great.

CHAPTER 89

The Top Seventeen Lies of CEOs

I'm not upset that you lied to me,

I'm upset that from now on I can't believe you.

~ FRIEDRICH NIETZSCHE

While asshole bosses are fresh in our minds, here is a list of the top lies of CEOs. Glenn Kelman of Redfin helped me compile this list of real-world fibs that come down from high places. If you are a CEO, you should perform a reality check with this list.

1. **"Working together, we've established our goals."** In other words, these are the goals that the CEO decided will make him look good. Few managers believe that these goals are doable, and yet they are the ones who are going to have to accomplish them. But that's what "working together" means: The CEO decides and the workers do.

2. **"It's like a startup around here."** This could mean that the place lacks adult supervision, money is running out, the product is behind schedule, investors have given up, and employees are paid below market rates. Or it could mean that the company is energized, entrepreneurial, making meaning, and kicking butt. Just double-check.

3. **"Your project will be a skunk works reporting directly to me."** This means that no one else at the management level buys into the idea. The

CEO might protect you, as this lie implies. Or, you may be fighting for your life against the naysayers when the CEO moves on to the next brilliant idea du jour.

4. **"I wanted to do this, but the board wouldn't let me."** This is a cop-out. A good CEO tells the board what she's doing. She doesn't seek permission—forgiveness maybe, but never permission. So this statement means one of two things: The CEO didn't really try her best to get something approved, or the board is losing confidence in her.

5. **"I expect you to figure this out."** This is a loaded, backhanded compliment. It's supposed to mean, "I have such confidence in you that I know you can do this." Sometimes it does mean this. Most times, though, it means that the CEO has no clue and is praying that you can save his butt.

6. **"Our sales pipeline looks good."** This means that the vice president of sales leaned on the regional sales manager who leaned on the regional sales rep to pump up the forecast, because the CEO doesn't want to look bad to the board of directors.

7. **"We will be profitable soon."** After he leaned on the sales organization and it "came through with a great pipeline," the CEO could then "reliably" predict profitability. He never did check with the CFO, though. If the company isn't profitable, then it's the fault of the vice president of sales or the CFO, anyway.

8. **"The stock price is not important; what's important is building a great company."** There are a handful of visionary CEOs who mean this when they say it. However, you don't work for one of them. If one could get an honest answer out of CEOs, most would tell you that they'd rather have a rising stock price than a great company. Very few have the courage to build a great company and trust that a rising stock price is a natural outcome of this accomplishment.

9. **"I've never worked with a better group of people."** This can be a legitimate morale-boosting statement when it is infrequently made.

However, if a CEO spouts this off more than once every five to ten years and you know there are clearly bozos on the team (often protected by the CEO), then you know that he's playing you.

10. **"I'm open to new ideas."** The CEO must have recently read a book by a management guru. She's certainly open to her own new ideas. She's probably open to new ideas from the consultants that she hired at $10,000/day. Maybe she read a new idea in a blog, God help us. But is she open to new ideas from the rank-and-file employees who really know how to fix the company?

11. **"I want to hear the truth; I don't want yes-men around me."** Maybe this is the truth: He doesn't want yes-men around—or maybe he wants yes-women. But it could be that he's so arrogant that he believes that he's always right, so there's nothing to disagree with. But most likely he's just lying, and he wants people to always agree with him.

12. **"I will gladly step aside when the time comes."** Sure, with a $10 million severance package, who wouldn't be glad to step aside?

13. **"This is how we did it at (name of previous company he was fired from), and it worked."** And that's why the company let him go. And that's why the employees at the previous company rejoiced when the news spread. And, unfortunately, that's why the directors of this company hired him: because he was a senior-level packaged-goods guy who was available, and the board thought that your tech products should be sold like laundry detergent.

14. **"I don't need to understand all that whiz-bang stuff to be a good CEO."** Absolutely. Your customers aren't that smart. Neither are your employees, vendors, and partners. The CEO just needs to stand there tall, white, and gray-haired and let everyone kiss his ring.

15. **"I don't need to rehearse my speech."** He's not going to gauge audience reaction, because his limo is waiting to whisk him away. He'll simply ask his handlers, Trixie and Biff, how they think he did. And they will tell him that the emperor has very fine clothes indeed.

16. **"We are a customer-focused company."** If only the CEO had appended two additional words: "this quarter." Because next quarter the company will be an innovation-driven company. And the quarter after that, a Six Sigma–driven company. And the quarter after that, the company will be producing purple cows. And the quarter after that, it will be evangelistic (depending on whether the CEO reads my book or Seth's first).

17. **"I can telecommute and still keep my house on the golf course in Carmel."** The CEO should be living and dying with the company. If anything, he should be there more than anyone else.

Rather than these lies, here are four things a CEO should say:

1. "I don't know."

2. "Thank you."

3. "Do what's right."

4. "It's my fault."

However, in all my interactions with dozens of CEOs, I can't remember many instances of any of them uttering such wisdom.

What's Your EQ (Entrepreneurial Quotient)?

I believe that the testing of the student's achievements in order to see if he meets some criterion held by the teacher is directly contrary to the implications of therapy for significant learning.

~ CARL ROGERS

We're coming to the end of this book. The last section will cover the reality of doing good, but before we get to that, here is a real-world quiz to determine your "entrepreneurial quotient." The intent is to test your knowledge of the subject of entrepreneurship, not to test how good an entrepreneur you are, because there's no way to measure that. Therefore, scoring high doesn't mean you're the next Steve Jobs, and scoring low doesn't mean you're not. This makes the EQ test as reliable as the IQ test, but it can't hurt to have a good working knowledge of the reality of entrepreneurship.

1. Your company is creating a new software product. The lead programmer has just shown you a working prototype and has promised that it will be done in six months. You should assume that it will really be completed in:
   a. 3 months
   b. 6 months
   c. 12 months
   d. 18 months
   e. Shortly after money runs out

2. When you're starting a new company, you shouldn't be afraid of polarizing people with a new product or service that flies in the face of convention.
   a. True
   b. False

3. Patents are the main way to make your company defensible and able to withstand the challenges of competitors.
   a. True
   b. False

4. The foundation of a successful brand is:
   a. Effective marketing
   b. Evangelistic customers
   c. Extensive advertising
   d. Attractive packaging
   e. An excellent product or service

5. Ultimately, who positions a product or service, establishing how customers will come to view it?
   a. The company that makes it
   b. The company's advertising agency
   c. The company's PR firm
   d. The customers themselves
   e. The press and industry analysts

6. If you want your company to be successful, it's most important to strive for which objective?
   a. To be the lowest-cost producer
   b. To be the best-known brand
   c. To be the most profitable company
   d. To be the sole provider of something people really want
   e. To have the largest customer base

7. When pitching potential investors, you should keep your presentation to how many slides?
   a. 0–5

    b. 10–15

    c. 30–40

    d. 1

    e. 60

8. As long as the founders own more than half of the company, they control the company.

    a. True

    b. False

9. Pick the statement that means a venture capitalist isn't interested in your business.

    a. "You're too early right now."

    b. "We don't have expertise in that area."

    c. "If you find other investors, come back to us."

    d. "Come back to us after you're shipped."

    e. All of the above.

10. Which part of a business plan is the most important?

    a. Financial projections

    b. Management biographies

    c. Competitive analysis

    d. Executive summary

    e. The product description

11. More than anything, you don't want your business model to be:

    a. Specific

    b. Simple

    c. Unique

    d. Scalable

    e. Proven

12. Which of the following key assumptions do you have to test when starting a company?

    a. Number of sales calls a salesperson can make

    b. Conversion rate of prospects to customers

    c. Length of sales cycle

d. Amount of technical support needed per unit sold

e. All of the above

13. A company that is bootstrapping should avoid which management practice?

    a. Managing for cash flow instead of profitability

    b. Trying to recruit a "dream" management team of proven executives

    c. Positioning against the industry leader

    d. Building a bottom-up forecast

    e. Collecting fast and paying slow

14. Many behemoth companies like Microsoft, General Electric, and 3M have broad and disparate product lines, but ironically started out with a focus on one specific product.

    a. True

    b. False

15. You've just met with reps of a key potential account. This could be a large sale and also bolster your company's credibility in the industry. However, they are afraid to do business with a startup. The best way to win them over is to:

    a. Ask your world-famous venture capitalist investor to call the customer.

    b. Arrange for the CEO of your company to meet with the buyer.

    c. Offer to do a pilot implementation at a deep discount.

    d. Tell the customer that you will contact them once your company is proven in the marketplace.

    e. Have your mom provide a character reference for you.

16. In the first sixty seconds of a presentation, you should:

    a. Furnish your biographical background

    b. Establish the size of the market you are addressing

    c. Provide a summary of your financial projections

    d. Summarize the technical foundation of your product or service

    e. Explain what your company does

17. What's the most important factor to consider when selecting the first employees at a startup?

a. The candidates' academic background

b. The candidates' work experience

c. The candidates' love of your product or service

d. The candidates' willingness to work for stock in lieu of salary

e. The candidates' prior personal relationship with you

18. Why should you never offer stock to an employee in lieu of salary?

a. Doing so sets an implicit price for your stock.

b. It could take a long time to raise venture capital, so the employee might amass a large amount of stock.

c. This practice is prohibited by law.

d. a and b

e. a, b, and c

19. The purpose of providing an offer letter to a job candidate is to:

a. Establish a starting point for negotiation

b. Demonstrate that the company is serious about an offer

c. Confirm what both parties have already verbally agreed to

d. Create an audit trail for the human resources department

e. All of the above

20. The best reason to form a partnership is to:

a. Increase revenues or decrease costs

b. Get the attention of analysts

c. Garner press coverage

d. Scare your competitors

e. Impress potential investors

21. The reason to put an out clause in a partnership agreement is

a. To enable you to get out of a bad deal

b. To make your lawyers happy

c. To enable both parties to work comfortably with each other

d. Because all agreements have out clauses

e. None of the above

22. The CEO of your company just told you that he and the CEO of another company have agreed to a partnership. Your first task, as vice president of strategic alliances, is to

  a. Contact the PR firms of both organizations to coordinate the announcement

  b. Contact the vice president of marketing of both organizations to coordinate the announcement

  c. Meet with the middle managers and individual contributors in your company who are going to have to make this partnership work

  d. Thoroughly research the other company to determine how best to work with it

  e. Begin drafting a rollout plan for the partnership

Answers: 1. c; 2. a; 3. b; 4. e; 5. d; 6. d; 7. b; 8. b; 9. e; 10. d; 11. c; 12. e; 13. b; 14. a; 15. c; 16. e; 17. c; 18. d; 19. c; 20. a; 21. c; 22. c.

What your score means:

• **0–5.** Your score is low, so you could use a little more knowledge about the subject of entrepreneurship. However, don't get discouraged or enroll in an MBA program, because this doesn't mean you won't be a great entrepreneur.

• **6–16.** You know just enough to know what you don't know. If you've got the passion for entrepreneurship, you're ready to roll.

• **17–22.** Your score is high, so you can now focus on doing, not learning.

The Reality of Doing Good

The final section of this book explains the reality of doing good. It's included because I believe that at the end of one's life, you are measured not by how much money you made, how many houses you own, or even how many books you wrote. Instead, you are measured by how much you've made the world a better place.

CHAPTER 90

The Six Lessons of Kiva

The deed is everything, the glory naught.

~ JOHANN WOLFGANG VON GOETHE

T he purpose of this chapter is to show you how nonprofits provide great lessons, too. Matt and Jessica Jackley Flannery created Kiva to enable people to make microloans to entrepreneurs around the world. The results are awesome: More than 123,000 people lent more than $12.4 million to 18,000 entrepreneurs as of 2008. There are so many lenders that limits have recently been placed on the number of individual lenders so that everyone can make a loan.

The process involves reading a short profile about each entrepreneur and then deciding which to fund. From beginning to end, you can make a loan in less than five minutes. Although lenders do not earn interest, the microfinance organizations that helped Kiva find the entrepreneurs do get a fee. To date, the entrepreneurs have repaid 99.67% of the loans.

These are the lessons that any entrepreneur can learn from Kiva:

1. **Create meaningful partnerships.** Most entrepreneurs create partnerships to impress investors, journalists, customers, and parents. Hence, most partnerships are bull shiitake. The best test of a partnership is whether its existence requires that you change revenues or costs in a spreadsheet. No changes mean a nonsense partnership. Kiva has sixty-seven

partnerships with microfinance organizations. It is these organizations that provide the leads to entrepreneurs for lenders to fund.

Also, Kiva has partnerships with PayPal (free transactions) and Google (free traffic), as well as with Yahoo!, Microsoft, MySpace, and YouTube. As you can imagine, these kinds of partnerships do make you change your spreadsheet.

2. **Catalyze and support evangelism.** Kiva has 250 active volunteers for its service. These folks want to help Kiva make the world a better place by fostering entrepreneurship. Evangelism starts with a great product or service, and that's why companies like Apple, Harley-Davidson, TiVo, and now Kiva have evangelists.

3. **Find a business model.** You'd be surprised how many people wave their hands or avoid the topic of business model completely. Kiva's model is a minimum $2.50 voluntary fee that lenders pay when checking out their "shopping cart." Yes, you read this right: Lenders receive no interest and pay a voluntary fee to Kiva in order to lend money. And you thought Google had a great business model.

4. **Bank on unproven people.** What would the ideal background be of the founder of Kiva? Investment banker from Goldman Sachs? Vice president of the World Bank? Vice president of the Peace Corps? Vice president of the Rockefeller Foundation? Partner at McKinsey? How about temporary administrative assistant at the Stanford Business School? Because that's how Jessica started her quest.

5. **Focus on free marketing.** Kiva launched in 2005 with seven businesses in Uganda. The first "marketing" was sending out an e-mail to Jessica and Matt's wedding invitation list. All seven businesses were funded in a weekend. Then the Daily Kos picked up their story from a hacked-together press release. Then PBS's *Frontline* covered the organization, and loan volume went from $3,000 to $30,000 overnight. No road show. No press tour. No conference circuit.

6. **Ignore the naysayers.** The Flannerys got advice that Kiva couldn't send money around the Internet without government approval, couldn't scale

beyond a few African villages, couldn't offer an investment product, and couldn't comply with the Patriot Act. As George Orwell should have said, "Ignoring is bliss."

Now do you think you're in a tough business? Because all Kiva had to do was deal with banking regulations around the world, find qualified borrowers thousands of miles from its home office, and convince people to loan money to those borrowers at zero interest and to pay a fee for this privilege. There's a lot we can learn from Kiva.

CHAPTER 91

Social Entrepreneurship

> Once social change begins, it cannot be reversed. You cannot
> uneducate the person who has learned to read. You cannot humiliate
> the person who feels pride. You cannot oppress the people who are
> not afraid anymore. We have seen the future, and the future is ours.
>
> ~ CÉSAR CHÁVEZ

David Bornstein is the author of *How to Change the World: Social Entrepreneurs and the Power of New Ideas* (Oxford University Press, rev. ed. 2007). No less than Nelson Mandela said the book is "wonderfully hopeful and enlightening." This interview explains social entrepreneurship and how this special kind of enterprise changes the world.

Q: Are there fundamental differences between social and for-profit organization founders?

A: Depends what you mean by fundamental. In terms of temperament, skills, drive, the way they ask questions and think about problems, social and business founders are very much the same creatures. We see more and more social founders who are using a business format to achieve their objectives. So a social founder doesn't have to run a nonprofit, and in the future you will see a lot more for-profit social entrepreneurship, as well as a lot of blending of legal formats.

The difference is really in what the founder seeks to maximize. What is the primary motivation behind building your organization, whatever form it takes? Are you trying to develop drugs for diseases that afflict large numbers of poor people in the developing world, as Victoria Hale is doing with One World Health, or are you trying to dominate the world market for sneakers or fashionable jockey shorts? For-profit entrepreneurs build all kinds of things. Social entrepreneurs are primarily motivated by an ethical imperative. They seek to respond to urgent needs. The question of why is paramount.

Q: Are there fundamental differences in the people who go to work for a social versus nonprofit startup?

A: The big difference is that the folks who go work for a startup focusing on creating a social change are less motivated to make a lot of money, because that usually isn't the upside. If you are phenomenally successful, you don't get rich—you change the world. That difference must somehow relate to the hierarchy of values that govern that person's decisions and what they feel they need to accomplish to be happy and feel good about themselves or, alternatively, to gain the approval of those whose esteem and admiration they are seeking.

Q: In the for-profit world, you keep score with sales revenue. How do you keep score in the not-for-profit world?

A: It is very tough, because it is all apples and oranges and plums. In business, you can compare the financial performance of companies whether they sell coffee or cars. How do you compare the success of an organization that helps disabled people to live more independent and dignified lives with that of an organization that provides after-school enrichment to low-income children? There is no single yardstick that is comparable to revenues or profits in business, but within subindustries—say college access or health-care access or environmental advocacy—there are clearly some organizations that achieve more impact per dollar spent than other organizations.

It isn't as simple as putting the data on a spreadsheet and doing a calculation. But by combining some well-thought-through metrics or proxies that relate to other forms of nonnumeric evidence or analysis, it is possible to make reasoned, reliable judgments about which organizations are doing the best work and which ones should, accordingly, have greater access at a lower cost to growth capital.

In the end, it's really not that different from what many investors and rating agencies do intuitively in business. Investors look at many intangibles—the team, the enthusiasm, the quality of the problem solving, the drive, the goodwill, the potential for growth—when they make decisions. You can do the same with social entrepreneurs.

Q: How can social entrepreneurs attract talent when there aren't high salaries and options?

A: By offering people employment opportunities that align with their talents, interests, and values. By inspiring them with a vision of changing the world, of being part of something bigger than themselves. We have to think about an assumption behind this question, namely the notion that people seek to maximize how much money they make. Certainly, we all care about making money. But choices that people make every day—becoming teachers, having children, giving money to charity—indicate that we are complex creatures motivated by many different things.

We are also at an interesting point in America's history. With all our wealth and freedom of choice, we seem to be obsessed with finding happiness. Every day it seems another book is published focusing on how we can make ourselves happy. Most Americans today are phenomenally wealthy compared to their grandparents, yet many studies show we are no happier, and we actually may be less so. At the very top of the list of things that make people feel happy and fulfilled is doing work that you find challenging and deeply meaningful with colleagues whom you respect and care for. Social entrepreneurship offers this.

Q: Is this why many prominent businesspeople move into social entrepreneurship?

A: Businesspeople are moving into social entrepreneurship for the same reasons that so many other people across society are moving into this field: They see new opportunities to solve problems in creative ways. As individuals, they have far more power to understand and address problems at scale than in the past. They see enormous needs to solve problems that aren't being addressed by traditional institutions, whether businesses, governments, or nonprofits, and they have lived through what may be described as the "failure of success"—the extraordinary accumulation of wealth and possessions over the past fifty years that has left people feeling dissatisfied and often empty.

When Bill Gates announced that he would be stepping down from Microsoft to run his foundation, he made it clear that he was not retiring but rather reordering his priorities. Why? It was through his research trips in the developing world that he came face-to-face with people suffering and dying—and he couldn't shake it. He saw that he could be more valuable to the world helping to develop AIDS or malaria vaccines, or expanding access to health-care systems, than helping to create more software tools, as valuable as those tools may be. Lots of people are coming to similar conclusions. It is like a global awakening.

Q: People celebrate when a corporate mogul ditches the big bucks and goes to work for a nonprofit, but has the opposite occurred, too?

A: What we're seeing today is much more interflow between business and social entrepreneurship. It's increasingly common to find people who have been working on social or environmental issues for many years who discover a business opportunity that will augment their impact.

The surge of entrepreneurship in CleanTech is a perfect example. It's driven by many people who cut their teeth working in the environmental field and who see business as a powerful engine to achieve their environmental goals. In the health arena, we are beginning to see more health professionals or people from public-health careers starting businesses that are aimed at solving problems well suited to a business model. More and more people are becoming "sector agnostics"; they are seeking impact and looking for the best tools to do the job. This trend looks likely to continue.

Q: What makes some people take action and others to just cogitate?

A: It's hard to say. Why do people who are procrastinating for months suddenly kick in gear and get their taxes done on April 14? At a certain point, the pain of not acting—getting hit with a penalty—overtakes the pain of actually doing your taxes. The same may apply to other aspects of life. There is emotional pain associated with inaction, especially if we care about something. So to the degree that we help people gain more and more exposures to problems in ways that make it more difficult to emotionally accept those problems, we will see more action.

On the other hand, there is the upside of action—the anticipated pleasure and satisfaction. So, to take the tax example again, if you know you're in for a big refund, you may be motivated to get your taxes done in January, so you can collect as soon as possible. The upside of taking action—the pleasure of collaboration, the feeling of satisfaction and the thrill of making a change happen, the joy in giving—are all potentially great motivators. But often we forget to talk about these aspects of change.

The bottom line is that we focus on the "doing good" aspects, on the sacrifice and ethical components, but we often forget to mention how wonderful it feels to take meaningful action in line with your core beliefs. Finally, people often delay because they just don't know where to go, what to do, or how to take the first step. So there is a big need for tools that help people find their place in the field of social entrepreneurship and social innovation. That is actually the subject of the current book I am working on.

Q: What are the things that keep potential social entrepreneurs from succeeding in fulfilling their potential?

A: The major blockage is the lack of rationally allocated growth funding that would allow people to build world-class institutions. Most of our major businesses are able to raise hundreds of millions of dollars in capital markets—through debt or by issuing stock. But social entrepreneurs have to raise considerable grant funding from foundations, which usually comes in small, short-term installments. Because the funding is so fragmented, social entrepreneurs end up spending 80 percent of their time fundraising rather than running their organizations.

This is a huge bottleneck. Social entrepreneurs who run "social enterprises" have a similar problem—the difficulty in finding patient growth capital targeted at businesses that seek to maximize social, environmental, and economic returns all at once. A corollary of this problem is the difficulty in recruiting and retaining highly talented people. Another blockage is the lack of two-way bridges between social entrepreneurs and both business entrepreneurs and governments.

Q: Then what could government or society do to encourage more social entrepreneurship?

A: There are many levels at which social entrepreneurship can and should be encouraged. At its essence, the goal is to help build a society in which many, many people have the confidence, skill, and desire to solve problems they see around them. The most important qualities in social entrepreneurship are empathy, the ability to collaborate well with others, and the stubborn belief that it's possible to make a difference—which motivates and stimulates people to act.

There are many ways to improve the education system so that young people have experiences that build these qualities and give them a sense of agency, a sense of their own power connected to an ethical framework. I would argue that this should be one of the fundamental goals of education. Once a child has had this experience, that child will never go back to being a passive member of society. She will always be asking the question—Why don't we fix this problem?—and causing waves of creative destruction wherever she goes.

We could build such experiences into the curriculum of every school and college. We could use our powerful media to make the field of social entrepreneurship more visible. At more advanced levels, social entrepreneurs need a variety of financial and structural supports—new laws, less fragmented and more rational capital markets, and stronger bridges with governments, business, and academia. There's lots of work for anyone who has some creativity and likes to be a positive deviant.

Q: Who is the Steve Jobs of social entrepreneurship?

A: The most famous social entrepreneur would be Muhammad Yunus, the founder of the Grameen Bank. Like Jobs, Yunus took a product—credit—that was once an exclusive item (like the first computers) and brought it to a mass audience. In so doing, his bank helped to democratize access to capital in a way that is similar to the way that Apple Computer democratized access to information. The effect is similar: more choice and self-determination in the hands of more people globally.

Q: Is the entrepreneur in the middle of Africa who gets a microloan and supports his or her family much different from Bill Gates or Steve Jobs?

A: Yes and no. In terms of vision and aspiration, the Bill Gateses and Steve Jobses of the world are pretty rare. Forget about Africa—there are many people born into the heart of privilege, with the best education, broad exposures, and lots of confidence, who don't become entrepreneurs. It's just not what draws them. Entrepreneurs are most excited by making their visions real. Other people derive their greatest satisfaction from different things—interpersonal relations, perhaps, or teaching or healing or making beautiful music.

There is not much difference between leading business entrepreneurs, like Bill Gates and Steve Jobs, and leading social entrepreneurs, like Jim Grant, Muhammad Yunus, Fazle Abed, and Bill Drayton. But clearly not everyone has the temperament and desire to be a for-profit entrepreneur—thank goodness!

There are also entrepreneurs at many different levels. Some people build small organizations, some build medium-size ones, and some build large ones. The difference is what's most important to them in life, how big they allow themselves to dream, and where they come to rest along the way. Without a doubt, millions of microentrepreneurs in Africa and Bangladesh and all around the developing world have massive pools of untapped and underutilized potential.

Given the right structural supports and exposures, including capital, many of them would go on to build very successful companies or social organizations; a subset of them would go on to build world-class firms, just as in the United States. But, lest we overemphasize the role of entrepreneurs, it's important to realize that they are only one ingredient in the change process.

Entrepreneurs are successful only to the degree that they can bring together other people with different talents and abilities who can, as a team, build things they could never do separately. Entrepreneurs are hubs or magnets: organizing forces. It takes many hands working together to produce any significant change.

I was on the board of a para-church organization called Hawaiian Islands Ministry, and a Montessori school called Bowman International School. From firsthand experience, I can tell you that social entrepreneurs and for-profit entrepreneurs share the same challenges: determining their organization's purpose, raising money, positioning, branding, and hiring. David is right on— so take what he's provided here and change the world.

CHAPTER 92

Making the Transition from the Corporate to Nonprofit World

Sympathy is no substitute for action.

~ DAVID LIVINGSTONE

R ichard Stearns is the president of World Vision. This is a "Christian relief and development organization dedicated to helping children and their communities worldwide reach their full potential by tackling the causes of poverty." He was the president and chief executive officer of Lenox Inc., overseeing $500 million in annual sales. He joined World Vision as president in 1998. His interview provides insights into the transition from the corporate to the nonprofit world and lessons to learn from an organization that raises billions of dollars every year.

Q: You had a nearly seven-figure salary and a corporate Jaguar, yet you moved and took a 75 percent cut in pay. Why did you leave the corporate sector in 1998 after twenty-three years to run an international Christian humanitarian organization?

A: It wasn't something I planned. At the time, I didn't even want the job. I had been a donor to World Vision for fifteen years when, through a long series of circumstances, I was approached by the group, interviewed, and offered the position. As a committed Christian, I felt I couldn't say no. When God gives you an opportunity to serve, you obey. I had talked the talk of being a Christian for many years, now I needed to walk the walk. It has turned out to be the greatest privilege of my life to serve the poorest of the poor in Christ's name.

Q: What was the biggest adjustment to your new role?

A: There have been lots of adjustments. Business travel now means getting shots and medicine for yellow fever, malaria, typhoid, and hepatitis. I used to travel to London, Paris, and Milan, sharing thousand-dollar dinners with the heads of other luxury-goods companies. Now I'm visiting desperate people in places like Ethiopia, India, Peru, and Uganda. I'm more likely to be visiting garbage dumps, brothels, and refugee camps than five-star hotels.

Q: What are the greatest differences and similarities between running a major corporation and running a large nonprofit?

A: They are both businesses with revenues, expenses, and a bottom line. Both have marketing, sales, finance, IT, HR, strategy, etc. Perhaps the biggest difference is that our bottom line is changed lives—money is simply a means to that end. Our shareholders are the poor, and our donors who make our work possible.

Q: How much money does World Vision raise every year?

A: Worldwide, World Vision raises about $2 billion annually; the U.S. office, which I head up, raises about half of the total.

Q: Is this the 80/20 rule—20 percent of the people send in 80 percent of the money—or are donations more spread out?

A: World Vision's strength is that we are supported by hundreds of thousands of faithful people who give us about a dollar a day by sponsoring children. Our major donors account for less than 5 percent of our total income. Also, for a nonprofit, we have quite a diversified portfolio of revenue. Just over 40 percent is cash from private citizens; 30 percent is government grants in food and cash; and about 30 percent is in the form of products donated from corporations—what we call gifts in kind.

Q: Are you trying to end poverty or evangelize Christianity?

A: As a Christian organization, we are motivated by our commitment to Christ to love our neighbors and care for the less fortunate. That's why we do what we do. We don't proselytize. We do not force our religious beliefs on anyone, and we don't discriminate in our delivery of aid in any way. If the people we serve want to know why we are there, we tell them. St. Francis once said, "Preach the gospel at all times. Use words if necessary." Love put into action is a compelling and attractive worldview.

Q: How can people who do not want to radically change their lives make a difference in the lives of the poor?

A: To really change the world, values must change. Consider the civil rights movement. Racial discrimination was once openly accepted in the United States. Today it is unacceptable to our mainstream culture. Very few of us are civil rights activists, but we let our values speak in our workplaces, in our schools, and to our elected officials.

Today we live in a world that tolerates extreme poverty much as racism was tolerated fifty-plus years ago. We can all become people determined to do something to change the world. We can speak up, we can volunteer, and we can give. Ending extreme poverty will take money, political and moral will, and a shift in our value system. When enough ordinary people embrace these issues, things will begin to change.

Q: In the eyes of God, do you think someone who goes to Africa and helps AIDS victims is better or worse than someone who writes a check every month?

A: I can't speak for God, but I believe God is pleased whenever anyone does something out of love to help the downtrodden. Hands, hearts, and checkbooks are all vital. If we all just did a little—our part—we could change the world.

Q: What keeps you awake at night as the CEO of World Vision?

A: If I thought every moment about the incredible suffering around the world,

I would never sleep. I worry about keeping the covenant we have with the poor and with our donors. It is a very sacred responsibility.

Q: What are the biggest hurdles to alleviating poverty?

A: One word: apathy. The very frustrating part is that we actually have the knowledge and the ability to end most extreme poverty. The world just doesn't care enough to do it. The U.S. government has spent more than $400 billion on the war in Iraq to date.

Our annual humanitarian assistance budget for the whole world is only about $21 billion. We spend less than a half percent of our federal budget on humanitarian assistance, and less than 2 percent of private charitable giving goes to international causes. People and governments make choices based on their priorities. Poverty is still not a high priority for the world.

Q: What's the biggest obstacle to getting rich people to care about poor people?

A: The obstacle is that poverty is often not personal. If your next-door neighbor's child was dying and you could save her for $100, you wouldn't think twice. But a child 10,000 miles away whom you have never met—that's just different.

About 29,000 kids die every day of preventable causes—29,000! These kids have names and faces, hopes and dreams. Their parents love them as much as we love our kids. We've got to make poverty personal. Stalin once said: "A single death is a tragedy, a million deaths is a statistic." We must try to see the face of the one child.

Q: Why is World Vision so successful at fund-raising?

A: The real secret of our fund-raising is the notion of child sponsorship. We allow people to see the face of that one child—we make that child real to them. It is very difficult to raise money for poverty eradication but much easier to raise money to help a specific child. That makes it personal.

Of course, we also have fiendishly clever and committed marketing people who really care about their cause. We also represent an amazingly compelling selling proposition: Where else can you spend your money and know that you may have saved a life or changed the world for the better?

Q: How has technology affected World Vision's work?

A: Not enough. I think we have just scratched the surface in using technology and the Internet to change the values of Americans and to raise money for our cause. Technology can make this abstract and faraway notion of global poverty real. We can take you straight to Africa via the Web and let you meet your sponsored child. We can show you the village celebration when a drilling rig strikes clean water for the first time, or a clinic or school is dedicated. We are beginning to experiment with techniques to bring this stuff to life for people. Maybe some of your readers could help us.

Q: What advice would you give to someone reading this who is considering leaving a corporate job to "change the world"?

A: There's a tendency among those uninformed about global poverty to say, "This ain't rocket science. People are hungry; let's feed them." What they don't realize is that the deeper you get into relief and development, you realize it really is rocket science. Problems like poverty, disease, and hunger are humanity's most intractable problems. They haven't been solved in 5,000 years, and they won't be solved overnight.

We need to systematically address a wide range of social, environmental, cultural, political, and religious issues. But the good news is that we do have the answers. Now, we just need the resolve to make poverty reduction a priority and persevere until we see results. We can fix this; we really can.

Q: Do the efforts of rock stars and movie stars really help alleviate poverty and AIDS, or are these people just seeking more publicity to sell albums?

A: They make a difference. Given the number of celebrities in our world, it is actually shocking that so few of them are using their celebrity to make a difference. Bono is amazing. He has perhaps done more for the poor than anyone in the last century. I call him Martin Luther Bono because he has really been the leader of our movement.

Bill and Melinda Gates are changing the global landscape for health and development. The media rarely want to talk to me about poverty, but many reporters gush at the chance to talk with Brad Pitt, Angelina Jolie, or Oprah. That's just the way it is. I welcome celebrities who really want to make a difference.

Q: How do you want World Vision to be perceived twenty-five years from now?

A: I want World Vision to be the best at what we do. There is too much at stake to be anything less. If it could be said of us that we gave the poor a voice, that we provoked the rich and the powerful to action, and that we gave hope to people trapped in hopelessness, I would be deeply gratified. My favorite Bible passage is from the book of Job. It would make a wonderful epigraph for World Vision:

Whoever heard me spoke well of me, and those who saw me commended me, because I rescued the poor who cried for help, and the fatherless who had none to assist him.

The man who was dying blessed me; I made the widow's heart sing. I put on righteousness as my clothing; justice was my robe and my turban.

I was eyes to the blind and feet to the lame. I was a father to the needy; I took up the case of the stranger. I broke the fangs of the wicked; and snatched the victims from their teeth. (Job 29: 11–17)

I must admit that "Martin Luther Bono" has a nice ring to it. Stearns provides powerful contrasts. On the one hand, he says that the key to fund-raising is to let every donor know that they are saving a particular child. Then he says that people like Bono and Angelina Jolie are also important to making a difference. My takeaway from this interview is that we should use all our tools and not get stuck thinking that the way people have done things in an industry is the only way to do them.

CHAPTER 93

The Art of Surviving

When the Japanese mend broken objects, they aggrandize the damage by filling the cracks with gold. They believe that when something's suffered damage and has a history it becomes more beautiful.

~ BARBARA BLOOM

Jerry White is the cofounder of Survivor Corps (formerly Landmine Survivors Network). His life changed in 1984 when he lost his leg in a land-mine explosion while visiting Israel. After this experience, he has championed the cause of survivorship and become a leader in the International Campaign to Ban Landmines. In 1997, this organization, Jerry, and Jody Williams shared the Nobel Peace Prize. He also wrote a book called *I Will Not Be Broken: Five Steps to Overcoming a Life Crisis* (St. Martin's Press, 2008).

Q: What do people who are undergoing a life crisis need most?

A. We crave empathy and support. We need to know that someone out there—anyone!—understands what we are going through. Yes, there are emergency *things* we need, like safety, food, shelter, direct assistance, but ultimately we are social beings in search of social connection and meaning.

Q: What do they need most from their government?

A: Governments add most value during emergency situations when they address macro issues, such as the rule of law, security, resource mobilization, strategic communications, respect for human rights without discrimination, and coordination of services. Unfortunately, recent examples like Hurricane Katrina and the current mortgage crisis suggest that government too often fails us and is slow to react to mass destruction.

It takes a village to survive emergencies, with help from the private sector, social sector, and public sector. No single government agency or sector can do it all. We need our neighbors and civil society to come through for us. It is always a mistake to wait passively for bureaucracies and government agencies to save us.

Q: What are the key stages of overcoming a crisis?

A: In the face of crisis and catastrophe, we are afraid. Our first temptation is to fight the facts or flee from the facts. But to overcome, we must get our mind around the truth of our lives and circumstances. Here are five steps that survivors worldwide have used to overcome a life crisis:

> **Face facts.** This awful thing has happened. I can't roll back the clock. This sucks.

> **Choose life, not death.** I want to find hope and create options for a positive future.

> **Reach out.** No one survives alone. Isolation will kill us. Let others into our lives.

> **Get moving.** You have to get up and out of the house. Do your "survivor sit-ups."

> **Give back.** Become a benefactor, not just a beneficiary. Yes, you will add value.

Q: How can people be expected to give back when so much has been taken from them?

A: The most generous can be found among the poorest of the poor, people who have experienced crisis and poverty themselves. Many have discovered that the key to finding joy lies in giving back to our communities. Many of us exert enormous effort just to survive life, but when we learn to give again, in small and big ways, we gain in strength. Giving keeps us from slipping back into a victim mentality.

None of the survivors I work with, from Bosnia, Vietnam, or Ethiopia, wants to be dependent on charity or pity. They want a chance to get back in the game. That's why each and every survivor we work with agrees to perform community service. For example, if we help a survivor get a fake leg or find a job, then he or she is obligated to help another survivor in their community. Sometimes it's as simple as a roof repair or sharing food. Everyone feels better after giving again. Does anyone out there feel good being in someone else's charitable debt?

Q: Is accepting the impact of such a crisis the best case, or can people go beyond and thrive or be stronger than before the crisis?

A: Acceptance is just the beginning. Slowly, we start to "face facts," to break through initial denial and fear. When life explodes, our first instinct is fight or flight. We rage at what has happened, or we run from it. These are short-term survival instincts, but not healthy long-term survivorship strategies needed to get through tough times. And just "getting through" is not our primary life objective.

We humans have an uncanny ability to reframe our thoughts and choose to find meaning in our scars. Thousands of survivors we have interviewed talk about growing stronger after a catastrophe. But they made healthy choices along the way; it was no accident that they rediscovered joy after debilitating loss.

Q: Still, even for the thrivers, do you think they would want whatever happened to happen to them again?

A: I never give good press to a bad thing. To this day, I wish I had never stepped on that land mine in Israel and lost my right leg. I don't romanticize the pain, nor do I give any credit for my thriving to land mines. They are lethal military litter that daily maims and kills innocent men, women, and children. I don't know any rape survivor who would put a positive spin on sexual violence, nor any cancer survivor who fancies cancer and chemotherapy.

The key to thriving is not the "thing" but our determination to choose the survivor path, en route to a healthy and positive future. Life can wound us terribly, but we, thankfully, are more than the sum of our wounds. We can choose our response to tragedy and trauma. As the cheerful but hackneyed saying goes, we can "make lemonade out of lemons." Still, lemons never stop being sour, do they?

Q: What differentiates someone who will overcome or even thrive from someone who will be defeated by a crisis?

A: People who overcome and thrive are those who have learned to rise above their injuries and give back to their communities. People are defeated by their crisis if they *become* their crisis, letting it rule their lives. The key is to recognize a crisis for what it is—a turning point and an opportunity.

I refused to let a land mine rob me of more than my leg. It couldn't make me less of a whole person unless I let it do so. I would never define myself by a piece of me or by one aspect of my past. I don't think of myself as "an amputee," just a regular guy who happens to be missing a leg. Survivors who believe they are more than their bodies have an advantage. Faith and a sense of humor are hallmarks of resilient personalities.

Q: Do you think there are fundamental differences between starting an organization like Survivor Corps and a for-profit company?

A: I don't see a big difference. The entrepreneurial impulse is the same across borders, even when there are different motives behind it. Some search for profits; others seek "higher profits." Still, a balance sheet is a balance sheet. Cash flow is what it is. Revenue and expenses are simple math for any company or nonprofit organization. I have spent my whole professional career as a social-sector guy because I am primarily motivated to address the mass market of growing numbers of marginalized people in need. I don't call them customers or clients, but others could.

As I earned my MBA from the University of Michigan, I was increasingly convinced that the dynamics of organizational development are the same for nonprofits and for-profits alike. I do think businesses could learn more from the nonprofit sector, particularly with regard to tapping into intrinsic motivation, mission drive, and passion. "Increasing shareholder value" is not a sustainable mission statement or business strategy. Employees want and deserve more.

Q: What are the challenges of starting an organization that serves people thousands of miles away from most of your supporters?

A: It is a challenge for people to feel empathy and compassion across oceans. It's a fact of life that most charitable giving, like politics, is local. Less than 3 percent of American private philanthropy goes to international causes or organizations. Americans are very generous, but most of their gifts go to churches, synagogues, hospitals, schools, and cultural institutions in their backyards.

I once sat in on a focus group and heard many participants admit they would be more likely to give to an international organization like Survivor Corps if they also knew we were helping survivors here at home, such as veterans returning from Afghanistan and Iraq. And we are. The United States is a very war-affected nation. We must have strategies to reach out and connect with conflict survivors to offer support and promote successful community reintegration after war and violence.

Q: What's your step-by-step recommendation for someone who wants to change the world as you have?

A: Look at your own life circumstances and take the Survivor Pledge: 1) I will not be a victim. 2) I will rise above. 3) I will give back. 4) I will change the world.

As His Holiness the Dalai Lama once told me, "We have to remove the land mines from our own hearts first, before we can fully demine the world and bring peace." So take a peek within, then gain some perspective to rise above self-centeredness and reach out to others in need. It can be scary at first, because it requires us to get out of our comfort zones and cross boundaries and barriers to meet people who seem different, marginalized, threatening at first.

The question becomes not whether to be a global citizen—we all are—but how best to become an active one. And it gets personal, because you have to get to know yourself and ask: Who am I? What do I care about? What am I good at? How can I help appropriately? And then align these things in your life, your work, your giving patterns. Give locally, act globally. Or give globally, act locally. Do it your way by mixing it up, have fun as you learn your unique value-added place in the world. It turns out that giving is simply good for you. Like exercise, it boosts your serotonin levels.

Q: What exactly happens when you win a Nobel Prize?

A: It was certainly exciting to be in Oslo in December 1997, joining with leaders of the International Campaign to Ban Landmines. A few weeks earlier, we had gathered together in D.C. to hear the news and jump for joy. The ceremonies are exquisite, replete with great musical performances and speeches and an audience with the Norwegian royal family. All heady stuff, and great fun.

But, as we raised our champagne glasses, I worried that this public attention would move on from land mines, even as our work had only just begun. Tens of millions of mines still had to be destroyed, and hundreds of thousands of mine victims and their families desperately needed our help. That was a big year for our survivor movement. We worked closely with Diana, Princess of Wales. We launched innovative survivor networks worldwide. We helped draft and negotiate the historic 1997 Mine Ban Treaty—the first arms-control treaty with specific obligations to help the victims of a weapon recover and reintegrate.

Ten years later, we reunited in Oslo to celebrate our progress. Today, casualty rates are down from 26,000 victims per year to fewer than 8,000—still too many, but progress nonetheless. Tens of millions of mines have been destroyed. Survivor rights are starting to be recognized worldwide. Still more is to be done, but it's a great survivor success story, worthy of the Nobel Prize for Peace. We are both proud and humbled to share this honor.

You and I may never win a Nobel Prize, but we will have to face difficult challenges. I hope these challenges are not as great as an exploding land mine, but because of Jerry's work there are (a) fewer land mines in the world and (b) a prescription for surviving.

CHAPTER 94

My Hindsights in Life

Commencement speeches were invented largely in the belief that outgoing college students should never be released into the world until they have been properly sedated.

⁓ G. B. TRUDEAU

Hindsights I

S ome people build houses, some people provide medical care, some people risk their lives; I make speeches to try to make the world a better place. In fact, one of the joys of my life is making baccalaureate and graduation speeches. I've given this Hindsights speech six times to high schools and colleges. This is the text of my speech from 1995. I hope that it doesn't sedate you.

Speaking to you today marks a milestone in my life. I am forty years old. Twenty-two or so years ago, when I was in your seat, I never, ever thought I would be forty years old.

The implications of being your speaker frighten me. For one thing, when a forty-year-old geezer spoke at my baccalaureate ceremony, he was about the last person I'd believe. I have no intention of giving you the boring speech that you are dreading. This speech will be short, sweet, and not boring.

I am going to talk about hindsights today. Hindsights that I've accumulated in the twenty-two years from where you are to where I am. Don't blindly believe me. Don't take what I say as "truth." Just listen. Perhaps my experience can help you out a tiny bit.

I will present them à la David Letterman. Yes, forty-year-old people can still stay up past 11:00 P.M.

1. Live off your parents as long as possible.

I was a diligent Oriental in high school and college. I took college-level classes in high school and earned college-level credits. I rushed through college in three and a half years. I never traveled or took time off because I thought it wouldn't prepare me for work and it would delay my graduation.

Frankly, I blew it.

You are going to work the rest of your lives, so don't be in a rush to start. Stretch out your college education. Now is the time to suck life into your lungs—before you have a mortgage, kids, and car payments.

Take whole semesters off to travel overseas. Take jobs and internships that pay less money or no money. Investigate your passions on your parents' nickel. Or dime, or quarter, or dollar. Your goal should be to extend college to at least six years.

Delay, as long as possible, the inevitable entry into the workplace and a lifetime of servitude to bozos who know less than you do but make more money. Your parents and grandparents worked very hard to get you and your family to this point. Do not deprive them of the pleasure of supporting you.

2. Pursue joy, not happiness.

This is probably the hardest lesson of all to learn. It probably seems to you that the goal in life is to be happy. Now you maybe have to sacrifice and study and work hard, but, by and large, happiness should be predictable. Nice house. Nice car. Nice material things.

Take my word for it, happiness is temporary and fleeting. Joy, by contrast, is unpredictable and intense. It comes from pursuing interests and passions that do not obviously result in happiness.

Pursuing joy, not happiness, will translate into one thing over the next few years for you: Study what you love. This may also not be popular with parents. When I went to college, I was "marketing driven." It's also an Oriental thing.

I looked at what fields had the greatest job opportunities and prepared myself for them. This was brain-dead. There are so many ways to make a living in the world, it doesn't matter that you've taken all the right courses. I don't think one person on the original Macintosh team had a classic computer science degree.

Parents, you have a responsibility in this area. Don't force your kids to follow in your footsteps or to live your dreams. My father was a senator in Hawaii. His dream was to be a lawyer, but he only had a high school education. He wanted me to be a lawyer.

For him, I went to law school. For me, I quit after two weeks. I view this as a terrific validation of my inherent intelligence.

3. Challenge the known and embrace the unknown.

One of the biggest mistakes you can make in life is to accept the known and resist the unknown. You should, in fact, do exactly the opposite: Challenge the known and embrace the unknown.

Let me tell you a short story about ice. In the late 1800s, there was a thriving ice industry in the Northeast. Companies would cut blocks of ice from frozen lakes and ponds and sell them around the world. The largest single shipment was 200 tons that was shipped to India. Only 100 tons got there unmelted, but this was enough to make a profit.

Ice harvesters, however, were put out of business by ice factories. It was no longer necessary to cut and ship ice, because companies could make it in any city during any season.

Ice factories were put out of business by refrigerator companies. If it was convenient to make ice at a manufacturing plant, imagine how much better it was to make ice and create cold storage in everyone's home.

You would think that the ice harvesters would see the advantages of ice making and adopt this technology. However, all they could think about was the known: better saws, better storage, better transportation.

Then you would think that the ice makers would see the advantages of refrigerators and adopt this technology. The truth is that the ice harvesters couldn't embrace the unknown and jump their curve to the next curve.

Challenge the known and embrace the unknown, or you'll be like the ice harvesters and ice makers.

4. Learn to speak a foreign language, play a musical instrument, and play noncontact sports.

Learn a foreign language. I studied Latin in high school because I thought it would help me increase my vocabulary. It did, but trust me when I tell you it's very difficult to have a conversation in Latin today other than at the Vatican. And despite all my efforts, the pope has yet to call for my advice. Latin has proven to be very valuable, but a live language would be nice, too.

Learn to play a musical instrument. My only connection to music today is that I was named after Guy Lombardo. Trust me: It's better than being named after Guy's brother, Carmen. Playing a musical instrument could be with me now and stay with me forever. Instead, I have to buy CDs at Tower.

I played football. I loved football. Football is macho. I was a middle linebacker—arguably one of the most macho positions in a macho game. But you should also learn to play a sport like hockey, basketball, or tennis. That is, a sport you can play when you're over the hill.

When you're fifty, it will be as difficult to get twenty-two guys together in a stadium to play football as it is to have a conversation in Latin, but all the people who wore cute white tennis outfits can still play tennis. And all the macho football players are sitting around watching television and drinking beer.

5. Continue to learn.

Learning is a process, not an event. I thought learning would be over when I got my degree. It's not true. You should never stop learning. Indeed, it gets easier to learn once you're out of school, because it's easier to see why you need to learn.

You're learning in a structured, dedicated environment right now. On your parents' nickel. But don't confuse school and learning. You can go to school and not learn a thing. You can also learn a tremendous amount without school.

6. **Learn to like yourself, or change yourself until you can like yourself.**

I know a forty-year-old woman who was a drug addict. She is a mother of three. She traced the start of her drug addiction to smoking dope in high school.

I'm not going to lecture you about not taking drugs. Hey, I smoked dope in high school. Unlike Bill Clinton, I inhaled. Also unlike Bill Clinton, I exhaled.

This woman told me that she started taking drugs because she hated herself when she was sober. She did not like drugs—she hated herself. Drugs were not the cause, though she thought they were the solution.

She turned her life around only after she realized that she was in a downward spiral. Fix your problem. Fix your life. Then you won't need to take drugs. Drugs are neither the solution nor the problem.

Frankly, smoking, drugs, alcohol—and using an IBM PC—are signs of stupidity. End of discussion.

7. **Don't get married too soon.**

I got married when I was thirty-two. That's about the right age. Until you're about that age, you may not know who you are. You also may not know whom you're marrying.

I don't know one person who got married too late. I know many people who got married too young. If you do decide to get married, just keep in mind that you need to accept the person for what he or she is right now.

8. **Play to win, and win to play.**

Playing to win is one of the finest things you can do. It enables you to fulfill your potential. It enables you to improve the world and, conveniently, develop high expectations for everyone else, too.

And what if you lose? Just make sure you lose while trying something grand. Avinash Dixit, an economics professor at Princeton, and Barry

Nalebuff, an economics and management professor at the Yale School of Organization and Management, say it this way: "If you are going to fail, you might as well fail at a difficult task. Failure causes others to downgrade their expectations of you in the future. The seriousness of this problem depends on what you attempt."

In its purest form, winning becomes a means, not an end, to improve yourself and your competition.

Winning is also a means to play again. The unexamined life may not be worth living, but the unlived life is not worth examining. The rewards of winning—money, power, satisfaction, and self-confidence—should not be squandered.

Thus, in addition to playing to win, you have a second, more important obligation: to compete again to the depth and breadth and height that your soul can reach. Ultimately, your greatest competition is yourself.

9. Obey the absolutes.

Playing to win, however, does not mean playing dirty. As you grow older and older, you will find that things change from absolute to relative. When you were very young, it was absolutely wrong to lie, cheat, or steal. As you get older, and particularly when you enter the workforce, you will be tempted by the system to think in relative terms. "I made more money." "I have a nicer car." "I went on a better vacation."

Worse, "I didn't cheat as much on my taxes as my partner." "I just have a few drinks. I don't take cocaine." "I don't pad my expense reports as much as others."

This is completely wrong. Preserve and obey the absolutes as much as you can. If you never lie, cheat, or steal, you will never have to remember whom you lied to, how you cheated, and what you stole.

There absolutely are absolute rights and wrongs.

10. Enjoy your family and friends before they are gone.

This is the most important hindsight. It doesn't need much explanation. I'll just repeat it: Enjoy your family and friends before they are gone. Nothing—not money, power, or fame—can replace your family and friends or bring them back once they are gone. Our greatest joy has been our baby, and I predict that children will bring you the greatest joy in your lives—especially if they graduate from college in four years.

And now, I'm going to give you one additional hindsight because I've probably cost your parents thousands of dollars today. It's something that I hate to admit, too.

By and large, the older you get, the more you're going to realize that your parents were right. More and more—until finally, you become your parents. I know you're all saying, "Yeah, right." Mark my words.

Remember these ten things. If just one of them helps just one of you, this speech will have been a success.

1. Live off your parents as long as possible.

2. Pursue joy, not happiness.

3. Challenge the known and embrace the unknown.

4. Learn to speak a foreign language, play a musical instrument, and play noncontact sports.

5. Continue to learn.

6. Learn to like yourself, or change yourself until you can like yourself.

7. Don't get married too soon.

8. Play to win and win to play.

9. Obey the absolutes.

10. Enjoy your family and friends before they are gone.

Hindsights II

It's been thirteen years since I first gave that Hindsights speech. During these years, a lot of water has gone under the bridge. I have four kids, two of them adopted from Guatemala. I've written nine books, counting this one. I've started four companies and endured two tours of duty at Apple. I've racked up 1.7 million miles on United Airlines: It's a bad sign when an immigration officer tells you, "There's no more space on your passport; you need to get a new one." But I am husband 1.0 still married to wife 1.0.

You'd think that I would have learned something beyond the original ten hindsights, and indeed I have. Therefore, here are the additional hindsights I will include in future commencement addresses.

1. **Things are never as good or as bad as they seem.** When I was working at Apple from 1983 to 1987, the company experienced fantastic highs and dismal lows. Shipping the Macintosh was one such high. Apple's first layoff a few years later was a dismal low. But I saw that when things were supposedly great, there were lots of problems that people chose to ignore. Then I saw that during the black days, things weren't that bad: Customers were still buying Macintoshes by the thousands, developers were fairly happy, and most employees weren't affected by the layoffs. (Some employees even thought the layoffs were a good method to clean house.) So I've learned to temper my optimism and my pessimism in my old age.

2. **You can love an adopted child as much as a biological one.** A man's contribution to a pregnancy lasts about ten seconds—five if he told the truth, three if you asked the mother. And yet I've met many men who were skeptical about adoption because they didn't think they could bond with a child who didn't have their DNA—i.e., the ten-second commitment. This is simply not true: When you hold your precious jewel for the first time, no one cares if none of those chromosomes came from you. Certainly not the baby. Certainly not your wife. So get over it. Your DNA isn't the Holy Grail—to mix several metaphors.

3. **The key to child delivery is one word: *epidural*.** We went to the delivery classes; we learned the relaxation techniques; we took the soothing music with us to the hospital. At the end of the day (or more accurately, twenty-six hours), we came to believe that if God wanted every delivery to be natural, She wouldn't have enabled doctors to invent the epidural shot.

4. **People act the way their last names sound.** People may start to look like their dogs, but I think that they act the way their last names sound. For example, I have a buddy named Will Mayall. He helps me with anything technical; when I ask him if he can make my Web site or blog do something, his initial response is, "I may be able to," and then two hours later he's done it, all. Hence, "may all." Similarly, there's Jean-Louis Gassée. He's a funny guy—always armed with a great (usually sexual) metaphor to explain anything. He is a gas for the things he says—hence, "gas say." Then there's Kawasaki: My high school football teammates told me that I was a "cow's ass sagging."

5. **If you think someone is an asshole, then everyone else does, too.** When I met people that I didn't like, I wondered if it was my fault or the person's. Perhaps I had gotten her all wrong, and other people adored and respected her. After much investigation, I formulated the Rule of Perfect Information About Orifices; that is, if you think someone is an orifice, pretty much everyone thinks she's an orifice, too. There is seldom disagreement about orifices. The same, however, is not true about good guys. If you think someone is a good guy, you should never assume most people agree with you.

6. **Life is too short to deal with assholes.** Continuing on the orifice track . . . I'm now fifty-one years old, so more than half my life is over. At this age, there's not enough time left to accommodate orifices—frankly, there's not enough time to take care of the people you like. Why should you waste time with people you don't? So no matter how great a customer, partner, or vendor someone could or should be, don't give that person part of your life. Orifices not only waste your time, they taint your soul for the time you spend with the people you like.

7. **Entrepreneurs are always a year late and ten times too high in their "conservative" forecast.** I've worked with entrepreneurs who were so green they couldn't run a lemonade stand, and I've worked with entrepreneurs with great track records in brand-name companies. Experience, age, gender, and educational background—nothing matters.

Entrepreneurs are a year late in delivering their product, and their financial results are 90 percent lower than their "conservative" forecast. This isn't necessarily bad—indeed it may be necessary for entrepreneurs to believe their own bull shiitake, but it is how things work.

8. **Judge others by their intentions and yourself by your results.** If you want to be at peace with the world, here's what you should do: When you judge others, look at what they intended to do. When you judge yourself, look at what you actually accomplished. This attitude is bound to keep you humble. By contrast, if you judge others by their accomplishments (which are usually shortfalls) and yourself by your intentions (which are usually lofty), you will be an angry, despised little man.

9. **You don't have to answer every e-mail.** I am compulsive about answering e-mail. Sometimes I simply can't answer e-mail for weeks, and I go crazy. However, there have been a couple of times where I lost my in-box because I copied the wrong file, the file got corrupted, or my computer completely died, and I was terrified that hundreds of people wouldn't get a response and would be furious. They'd be thinking, "Guy thinks he's such a big shot that he doesn't need to answer e-mail anymore." I expected to get hate mail for weeks. Do you know what happened? Nothing. Not one pissed-off e-mail. I was amazed. But I am still compulsive about e-mail.

10. **Don't ask people to do something that you wouldn't do.** This is the ultimate test for every sales promotion, marketing campaign, engineering design, and employee directive. In reality, it's as powerful as the Golden Rule ("Do unto others as you would have them do unto you," not "He who has the gold makes the rules.")

If you won't do something, don't ask anyone else to do it.

I don't care how great your nuclear-powered mousetrap is: You wouldn't pay $500,000 for it, go back to school for a PhD in physics to learn to arm it, and drive to the middle of Utah to drop off dead, toxic mice. On the flip side, if you do the tough, dirty, stuff then (a) employees can't complain, and (b) employees will follow you to the ends of the earth.

Mathematically, I gained approximately one hindsight per year. I guess that's a pretty good rate. Here's the mother of all hindsights for you: My family has brought me by far the greatest joy. This did not occur to me when I was younger—I thought acquiring money, cars, power, or fame (not that I have all these) was the goal. I thank God every day for my four children and my wife.

The *Reality Check* Checklist

**If you wanna be a good archaeologist,
you've gotta get out of the library!**

~ INDIANA JONES IN *INDIANA JONES AND
THE KINGDOM OF THE CRYSTAL SKULL*

In reality, no one can implement all the recommendations in a book, so I'm providing a list of the ten most important ones. Success isn't as simple as this list, but it will put you on the right path for the journey.

1. Are you making meaning?

2. Does your product jump to, or create, the next curve?

3. Is your product Deep, Intelligent, Complete, Elegant, and Emotive?

4. Do you have a mantra for what you do?

5. Do you have a 10-slide pitch with no font smaller than 30 points that you can give in 20 minutes?

6. Have you figured out a way to take your product to market with no budget?

7. Are you helping people who cannot help you?

8. Can you blow away any audience with a demonstration of your product?

9. Would you hire "imperfect" job candidates who love what you do, as well as people who are better than you are?

10. Are you only asking people to do things that you would do, too?

This is what you have to do so that you can do what you want to do. I hope, in the words of Henry David Thoreau, that *Reality Check* is a "truly good book" that helps you change the world.

GUY KAWASAKI

Index